To John –
and the Asia
Anne Park Shan

Finding

JAPAN

EARLY CANADIAN ENCOUNTERS

with ASIA

Anne Shannon

VANCOUVER • VICTORIA • CALGARY

Heritage House Publishing Company Ltd.
heritagehouse.ca

Library and Archives Canada Cataloguing in Publication

Shannon, Anne Park

Finding Japan: early Canadian encounters with Asia / Anne Shannon.

Includes bibliographical references and an index.
Issued also in electronic format. ISBN 978-1-927051-55-9

    1. Canadians—Japan—History. 2. Japan—Relations—Canada. 3. Canada—Relations—Japan. 4. Japan—Civilization—Western influences. 5. Japan—History—1868-. I. Title.

DS832.7.C3S43 2012   952.03   C2012-904128-9

Edited by Lana Okerlund
Proofread by Renate Preuss
Cover design by Jacqui Thomas
Interior design by Kate Moore

Front cover image credits clockwise from top: Library and Archives Canada (C-00283101); Vancouver Maritime Museum; Library and Archives Canada, (PA-206846); Art Gallery of Greater Victoria (AGGV 1977.235.001); BC Archives (A-02284); United Church of Canada Archives (1989.054 P45N); Royal Ontario Museum, (926.18.609); bamboo by rusm/iStockphoto.com
Back cover: Art Gallery of Greater Victoria (AGGV 1977.235.001); bamboo by rusm/iStockphoto.com

 The interior of this book was produced on 100% post-consumer recycled paper, processed chlorine free and printed with vegetable-based inks.

Heritage House acknowledges the financial support for its publishing program from the Government of Canada through the Canada Book Fund (CBF), Canada Council for the Arts and the province of British Columbia through the British Columbia Arts Council and the Book Publishing Tax Credit.

16 15 14 13 12 1 2 3 4 5

Printed in Canada

CONTENTS

Introduction 5

PART 1: ARRIVING (1848–1900) 9
    Inspired Madness 11
    Those Seductive Treaty Ports 30
    Missions and Mountains 42
    No Geisha 61
    Highway to the East 77

PART 2: GROWING (1900–30) 95
    Myths and Markets 96
    King's Japan 113
    Flaming Passion 130
    The Great Quake and Commerce 141
    Sir Herbert and the Legation 154

PART 3: STRUGGLING (1930–50) 173
    The Dark Valley 174
    War and Reconciliation 190
    Norman *Sensei* 208

Sources and Further Reading 224

Index 234

Acknowledgments 238

INTRODUCTION

This book is about early encounters with Japan, the first place Canadians found when they crossed the Pacific. In contrast to the widely known experience of Japanese who came to Canada, it looks at movement the other way.

It began in Tokyo, where I worked during the 1980s and, like many foreigners, became intrigued with the society around me. Only in my case the object of fascination was not simply the Japan I was in; it was also other, earlier Japans I might have experienced had I only arrived there sooner. A chance visit to a local book fair led to Ranald MacDonald, the young half-Aboriginal son of a Hudson's Bay trader who dared to smuggle himself into Japan in 1848 when it was still closed to the outside world—quite possibly the first person of Canadian origin to reach the shores of Asia. I was hooked. I began ransacking second-hand bookshops, libraries and archives, and asked friends and colleagues for their recollections.

The result is the colourful and disparate cast of characters who inhabit these pages—adventurers, military and technical advisers, missionary educators and social workers, businessmen and art collectors, politicians, diplomats and soldiers, as well as the occasional misfit.

Their stories took place during the tumultuous 100 years roughly between 1850 and 1950, when Japan made its spectacular leap from a closed and largely feudal society to a major power—an arc that coincidentally also mirrors Canada's own rise to nationhood. Part 1 (1848–1900) tracks early arrivals during the half century when Japanese began bootstrapping their country into the modern world. Part 2 (1900–30) is about expanding economic, government and other connections during the early 20th century against the backdrop of growing international tensions over competing interests in China. Part 3 (1930–50) is about struggling through the deteriorating decade of the 1930s and the Pacific War.

The stories provided the feeling and texture of earlier Japans that I was looking for. I could imagine MacDonald alone in his boat off the northern island of Hokkaido, counting on goodwill and a collection of books to save him from the terrible fate that awaited any foreigner who showed up on Japan's shores. Picture eager young missionary Alexander Shaw sneaking out of Tokyo's treaty port in 1873 and setting up camp in a corner of a Buddhist temple—and sense his relief at being discovered by the era's great modernizer, Fukuzawa Yukichi. See budding British Columbia lumber magnate H.R. MacMillan pacing the docks of Yokohama, pursuing sales and dodging dubious middlemen as Canadian exports to Japan exploded during the 1920s. Identify with diplomat Hugh Keenleyside in Canada's new legation in Tokyo in the early 1930s, comparing notes with Herbert Marler, Canada's first minister to Japan, over the latest incident in Japan's growing confrontation with China—possibly after a morning of duck-netting at the Hama Detached Palace.

The discoveries were not only of young men. As a foreign woman working in the economic and financial field in Tokyo at the time, I was struck by the independent professional women who had boldly set off for Japan a hundred years before and prospered building schools and other social institutions. The notion that foreign women cannot operate effectively in "male-oriented Japan" not only was outmoded, but apparently less than accurate to begin with.

An unanticipated dividend was the leading Japanese personalities of the era who popped up. In addition to Fukuzawa, now immortalized on the 10,000-yen note, there was revolutionary hero Katsu Kaishū, illustrious late-19th-century prime minister and statesman Itō Hirobumi, leading female educator Tsuda Ume, early-20th-century foreign minister Komura Jutarō, *Bushido* author and controversial internationalist Nitobe Inazō, and business giant Baron Sumitomo, among others. The remarkable social activist and prison reformer Caroline Macdonald—said to have been the best-known foreigner in Japan in the 1920s—seems to have connected with everyone, from convicts to businessmen to bureaucrats to academics to labour organizers. There were also names that should be better known, notably Tamura Shinkichi, the Kobe businessman who went to Vancouver and pioneered early development of Canada–Japan trade.

At the same time, some stories also illuminated more troubling passages in Canada's history with Japan. William Lyon Mackenzie King will be forever remembered for his government's egregious treatment of Japanese Canadians during the Pacific War. But the image of an earlier King—one who made a little-known visit to Japan in 1909 and established a diplomatic legation in Tokyo in 1929 as part of Canada's international coming of age—adds dimension to a complex persona. In another vein, the shafts of human light that emerge in the recollections of Canadian prisoners of war in Japan give nuance to an episode that is otherwise grimly dark.

Indeed, what leaps out of many pages is the sheer power of human connection, the sparks of energy that transcended seemingly impossible cultural barriers and ignited some remarkably productive relationships. There was also the foreign tendency to misread Asian cultures by exoticizing them on one hand and stereotyping them on another. Early modern Japan was certainly different, but it was neither as enticing nor as frightening as it was sometimes made out to be. And there were many different Japans and different kinds of Japanese. To paraphrase Herbert Norman, the brilliant born-in-Japan Canadian scholar-diplomat whose tragic story concludes the book, it is possible to prove that virtually any set of qualities is inherent in the Japanese character—and come away none the wiser for it.

Ultimately, however, the book is about more than Japan. It is also about the role Asia played in the Canadian historical imagination. Lachine on the St. Lawrence River, it should be remembered, was named in the 1600s for the early explorers who set off westward into the interior of North America in the belief they were on their way to China.

Author Pierre Berton did Canadians a tremendous service when he highlighted the key role the Canadian Pacific Railway played in the making of Canada—the fulfillment, in the words of his well-known volume, of the "National Dream." In the process, however, something tended to get lost along the way—the role Canadian Pacific also played in fulfilling the older "International Dream" of a fast rail-and-ocean route from Europe across North America to Asia. The image of the legendary William Van Horne collecting Japanese ceramics while designing Asia-inspired travel advertising that urged passengers to take "The New Highway to the East"—that is, the Far East—provides a context for the enterprise that goes beyond the popular metaphor for Canadian nation building it has become.

Similarly, present-day visions of vast market opportunities in China, India and other rising Asian economies are not entirely new, but hark back to Wilfrid Laurier's tantalizing 20th-century vision of wheat as "the tea of the Orient," which rallied support for the opening of the Canadian Northwest and heralded Japan's emergence as a major Canadian trade and economic partner in the 1920s.

During most of the last century, attention focussed on nation building and realizing opportunity within North America. Now, as global dynamics shift in Asia's direction, it is time to reset the compass and to recognize that Canada has long been a Pacific, as well as an Atlantic and North American country. And while it may be best known as a land of opportunity and immigration, Canada's west coast has also been a gateway for adventurers to explore the Pacific Rim. This is a story of women and men who have demonstrated that great things can be achieved by those with the courage to look beyond their own boundaries, both geographic and cultural.

Finding Japan is offered in this spirit, in the hope that it may help to inspire new and productive connections across the Pacific in the years ahead.

A Note on Japanese Names

In the interest of simplicity, Japanese names are rendered in the traditional Japanese way—that is, family name first. Exceptions are when the person is best known by an honorific or artist's name.

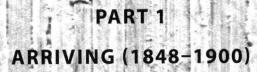

PART 1

ARRIVING (1848–1900)

INSPIRED MADNESS

In the early hours of a July morning, a small boat drifted forlornly off a remote corner of northern Japan. The sky above was overcast and dismal, with glimmers of daylight just beginning to pierce the cloud cover.

In the boat a man stood, motionless, staring into the gloom. He was young, heavy-set and dressed in sailor's clothes, which he occasionally tried to wring out without success, for the air was almost as sodden as the sea itself. The boat was in even worse shape, its mast snapped in two. A few sad belongings lay strewn haphazardly around the tiny deck, while seawater sloshed from side to side in the hold below.

He had the appearance of a sailor in distress, anxiously scanning the horizon in hope of rescue. That, certainly, was what he wished for. But there was more to it than that. Three days earlier he and the boat were lowered from the side of a whaling ship, the *Plymouth*. After spending the night in the shelter of a deserted island, he furtively sailed out of the bay and capsized the boat, losing the rudder and an oar in the process. The following day he repeated the same odd ritual, although this time he had forgotten to lock his sea-chest and some of its contents were lost. His last "accident" was truly accidental; caught off balance by a huge wave, he and the sea-chest had both gone overboard. He had retrieved what he could, but the compass was gone for good.

He had passed the night fitfully, struggling to keep the boat from drifting onto the rocks while wrestling with the voices in his head. There were the words of his captain and shipmates, pleading with him to remain aboard the whaler. There were also the tales, familiar to every sailor in every port, of the cruel fate that awaited anyone unfortunate enough to wash up on Japan's shores: at best, hideous punishment; at worst, gruesome death. Two years earlier, the crew of an American whaler, the *Lawrence*, had mysteriously gone missing in the same waters, as had that of a British brig, the *Catherine*. Only two months ago, 15 mutineers from the *Lagoda*, another American whaler, had vanished without a trace.

For the year was 1848, and Japan was still locked in the tight seclusion into which it had consigned itself two centuries earlier when the Tokugawa shogun issued his famous edict forbidding foreigners to enter Japan, or Japanese to leave, on penalty of death. For over 200 years Japan's only peephole on the outside world had been tiny Deshima Island in Nagasaki harbour, where the Dutch were permitted to maintain a presence, and through occasional contact with Chinese and Korean traders. US Commodore Matthew Perry and his famous black ships would not open Japan to the Western world for five more years, in 1853.

"Japan was our next neighbour across the way—only the placid sea, the Pacific, between us." Ranald MacDonald ca. 1853, five years after he smuggled himself into Japan disguised as a shipwrecked sailor. *From daguerreotype, BC Archives, H-02773*

If the sailor had doubts, however, the moment for them had passed. There was no turning back; the loss of the mast and the compass had seen to that. He also had a plan. Suddenly, his eyes fixed on a thin wisp of smoke on shore and a group of boatmen slowly making their way toward him.

He then did the strangest thing of all. Wresting the plug from the bottom of the boat, he watched the seawater swirl in around his ankles and waited for his would-be rescuers to arrive.

• • •

While Ranald MacDonald has a modest foothold in history as the first American teacher of English in Japan, his origins are at least as much Canadian as American.

He was a child of the Pacific Slope, the vast territory bounded by the Rocky Mountains, the Pacific Ocean and the Columbia River that was the western bastion of the formidable Hudson's Bay Company, which nominally controlled much of northern North America. Born in 1824 near the mouth of the mighty Columbia in what later became the US state of Oregon, he grew up at his father's forts at Kamloops on the northern end of the Okanagan Trail and at Langley on the lower Fraser River east of what became Vancouver, British Columbia.

His father, Archibald McDonald (he spelled the family name "Mc" while Ranald spelled it "Mac"), was a distinguished fur trader. Like most Scots, McDonald was also a stickler for education. At 10, after a year's schooling at company headquarters on Thompson's River (Kamloops), Ranald was taken on the 3,000-mile journey east up the long loops of the Columbia by canoe, over the freezing snows of the Athabasca Pass and across the prairies to a school at what became the Red River Settlement in Manitoba. At 15, he was sent farther east on a 1,500-mile journey by canoe to St. Thomas near the shores of Lake Ontario in then Upper Canada, where he was placed under the wing of a retired Swiss fur trader turned banker named Thomas Ermatinger.

What began with the best of intentions, however, soon went awry. After demonstrating such promise at Red River, Ranald showed little aptitude for banking. As the months went by, Archibald McDonald received increasingly worrisome reports from Ermatinger. "About my son," he replied apologetically, "I am truly at a loss what to say."

What happened is not entirely clear. Perhaps the adventurous young man from the west was uncomfortable in more settled town society. It also may be, however, that Ranald was finally forced to come to grips with the implications of his birth, after his interest in a young woman was thwarted by her parents on racial grounds.

In Ranald's mind he was the equivalent of frontier aristocracy. His father was not only a powerful fur trader but a descendant of Scottish Highlanders, a gentleman. His mother was Princess Raven, the youngest daughter of Comcomly, chief of the powerful Chinook tribe on the Pacific coast.

There was nothing unusual at the time about mixed or "Métis" parentage; many Hudson's Bay men had Aboriginal or "country" wives. When Ranald's mother died soon after he was born, his father married Jane Klyne, the daughter of the French Canadian postmaster at Jasper House and a Métis mother. Red River was a thriving and, for its time, relatively cosmopolitan community of Métis and Europeans. Intermarriage was also not unknown around St. Thomas. By the 1840s, however, it was becoming increasingly less acceptable socially and professionally, and Ranald was not the only unhappy mixed-blood son of a Hudson's Bay trader.

Archibald McDonald's letters grew more anxious, the last ending in a final heart-wrenching parental plea: "For God's sake, don't lose sight of my son." But it was too late. In 1842 Ranald left his banker's stool and set off for Japan.

• • •

It was an extraordinary idea. Japan in the mid-1800s was not only closed, but also on the opposite side of the globe.

It was not, however, as far from Ranald MacDonald's world as might be imagined. The great North American fur empire was oriented eastward to Europe, with its insatiable appetite for beaver pelts, used in making gentlemen's hats. For the handful of traders perched on the great saucer lip of the Pacific, however, the outlook also lay westward—to China, a destination for sea otter skins used to decorate the robes of mandarins, and to Japan, where foreigners were forbidden to go. It is easy to imagine a young man, unhappy and far from home, casting back to long evenings by the fireside in his father's forts where traders tantalized themselves with visions of enticing lands across the sea.

Evidence of Japan also haunted the North Pacific in the form of shipwrecks, remains of vessels caught up in the *Kuro Shiwo*, the powerful "black current" that sweeps northward from Japan across the Aleutians and down the coast of North America. While recorded wrecks are few, in 1833 three Japanese—Iwakichi, Kiukichi and Otokichi, survivors of the *Hojun Maru*, which had set out from the Ise peninsula to bring the Owari clan's annual tribute to the shogun in Edo—were rescued at Cape Flattery near the mouth of the Strait of Juan de Fuca. They were taken to Hudson's Bay headquarters on the Columbia, where the chief factor, a Scot from Quebec named John McLoughlin, treated them well, enrolling them in the local school.

MacDonald had never met "the three *kichis*," as they came to be known, but he knew their story, which sent the equivalent of a rocket through Hudson's Bay circles. Inspired by their experience he decided to smuggle himself into Japan disguised as a shipwrecked sailor in the hope that he, too, would be treated humanely. Dressed in buckskin, fur cap and leggings, he made his way south to Long Island's Sag Harbor.

If Nagasaki was Japan's peephole on the Western world, Sag Harbor was America's on Japan. Like Nantucket and other New England ports, it was home to America's booming whaling economy, a magnet for footloose men prepared to engage in the dirty, dangerous business of killing whales for the immense profit to be made in whale oil and bone. In Sag Harbor MacDonald entered the world of *Moby Dick*, Herman Melville's 1851 novel that contains Ishmael's fateful prophecy: "If that double-bolted land, Japan, is ever to become hospitable, it is the whale-ship alone to whom the credit will be due; for already she is on the threshold."

In 1845 MacDonald signed on to the *Plymouth*, a whaler headed for the Sandwich Islands (Hawaii), then the crossroads for trans-Pacific trade. The place was not entirely unfamiliar: Hawaiians (Owyhees) had long been employed by the Hudson's Bay Company on the Columbia River, and his father's fort at Langley on the Lower Fraser River exported salmon and lumber to the islands from 1830 onward. In 1834 the Hudson's Bay Company established its own agent in Honolulu, and by the 1840s was engaged in a bustling trade across the Pacific to and from the Sandwich Islands as well as up and down the coast to San Francisco and Alaska.

Lahaina, where the *Plymouth* landed, was more than a whaling port; it was a repository of the little then known about Japan. In the local seamen's library MacDonald could read about Japan. In the taverns he would have heard worried talk about the dangers of being caught up in tricky Japanese waters. He would have known about Japan's refusal to allow US Commodore Biddle's attempt to enter the country in 1846.

In the islands, Japan seemed closer and the prospect of its opening not so far-fetched. What MacDonald planned to do when he got there is unclear, but it seems he may have had ambitions to become an interpreter or engage in trade, or otherwise make something of himself in much the same way his father had done in the Pacific Northwest. Locating a whaler bound for the Japan Sea, he arranged with the captain to be given a small boat at the end of the whaling season in lieu of his share of the whaling profits. He also carried with him an insurance policy in the form of a sea-chest full of books. "I knew that such freight—so strange for a mere castaway from a whaling ship—would naturally excite suspicion; but I had my story, ready, for the nonce. Themselves even of the middle and lower classes, being a people of literature and books, I thought I might pass on this score. The sequel proved so."

• • •

In his sinking boat MacDonald was greeted by his rescuers with deep bows, to which he responded with a polite "how do you do?" and a respectful right-armed salute. "They did not seem afraid of me, but to be wonderstruck as to who or what I was."

On a rocky beach a hundred men, women and children awaited him, kneeling. Provided with a pair of sandals, he was led up a path toward a man with a shaved head and topknot, dressed in a long cotton gown cinched by a wide belt; MacDonald touched his hat in deference. After first admonishing him to remove the sandals, the man showed him into a large paper-windowed dwelling where a clean gown and a breakfast of rice, broiled fish, ginger, preserved shellfish and pickles awaited, as well as something called "grog, yes?"—evidence, MacDonald surmised, that he was not the first English-speaking sailor to arrive in the area. After a short walk he returned to find a large, thickly padded cotton gown on the floor. He went to sleep while his hosts washed his clothes.

Having experienced Japanese courtesy, he was next introduced to the innate Japanese sense of curiosity. Detailed inventory was taken of what remained of his belongings, each item exciting great interest, especially the books. A keg of dried meat, on the other hand, was greeted with horror and examined at a distance with a long fork.

One man in particular peppered him with questions: "Tangaro [Tajiro], a very intelligent Japanese . . . was my constant companion. His desire to learn English seemed to be intense." One day Tangaro led him away from the village into the tall grasses, where, squatting to avoid detection, he brought out a map of Japan with distances marked in terms of a day's travel from Edo, the capital. For the first time MacDonald realized that the village, which he called "Nootska" (Notsuka), was on Rishiri Island off the northwest corner of "Yesso" (Hokkaido), not yet part of Japan proper but a territory under Japanese control. The heavily bearded people around him were Ainu, the indigenous people of the region.

The Notsuka idyll was soon interrupted by the long reach of official Japan, which arrived one day in the form of two junks. Seated on a stool, MacDonald was subjected to a lengthy questioning: who was he and why had he left the whaler? His belongings were again examined in detail, his stores minutely inventoried, a sketch made of every article of interest. Everything was measured, even his own person.

The interrogation over, he was marched off to a larger village, flanked by two officers and two lines of Ainu. As the procession neared "Tootoomari" (Hontomari), it took on a sense of theatre as the path gave way to a road curtained by strips of black, blue and red cloth. Whether their purpose was to keep him from sight of the villagers, or vice versa, MacDonald was unsure, though it did not matter much as he towered over the curtain top. He was more perturbed by his own appearance. "As to myself, I felt in an awful state. I wore a cotton gown, which being too short by several inches was a poor shift for a dress of ceremony."

Until that point MacDonald had rather enjoyed himself. But in Hontomari, the atmosphere tightened. There he was put into what he described as a "cage," a wooden barred space about 12 feet square. Still, he had little complaint, especially as he was kept amply supplied with tea and tobacco. Thirty days later his journey resumed, the path lined this time with curious onlookers. Boarding a small junk, he joined the crew for a meal of rice and fish served in lacquered bowls. He stayed on deck for the remainder of the voyage.

In Soya on Hokkaido's northern tip, where military had been installed to ward off Russian incursions, the atmosphere turned distinctly more ominous. MacDonald exited the junk behind 18 men marching 2 abreast, followed by more soldiers and officers. The streets were again curtained off, some painted in the imitation of forts. The square held still more soldiers holding flags and lances, to whom others bent in passing. "Not wishing to follow their manner, I only touched my hat. The officers, seeing this, sent word to Tangaro to tell me to take off my cap, which I did."

This time MacDonald objected to his confinement, complaining about the lack of air in his tiny wooden-grated room and refusing to communicate. In response he was given freedom to exercise in an adjoining cell and was supplied with a bench to sit on, as well as plenty of sweets, tea, a pipe and tobacco. He was also permitted access to his books, though not the key to his sea-chest. Curiosity about him was intense and he received daily visitors, many of whom expressed disbelief that America, England and France were bigger than Japan.

The next junk he boarded was large, its appearance chilling, with painted portholes that in his imagination took on the grin of war. Worst of all was an enormous hairy swab suspended from the prow, presumably some sort of talisman.

> I am not imaginative—at least not abnormally so—but I must confess that that huge black swab of hair, etc.—large as a tar barrel—did puzzle me not a little . . . Painted portholes for imaginary cannon, and uncovered spear heads were plain enough and spoke for themselves; but an enormous dangling "what you may call it," swinging and dipping with the motion of the waves, into the limpid sea, was beyond my comprehension . . . I often, idly, thought of it, when lying in my cabin . . . To ask about it I knew, from experience, would be useless—so there, I left it, hanging.

He spent a lonely 15 days in the stern.

The next stop was "Matsmai" (Matsumae), a castle town on the southwest corner of Hokkaido from which the Matsumae clan administered the northern frontier. As the junk entered the harbour, MacDonald was ordered below. All was silent except for occasional sounds of arriving boats. Through a small chink in the wall he spied two camp stools going up, then two officers, followed by 30 or 40 officers and soldiers who knelt on mats on deck. Suddenly a partition was removed and he found himself dramatically on exhibit.

> I felt . . . I had to do something; though no one spoke, nor moved, in the way of formal presentation or direction to me. Rising with

as much dignity as I could command to one knee, I made my compliments . . . with wave of hand and dignified respect to the assemblage generally. It was received stoically.

A large man in black silk and what looked like white linen moccasins stared in amazement and let out a single word: *"Nipongin!"* (*Nihonjin*). To him, MacDonald looked like a Japanese. Told he would be sent to Nagasaki, MacDonald seized the moment and asked whether he might remain with them instead. The response was a loud laugh: "No! No! Nagasaki! Go away!"

For the first time he felt the precariousness of his situation. Crowds who previously seemed merely curious now took on a menacing air. "The whole neighbourhood was crowded with human beings [trying] to catch a glimpse of me. I really believe that every person had a lantern; it looked so. They gazed at me as if I were a wild beast, I could not stand it."

Grateful to retreat into the safety of a tightly lashed "box" held aloft by bearers and flanked by columns of soldiers, MacDonald bobbled off into the countryside. Uncharacteristically, he refused both conversation and food.

It was after midnight when the procession reached "Erametz" (Eramachi, a fishing village a few miles north of Matsumae), where he was shown into a dwelling with a mat-covered floor and a glowing fire. His host gave him to understand the room had housed 15 Americans who had been caught while attempting escape; pointing to the ceiling and drawing a sword, he made a sign of cutting the throat. Casting his eyes upward, MacDonald spotted patches over a hole in the roof and a beam bearing foreign names, apparently those of the vanished *Lagoda* crew. The message was clear: try to escape and he could expect a similar fate. In other respects, however, he might as well have been staying in a *ryokan*, or inn. A tray arrived with a bowl of rice, fish, pickles and boiled kelp, accompanied by chopsticks, a bamboo spoon and a wooden fork. Interest in him was intense: "Whilst I devoured the viands they devoured me with their eyes."

After supper he received four gowns, trousers, two knives and a box of confectionery with a presentation card. He was then shown to a mat, a thickly padded gown and a traditional Japanese pillow—a lacquered wooden box with a drawer, topped by a tiny rice-husk cushion. "Then the Governor kindly made a sign to me to sleep, and said 'Noo'—the Japanese word apparently for snooze . . ."

As before, his sea-chest was treated with great respect, sealed on top and sides with strips of paper so it could not be opened without discovery. "When opened—as it had to be, when I got anything out of it—it was always in the presence of a large number of persons, and was sealed, when closed before the same." Some 20 days later he was presented with a gift of apples by the officer in charge and seen off by another large contingent of colourfully arrayed soldiers.

The junk this time was a larger version of the last forbidding vessel, with a similarly unnerving great hairy swab. But the thousand-mile voyage south proved uneventful. Forced to remain below, MacDonald saw nothing of the closely guarded coast of Japan.

• • •

Much about Ranald MacDonald is reminiscent of the adventures of Will Adams, the English captain who inspired James Clavell's well-known novel *Shogun*. There are also echoes of Vasili Mikhailovich Golovnin, a Russian naval captain captured off Hokkaido, who reported similar curtained processions and imprisonment in tiny wooden "birdcages."

Adams, however, was a genuine shipwrecked sailor, marooned with his crew on Japan's storm-tossed southern coast in the early 1600s. And Golovnin arrived in the early 1800s with ships, men and guns. Of the few who entered Japan during its 200 years of self-imposed seclusion, Ranald MacDonald is the only one who entered deliberately, alone and unarmed.

He also differed from the rest in the warmth of his reception. Though imprisoned, he was treated with great courtesy, which he happily reciprocated. Compared to Adams's crew, who were thrown into a pit, or to two luckless young Russians, whose heads were returned, pickled, after they were caught pillaging the coast of Hokkaido, his treatment was positively benign.

Quite likely this had much to do with MacDonald himself, whose physical appearance and genial manner was nothing like the rude, red-haired foreign barbarians of Japanese imagination. But it was also a function of timing. With Russia expanding in the North Pacific, the Opium Wars in China and the US navy knocking at its door, Japan in the 1840s was beset by a mounting sense of encirclement—one heightened by growing numbers of whaling ships, their sails visible from shore.

The whalers also brought a new problem: increasing numbers of shipwrecked sailors. To avoid providing a pretext for rescue missions, the shogunate quietly modified its seclusion laws in the 1840s to encourage their return via Nagasaki on the southern island of Kyushū. In short, MacDonald was being passed down the line.

Nagasaki, however, was far more than an exit chute for unwanted foreigners. Two hundred years earlier it had been a focal point for anti-foreign sentiment, the site of terrible anti-Christian purges in which thousands of Roman Catholic converts were tortured, killed or both. Now it was home to a small group of scholars with a growing thirst for Western knowledge, desperate to learn English. Officially, anything Western remained dangerous and any foreigner was automatically suspected of being a spy. But beneath the surface ran mounting curiosity about the outside world, which some Japanese recognized they would soon be dealing with whether they wanted to or not. For them, the intelligent young man with the enticing sea-chest full of books was a catch.

Entering the city's long, green, island-dotted harbour, MacDonald was greeted by Murayama (Moriyama) Einosuke, a leading member of the school of Dutch-language interpreters. After initial questioning, he was taken to see the local Nagasaki magistrate. As they entered the building, Moriyama pointed to a small bronze plate on the floor that depicted the virgin and child, and urged MacDonald to step on it, which he did; this was the *fumi-e*, the test that had been used to ferret out Christians.

As the magistrate entered, Moriyama urged MacDonald to bow low, which he initially resisted; the two briefly stared each other in the eye before he went down on one knee. Then, when the interrogation turned to religion, Moriyama leaped in with a quick "that will do!" before his charge could get into real trouble. Afterward MacDonald was told that the magistrate had said he "had a big heart"—in other words, he was gutsy. He was also informed that a house would be provided for him and that, "if I was good, I should live better and better." The official record of the interrogation simply listed him as "a fisherman from Canada."

The house, part of a former Buddhist retreat, turned out to be a dwelling measuring seven by nine feet, with a barred opening along one side; it was furnished with a mat, a mosquito net, a hibachi, tea utensils and a table. In the evenings he received soup, rice and tea. No one spoke to him.

Three weeks later he was summoned to a second interrogation: Why did MacDonald leave the whaler? Had he intended to survey the coast with his quadrant? What was the position of his family, and was an inquiry likely to be launched after him? In response MacDonald gave his name, birthplace (Oregon), age (24), country (Canada in North America) and occupation (pilot or navigator), while hedging his bets about rescue prospects by claiming connections to both England and the United States. About his presence in Japan he held back nothing, except his bargain with the whaling captain and his self-inflicted shipwreck.

One day the magistrate arrived with an English atlas. What route had MacDonald taken, what other places had he visited, how many vessels were engaged in whaling? "I gave them to understand, as delicately as possible in the way of suggestion, that for such business particularly, Japan would be a good place for supplies, and that if Japan were to furnish them there would be no necessity for going to the Sandwich Islands or Hong Kong." He also cautiously broached the forbidden subject of opening trade. "They said No! Murayama, with some emphasis, stating—'No ship can approach the Coast: No ship can enter our harbours: It is against the law.' I often, after that, spoke to him on the subject. His answer was invariably the same."

Soon MacDonald was giving daily English lessons to 14 eager Japanese, who until then were making do with awkward Dutch translations. Their habit was to read English to him, which he corrected as best he could using the smattering of Japanese he had managed to pick up. His students' biggest problem was with some of the sounds, especially the consonants. "For instance: they cannot pronounce, except very imperfectly, the letter 'l'," MacDonald noted. "They pronounce it 'r' so that they rendered my name Ranardo Macdonardo."

Some things troubled him. In particular he was appalled by *seppuku*, or ritual suicide, when he heard of it. He was also alarmed to hear that a guard who brought his wife and daughter for a visit was punished by having "his head chopped off"—although this may simply have meant the man was punished.

But, with the exception of personal liberty, he had everything he wanted. "They even gave me up my Bible; and seeing—as they expressed—that 'I had made a God of it,' they made a neat shelf (*tokiwari*) at a corner of my room, to put it on, as a place of honor." A gift of pork arrived every seventh day from the Dutch on Deshima, and by deeming pork days his "Sundays," he kept track of time. His only real complaint was the smallness of his "cage," but in this he received no satisfaction. It was, "according to their ideas, a house to live in."

As the weeks slipped by he also increasingly came to think of those around him more as his friends than his keepers.

The Japanese, I would observe, are naturally chatty; always in a good vein of humour. In this respect I was en rapport with them. In look, facial features etc., I was not unlike them; my sea life and rather dark complexion, moreover, giving me their general color—a healthy bronze. I never had a cross word with any of them.

The person who made the most lasting impression was his rescuer, the astute 29-year-old Moriyama.

He had a pale cast of thought, piercing black eyes which seemed to search into the very soul, and read its every emotion. He spoke English pretty fluently, and even grammatically. His pronunciation was peculiar, but it was surprisingly in command of combinations of letters and syllables foreign to the Japanese tongue. He was my daily companion—a lovable one—ever afterwards, during my sojourn in Japan.

One day MacDonald heard cannons signalling the arrival of a ship in the harbour. It was the USS *Preble* come to rescue the 13 remaining *Lagoda* survivors. The difference he observed between the rough and unruly American sailors and himself was striking. "They had on their ordinary sailor dress. I had on my best Japanese dress, plain and respectable. They appeared very pale and thin. We all appeared, at the same time, before the Governors. They made me kneel apart from the rest."

With that, Ranald MacDonald departed Nagasaki after nine months in Japan, with the magistrate's final warning ringing in his ears: "Never to put my foot on Japan's soil again, or it would be the worse for me."

• • •

Aboard the *Preble*, MacDonald made a brief statement to the captain that later appeared in the US Congressional Record. Otherwise he received little attention. Far more to public taste were the *Lagoda* survivors' tales of harsh treatment and wild derring-do, which bolstered support for Commodore Perry's famous mission to open Japan to the outside world a few years later. By allowing MacDonald to slip through its fingers, however, the United States lost something more valuable than anything the rough-and-tumble *Lagoda*

Ranald MacDonald's companion Moriyama Einosuke (left) served as chief interpreter for Japan during the negotiations that followed US Commodore Matthew Perry's return to Japan in 1854. *From Perry and Hawks,* Narrative of the Expedition of an American Squadon i. 348

sailors could possibly have provided. A careful observer, MacDonald had kept careful track of Japanese manners, customs and military organization. He had also developed a facility in Japanese—something the Western world at the time was most anxious to acquire—even surreptitiously compiling a rudimentary vocabulary with a quill pen.

The United States conceivably lost more than that. The chief interpreter for Japan in the tense negotiations that followed Perry's second mission to Japan, in 1854, turned out to be none other than the capable Moriyama Einosuke. Who knows what might have happened had MacDonald and Moriyama faced each other across the negotiating table. As it was, history was captured by the spectre of Perry and his black ships forcing a recalcitrant Japan to open its doors, and lost sight of the brave young man who risked his life smuggling himself into the country with little more than a bold plan and a flair for making friends.

As for MacDonald, after knocking about the world for a few years he simply went home. In 1853, the same year Perry first sailed into Edo (Tokyo) Bay, he arrived in St. Andrews East (St. André d'Argenteuil) on the lower Ottawa River near Montreal, where his father had retired and recently died. With nothing to hold him there, he headed south to Panama, then up to San Francisco and farther north to Fort Victoria, where he visited Governor James Douglas, who had been a colleague of his father's.

From there he melted into the interior of what became the province of British Columbia. For a while he and a half-brother ran a store and pack trains supplying the hopeful hordes who poured into the Upper Fraser and Cariboo district during the gold rush. He tried prospecting himself and was said to have both made and lost a good deal of money. At various times he owned a ranch at Bonaparte Creek, managed the hotel at Hat Creek and ran a ferry across the river at Lillooet. In the early 1860s he explored the little-known territory between the Upper Fraser and the coast near Bella Coola in an effort to identify a viable shorter route to the gold fields. He was also a member of early government expeditions to explore Vancouver Island.

His Japan adventure was all but forgotten—or would have been except for an unusual series of events. Before departing central Canada, MacDonald had left a copy of his Japan notes with Malcolm McLeod, the family lawyer. Another mixed-race son of a Hudson's Bay trader, McLeod was fascinated by the story and tried, unsuccessfully, to have it published in the 1850s. There the matter might have rested, except that McLeod was a fervent early champion of the case for a transcontinental railway, a vociferous speechmaker and pamphleteer who peppered anyone and everyone with the case for his preferred route, a northerly one that constituted the shortest distance across the Pacific to Japan.

Several decades later, McLeod happened upon the name Murayama, proprietor of the *Asahi Shimbun* (Rising Sun), a leading Japanese newspaper. Thinking he and MacDonald's Murayama (Moriyama) might be one and the same, McLeod wrote to him. They were not; the man had also recently died. His son, however, was convinced of the authenticity of MacDonald's story and published a brief account of it. McLeod was then astonished to receive a visit from one of Moriyama's friends, a British-educated editor and translator named Oda Junichiro, who arrived in Ottawa in 1888 en route to London bearing two beautifully inlaid boxes and a scroll for MacDonald.

By another twist of fortune, MacDonald caught wind of Oda's visit and reconnected with McLeod, and together they began plotting to publish in earnest. K.T. Takahashi, a Presbyterian minister in Montreal and one of the few Japanese nationals in central Canada at the time, pronounced the story one of great significance. Ranald MacDonald, he affirmed, was fully entitled to lay claim to being the first instructor and propagator of the English language in Japan.

For help with publication they turned to that 19th-century Canadian of many hats, Sandford Fleming, who—when he was not surveying the route for the Canadian Pacific Railway, inventing Greenwich Mean Time or designing Canada's first postage stamp—headed the Canadian Literary Society. An advertisement for the book headed *A Canadian in Japan* was circulated under Fleming's name in 1891.

Their elation was short-lived: interest proved insufficient to justify publication. MacDonald, in a letter to McLeod, was dejected.

> It is a wonder that the Literary Institute of Canada with Sandford Fleming as President doesn't encourage with an advance—I would think they would take a pride to think that one of their sons was able to get up such a work that would be a lasting credit to Canada . . . Mr. Fleming ought to take the whole matter off your hands and publish it for the credit of Canada. Ah—our experience tells us that corporations have no souls.

• • •

On the face of it, MacDonald's story ought to have been a publisher's dream. The world by the early 1890s could not get enough of Japan—or the romanticized version of it. Gilbert and Sullivan's *The Mikado* premiered in Montreal in 1886. Basil Hall Chamberlain's brilliant one-volume encyclopedia, *Things Japanese,* was released in 1890. The travelling classes were beating a path across the Pacific on the recently inaugurated Canadian Pacific rail and ocean service to Japan.

Various further attempts were made at publication, with similar unhappy results. Part of the problem lay with McLeod, the manuscript's self-styled author, who injected his own views and muddled facts while clogging the text with archaic references and literary frills and furbelows—though MacDonald's own straightforward prose is clearly discernible. McLeod was a liability, although without him MacDonald's story would have been lost.

Far from the world of cities and publishing, MacDonald did what he could, mortgaging his homestead and tapping family and friends for loans. By then a US citizen living in the Colville Valley near the site of his father's last fort on the Columbia in northern Washington State, he cut an elegant and imposing figure, a muscular man in a light-blue army overcoat, probably of American Civil War origin, with cape and brass buttons, his curly, grey hair topped with a wide-brimmed, black felt hat. It is said that he rarely made calls without carrying a handsome ivory-headed cane and the scroll box sent by Oda Junichiro. Locally he was a much-admired patriarch, with the aura of an upper-class gentleman of the old Hudson's Bay aristocracy. To the outside world, however, he was a relic of a bygone era—something that became abundantly clear in an incongruous encounter with Elizabeth Custer, wife of General Custer, recently killed in the Battle of the Little Bighorn.

On a tour of the west following her husband's death, Custer showed up at the fort one day in 1891 in search of local colour. MacDonald graciously obliged, showing her around and telling her of the old days. His thank you was a viciously patronizing article in *Harper's Bazar* portraying him as "the Prince of Paupers"—a quaint old man with pretensions to grandeur, living in destitution in a tangle of half-breed children, chickens and dogs. "I suddenly said: Oh, Mr. MacDonald, how I should like to take you home with me!" she wrote. "In return I received such an impressive bow, and his hand went instinctively over his heart as he said: Oh, madam, take possession of me. I am yours."

Perhaps she thought the article clever, the sort of thing that would amuse the sophisticated *Harper's* readership. MacDonald was deeply insulted. He had done his best to play along; when she had mentioned going to New York, for instance, he thought she had been joking. "Then it struck me that she had come to the woolly west to pull wool over me and exhibit me on show as Barnum would his Woolly Horses."

In a letter to his local newspaper, he let rip. He was especially indignant about the slights to himself and a cousin's family; "Mrs. Mustard Custer" had violated all the rules of decency and common politeness. He and his family were not poor but rich in the abundance of the Pacific Northwest, including cattle and horses. If he was wearing working clothes it was because she had arrived at the fort unannounced. The "squaw" she referred to was the wife of a cousin, an educated woman of highly respectable lineage that included a part-Aboriginal grandmother. And his adventure, thank you, had been in Japan, not China.

Custer's behaviour was inexcusable, but it spoke to a wider phenomenon: the growing social, as well as geographic, marginalization of mixed-race people like MacDonald in the rapidly settling North American West—which conceivably was another factor in the lack of response to the manuscript, though MacDonald was too proud to see things that way. The prospect of publishing his story, however, clearly opened a window on a happier time of inter-racial connection, as a letter he wrote to McLeod in 1889 suggests.

> Even now in the vicissitudes of life many and varied during that forty years and more since I parted from those friends at the Port of Nagasaki I have never ceased to feel most kindly and ever grateful to them for the manner of their treatment of me . . . Truly I liked them in that congenial empathy which, left to itself—unmarred by antagonism of race, creed or worldly selfishness—makes us all, of Adam's race, "wondrous kin."

The same letter reflected the justifiable pride MacDonald felt in his achievement; he knew what he had done was remarkable, even if the world did not.

> In all this I flatter myself that I have broken the seal that made Japan a sealed Empire to the West—at all events cracked it so bad that it made it easy for Commodore Perry to do the rest of the business and secure a commercial treaty . . . I in the meantime to wait my reward from government.

This last reference was a wry nod to part of MacDonald's statement aboard the *Preble* that was omitted from the US Congressional Record, a suggestion that future visitors should bring with them models of Western ingenuity—the very approach Perry used when he returned to Japan in 1854 with a small-scale model railway that Japanese dignitaries rode around a track, to their intense delight.

Ranald MacDonald in 1891, three years before he died. He is buried at Toroda, Washington, a few miles south of Grand Forks, British Columbia. There are monuments to him on Rishiri Island, in Nagasaki and in Astoria, Oregon. *BC Archives, PA-02284*

In August 1894 he mounted his horse and rode off into the purple mountains to the nearby Colville Reservation, where he died. His last words, as he lay in his niece's arms, reportedly were, "*Sayonara*, my dear, *sayonara*." It was many years before anyone could tell her what they meant.

He had lived long enough to see part of his story printed in the local *Kettle Falls Pioneer* the previous year. The full version did not appear for three more decades, when it was published by the Eastern Washington State Historical Society in 1923.

THOSE SEDUCTIVE TREATY PORTS

About the same time that Ranald MacDonald arrived in Japan, a young Japanese man was travelling about calling on his country to shore up defences against the impending arrival of the barbarians.

Yoshida Shōin, or Shōin as he is generally known, was one of the restless, lower-ranking young samurai from southern Japan who spearheaded opposition to the 200-year-old hegemony of the country's military rulers, the Tokugawa shoguns. Physically scrawny and unkempt, with lofty plans that never quite seemed to work out, he may seem an unlikely champion. But there was something about his passion and sheer audacity that appealed.

The son of a military instructor in Choshu in southern Japan, he grew up in a world of military tactics, Chinese classics and the virtues of willpower and self-control. In 1851 he went to Edo to study with the celebrated scholar Sakuma Shozan, from whom he absorbed the crucial lesson that Japan could not expect to meet the foreign threat without matching the foreigners' superior military strength.

The arrival of US Commodore Matthew Perry in Edo (Tokyo) Bay in 1853—all those black monsters belching black smoke—struck Shōin and his contemporaries as an outrage. It confirmed their worst nightmares. At the same time, it also presented an opportunity. Anxious to learn what they could about the Americans, Shōin and a companion attempted to sneak aboard one of Perry's ships in 1854, bringing with them a farewell poem from Sakuma and a letter in Chinese addressed to the US fleet's senior officer. Discovered and put ashore, they were spotted the next day in a small cage awaiting transport back to Edo. From there Shōin was sent back to the walled city of Hagi in the domain of the powerful Choshu clan, where he was put under house arrest and out of further trouble.

He could not be counted on, however, to remain quiet for long. He soon opened a small village school, where he taught military arts along with the Doctrine of Imperial Loyalty, the dangerous but growing view that supreme authority in Japan rested not with the shogun in Edo and his retainers—who had patently failed to keep the foreigner out—but with the country's divine ruler, the emperor in Kyoto.

On hearing of the shogunate's plans to enter into a commercial treaty with the United States, an enraged Shōin plotted to kill an official. But the plot was discovered, and in 1859 he was executed; he was 29. His name went on to become synonymous with impulsiveness, revolutionary zeal, hatred of the shogunate and extreme loyalty to the emperor.

• • •

The international agreement that so troubled Yoshida Shōin was one of the so-called unequal treaties struck between the European powers and Japan at the end of the 1850s that opened the treaty ports—principally Yokohama, Nagasaki, Kobe, Osaka, Tsukiji (Tokyo) and Hakodate, places where foreigners could live and do business without intruding into the rest of the country. In Japan but not really of it, the treaty ports were instant magnets for the human flotsam and jetsam of the Far East: merchants looking for a good deal, sailors interested in a good time, as well as crowds of curious Japanese. It was there that foreigners and Japanese really encountered each other for the first time, with results that were sometimes fruitful, quite often comic and occasionally distressing. Foreigners gaped and twittered over exotically dressed men and women who ate raw fish and bathed together naked in public, while Japanese were put off by the hook-nosed, rude-mannered, smelly butter-eaters, who displayed affection publicly.

The attraction was erotic as well as exotic, as more open Japanese attitudes toward sex provided a welcome release from the Victorian era's repressed morality. As word spread around the world, the treaty ports became synonymous with guiltless fun. Sailors dreamed of the day their ship would dock in Yokohama with its fabulous Gankiroo, an exotic setting of buildings and gardens where women awaited visitors down the length of a wooden veranda. Another star attraction, called simply No. 9, was known for providing not only sexual amenities but also the best ham and eggs in town after midnight.

Initially the foreign settlements had the aura of unruly frontier boomtowns—especially Yokohama, the "Wild West of the Far East." Horses and riders raced up and down the streets in clouds of dust, pistols firing, while foreigners' houses were surrounded by wooden palisades against risk of attack from samurai still bitterly opposed to foreign intrusion. British and French garrisons arrived in the early 1860s to keep order. As time went on, the settlements came to resemble their counterparts on the coast of China, with white clapboard houses, clubs and hotels, cricket pitches and tennis courts. Inwardly, however, they remained culturally ambiguous places where the rules of neither Western nor Japanese society ever quite applied. In the treaty ports a foreigner could get away with a lot.

Their foreign denizens were mainly American, British and European. In a Nagasaki foreign cemetery, however, lies one Jean Couder, born in Quebec. After his father's death, Couder went with his mother to France and from there to sea. In 1862 he arrived in Nagasaki, where he opened a French restaurant and pastry shop. He remained for the rest of his life, becoming a bookkeeper for a foreign company and honorary secretary of the Nagasaki Bowling Club.

• • •

The 1860s were a tumultuous time, as Japanese grappled with how to respond to the shocking reality of foreigners on their doorstep. In 1868, to growing cries of *"Sonno Joi"* ("Revere the emperor and expel the barbarian"), young lower -ranking samurai from the southern clans rose in favour of what Shōin had been advocating: the supremacy of Japan's divine authority, the emperor, over its military ruler, the shogun. In the historic watershed that came to be known as the Meiji Restoration, the last shogun, Tokugawa Yoshinobu, was replaced by the Emperor Meiji, then a boy of 16 who was taken out of the seclusion in which he was kept in Kyoto and brought to Edo, the capital, newly named Tokyo.

The barbarian, however, was not expelled. Instead, everything was soon turned upside down as Japan's new Meiji leaders began bootstrapping their country into the modern world in the interests of self-preservation.

By the early 1870s, previously forbidden foreign ways were suddenly *de rigueur* as fashionable Japanese eagerly exchanged topknots for top hats, loose *haori* jackets for waistcoats, and wooden *geta* for lace-up shoes. Married women stopped blackening their teeth. And nothing became a Meiji dandy so much as a pocket watch, a pair of round, wire-rimmed glasses and a *kasa*, or umbrella.

Tokyo's Ginza district, with its newly erected red brick buildings, sidewalks and streetlamps, took on a distinct Boston and London air. The *kago*, or sedan chair, was edged out by Japan's first wheeled transportation, the *jinricksha*, while the new emperor made the first trip on the new railway line from Tokyo's Shinagawa station to Yokohama in 1872. New customs appeared as daring students downed beef in new Ginza restaurants. Beer challenged sake as the national drink and baseball began competing with sumo as the national sport. Western books flooded Tokyo bookstores as Japanese eagerly sought out the secrets of modern success.

Beneath the froth lay real change, as Japan's leaders set in motion an astonishing transformation of everything from the country's social structure, to its economy, to its place in the world. It was all a little too breathtaking for some, especially many former samurai who suddenly found themselves bereft of swords, status and function vis-à-vis the rising merchant class.

The process rattled along to an unsteady climax in 1887, when the prime minister, the charismatic Itō Hirobumi—another former Choshu samurai and one of the students who had removed Yoshida Shōin's body from the execution ground—gave a notorious masked ball at his large Western-style mansion. This so scandalized the public that a new mood of reaction and growing nationalism set in.

In the end much did change, although much also remained the same. And as the push-pull of modernization and tradition see-sawed through the Meiji era, it produced something the Western world had not seen before: a rapidly industrializing Asian power.

● ● ●

At the top of the Meiji wish list, not surprisingly, was a modern navy. Navies were the instruments of foreign encroachment. China had been opened by the British navy. Perry had entered Edo (Tokyo) Bay unimpeded because Japan did not have a navy capable of defending itself. For a model, Japan naturally turned to England, a small island nation that successfully ruled the seas—which was how Commander Archibald Lucius Douglas came to head a 35-man British mission invited to assist in modernizing the Japanese navy.

Douglas grew up on the broad expanse of the lower St. Lawrence River near Quebec City, where his Scottish-born father was in charge of the immigrant quarantine station on Grosse Isle. When Douglas was 14, his parents allowed him to enter training for the British Royal Navy. In 1873 31-year-old Commander Douglas arrived in Tokyo accompanied by his English wife, Constance ("Chum"), their two young children and a nanny, and set up housekeeping in *Mikawa-dai* or Riverside, their house in Tsukiji, Tokyo's foreign settlement.

From the beginning the Douglases were treated with great courtesy. He was received personally by the young Emperor Meiji, and when Chum produced a third child a few months later, they were presented with a Satsuma font, thoughtfully embellished with a salamander copied from the Douglas family crest. All the same, their first days were fraught with apprehension. Despite the vogue for things Western, anti-foreign feeling still ran high, and they frequently found themselves hissed at in the streets. Foreign women in particular were a great novelty, and Chum was disconcerted to feel her clothes being touched in the shops and streets, although she came to understand this had more to do with curiosity than hostility. Nonetheless, soon after their arrival Douglas wrote to the Admiralty requesting 34 revolvers. Whether he ever received them is unrecorded, but he is known to have slept with a loaded shotgun.

The Imperial Naval College, also located in Tsukiji with a branch farther down the coast at Yokosuka, was the brainchild of Katsu Kaishū. Another lower-ranking samurai, though from Edo rather than southern Japan, Katsu was as streetwise as Shōin had been headstrong. In 1855 he entered an elite naval academy in Nagasaki, where he soon came to the view that the answer to Perry's arrival was to build naval academies, hire men based on ability rather than birthright and lift the existing ban on construction of warships. In 1860 he captained the famed *Kanrin Maru*, the schooner that preceded the first official visit of a Japanese delegation abroad, to San Francisco. In the early 1860s he established a short-lived private naval academy in Kobe.

By the time Douglas met "Kats," as he knew him, the latter had become a national hero for the critical role he played in negotiating the bloodless surrender of Edo Castle to the emperor's supporters, thereby averting a bloody civil war. He then switched horses, taking the key role of navy minister in the new Meiji government.

British navy spit and polish and the code of the samurai did not initially mesh as well as might be supposed. "It is almost impossible," Douglas noted in a report to the British Admiralty at the end of the first year, "to establish and carry out a complete system with a people like the Japanese, to whom

LEFT Commander Archibald Lucius Douglas, who grew up in Quebec, led a British mission to modernize the Japanese navy in 1873. *Japanese paper cut in* Archibald C. Douglas, Life of Admiral Sir Archibald Lucius Douglas, *p. 79*

RIGHT Katsu Kaishū, hero of the Meiji Restoration and the minister of the navy in the new Meiji government. *Yokohama Archives of History, album of E. Sato, PA-106-13-8*

anything like Western order or discipline is so foreign." In an effort to establish common ground, he drew on the great British naval hero Admiral Horatio Nelson. "What would Nelson have done?" became the college's unofficial credo. An address given by one of Douglas's students shows how readily the Nelson spirit was absorbed.

> Therefore will we naval men one and all be diligent and work for our country's sake with the hope that there will arise in our midst many commanders as heroic as Nelson, that our navy may grow in size and importance, that true to her name, the England of the East, Japan, may indeed place herself on a par with England and send out hundreds of ships to all countries of the world; and that thus the glory of Japan may be made to shine like a light above the Universe.

Admiral Tōgō Heihachirō, shown inspecting the Seaforth Highlanders during a visit to Vancouver in 1911, was one of Archibald Douglas's pupils. *UBC Library, Rare Books and Special Collections, JCPC 1296*

Tōgō Heihachirō, one of Douglas's most promising pupils, went on to do just that, earning the title "Nelson of the East" for his decisive victory at the Battle of Tsushima in 1905, the defining moment of the Russo–Japanese War. Admiral Tōgō's rallying cry—"The fate of the empire depends upon this event. Let every man do his utmost!"—was an echo of Nelson's famous "England expects that every man will do his duty" on the eve of the Battle of Trafalgar.

Not all of Douglas's techniques were so well received. A college sports day provoked outrage in a country accustomed to thinking of traditional sports like archery and judo more as spiritual tests than games, as reflected in a skeptical letter to the newspaper from a well-versed English speaker who signed himself "Man on the Mountain."

> What outrageous thing is this item marked No. 9 in the programme? This two-headed, three-legged affair? Is this a prospective punishment for lads who may behave in a dissipated or wicked way hereafter, or is it perhaps a method for patching up two cripples from the war into one soldier . . . And again this 12th event, binding both a man's eyes and making him run a race in the dark? If it is desired to give the cadets some recreation after the examination, hire a few hundred ponies and let your pupils whip away gallantly for a good ride, or put them into a few score boats and let them disport themselves upon the sea.

Douglas had better luck introducing the game of soccer. The mission, however, soon ran into more serious difficulties. For one, it had problems being paid, as foreigners were reluctant to accept the newly minted Japanese yen, preferring instead the old common currency of the Pacific, the Mexican silver dollar. More fundamentally, the role of the mission itself was ambiguous. In his own British Empire–clouded mind, Douglas was "creating the modern Japanese navy." To his Japanese counterparts, still deeply suspicious of foreign intentions, he was a valued adviser, there to help develop curriculum and little more.

After two years, Douglas left for England to pursue his naval career, stopping off in Canada en route to visit family. The mission was dissolved and its members subsequently rehired on contract to the Japanese government, thereby dispelling any doubt as to who was in charge. This turn of events was deeply disappointing to the British minister to Japan, Harry Parkes. An old-school diplomat who had made his mark in China, the high-handed Sir Harry was the imperious representative of an imperial government that viewed placement of its nationals in key positions in the Meiji bureaucracy as a pathway to influence and commercial advantage.

Douglas ran into Parkes one hot summer day when he went to pay his farewell respects to the Japanese foreign minister.

> Go to the Foreign Office. Sir Harry not being there, sent in my card. While I am waiting the great little man comes in and flies into a passion and says he "won't present me in that dress—I ought to be in uniform" . . . I was properly dressed all in clean white, like everybody else, and I explained this to him, or tried to do so, but he was in such a rage that I could not get him to listen to me. The Foreign Minister then appeared and I see him, but when he sees me Parkes jumps out of the room. I make the interview as short as possible, and am met at the door by Parkes, white with rage and calling to me "begone sir, begone!"

Douglas went.

• • •

Japan and Canada in the last quarter of the 19th century could hardly have been more different—but they both attracted a similar kind of foreigner.

Archibald Douglas was an *oyatoi*, one of the hundreds of hired foreign advisers—military men and bureaucrats, engineers and architects, scientists and jurists—who poured into Japan during the 1870s and '80s in an unprecedented frenzy of cross-cultural borrowing.

Japan had, of course, actively borrowed for centuries, most notably from China. But its self-imposed seclusion policy came at a cost of missing out on the industrial revolution and Western technology, to which Perry's arrival provided an irrevocable introduction. There was a huge premium on playing catch-up. What was distinctive about the borrowing process this time was the alacrity with which Japan opened itself to foreign knowledge and expertise. It was Japan that sought out and hired foreign experts, and Japan that paid. Indeed, one of the main attractions for foreigners was that they were well remunerated, often receiving double what they could expect at home.

Those who responded were part of the larger phenomenon that saw thousands of people charge off to far-flung parts of the world, confident in the superiority of their own culture and determined to spread it. Typical of the breed was Henry Spencer Palmer, who cut his teeth in Canada before going on to modernize the port of Yokohama.

Born into a military family in Bangalore, Palmer was a child of empire. In 1858 he arrived in Victoria as part of an expedition of Royal Engineers, dispatched after the colony's governor, James Douglas, became alarmed by the number of Americans showing up in response to the gold rush. Designed to show the flag, establish order and prepare for future settlement, the force comprised experts of every trade and calling who laid the basis for transportation routes and townsites, as well as the first hospital, a printing office, public works and a meteorological observatory.

Described by his superiors as "an exceedingly clever young officer" and by a contemporary as "a regular swell," Palmer cut a swath through what would soon become the province of British Columbia. Over the course of five years he surveyed much of the Lower Mainland: the old Hudson's Bay Trail east from Fort Langley to Fort Colville in future Washington State via Lake Osoyoos; north from Harrington Lake to Lillooet and on to the gold fields of the Cariboo; as well as a possible alternative route to them from North Bentinck Arm via the Bella Coola River (incidentally the same general territory Ranald MacDonald explored at about the same time). When not on trails or wagon roads, he took part in local theatricals, contributed papers to the Royal Geographical Society and organized products for the colony's exhibit at the huge London International Exhibition in 1862.

One of the multi-talented Victorians who made the Empire tick, Palmer moved on to Sinai, where he surveyed the desert and became an Arabist. From there he went to New Zealand, where he transformed himself into an astronomer for observation of the Transit of Venus (which proved too cloudy to see); to Barbados, where he was bored; and to Hong Kong, where he drew up plans for the astronomical observatory.

While in Hong Kong he was approached by the Japanese government to assist with the design and construction of the first modern pressurized waterworks in Yokohama. He left the Royal Engineers and settled in Japan.

Built to Palmer's designs by Japanese engineers using metal pipe

Henry Spencer Palmer surveyed the future province of British Columbia in the late 1850s before modernizing the port of Yokohama in the 1880s.
BC Archives, HP003966

from England, the new system was a major feat in a city that stood in large part on land reclaimed from the sea. In 1887 Yokohama citizens let out a loud cheer as water poured from lion-headed cast-metal faucets along the roadways. The following year Palmer received a commission to turn Yokohama Harbour into a modern port, as well as requests to design water systems for other cities, including Osaka and Hakodate.

As useful as he was as an engineer, however, Palmer may have been even more valuable to his Meiji mentors as a journalist. An article he wrote for a British journal extolled Japan's progress in areas like law and the judiciary, while sympathizing with growing Japanese frustration over foreign unwillingness to reopen the unequal treaties struck at the end of the 1850s. Initially these had served both sides well, but their continued existence increasingly stuck in the Japanese craw, particularly the requirement to maintain low import tariffs, which undermined the government's capacity to raise revenue, as well as the inability to exercise legal jurisdiction over foreigners in the ports.

Palmer's article caught the eye of Japan's foreign minister, Count Inoue Kaoru, a man so seized of Japan's aspirations to be recognized as an equal that he built the extraordinary Rokumeikan, or Deer Cry Pavilion, a large Western-style building that opened near Hibiya Park in 1877. There, in an atmosphere resembling the elegant clubs of London and Paris, upper-class Japanese men in suits and women in flounces and bustles cavorted with foreigners in a steady round of dances, garden parties and charity bazaars designed to demonstrate just how "Westernized" Japanese society had become.

With Inoue's encouragement, Palmer became special Japan correspondent for the influential *Times* of London. While struggling with pipes and cement, he produced "Letters from the Land of the Rising Sun," a series of articles that gave the British their first real introduction to Japan while propagating the view that the treaties not only were fundamentally unfair but had long since served their purpose. In 1894 the British treaty was finally abandoned, replaced by a cozy alliance designed to counter growing Russian power in the Far East.

Palmer's story has an intriguing postscript. In 1987 his Canadian descendants went to Yokohama for the unveiling of a bust in his memory at the harbour. Taking advantage of the opportunity to visit Palmer's grave in the old foreign section of Tokyo's Aoyama Cemetery, they were surprised to find it decorated with fresh flowers. They then learned that Palmer had had two families: one with Mary Jane Pearson Wright, the young daughter of a Victoria archdeacon who had remained behind in England, and another with a Japanese woman, Saito Uta.

In the Meiji era, where the practice of second households existed among the upper classes well into the late 19th century, no one would have batted an eye. Descendants of the two families became friends.

• • •

Through all the upheaval, the underlying eccentricity and just plain whimsy of the treaty ports endured. For every hard-working *oyatoi* like Douglas and Palmer was an eccentric, a misfit, a drifter on the lam, a "remittance man" dispatched abroad with the best wishes of his family and a regular cheque, come to seek his fortune or simply find a new life in faraway Japan.

Richard Gordon Smith was a "huntin', shootin', fishin'" kind of Englishman who was sent abroad by his family after he failed the entrance examination for Sandhurst. He arrived in Quebec in the 1870s, where he is said to have roared through the winter landscape killing anything and everything in sight. After he returned to England, his marriage to a Montreal woman foundered and he decamped farther afield, this time finding his way to Japan.

By the time he arrived in Kobe in the late 1890s, there was a growing feeling that the treaty ports were no longer sufficiently Japanese to be interesting. Instead, he found himself what he called "a paper house" in the hills overlooking the bay. There he lived the life of an English country gentleman, even importing hunting dogs and training the local peasantry to serve as beaters. When not off shooting elephants in Burma and tigers in Johore, dallying with the tea-house girls or having himself tattooed, he set upon the local wildlife.

Amazingly, local authorities seem to have gone along with it all, requiring only that he keep track of the carnage.

"I wrote farewell letters to the Governor and Chief of Police," Gordon Smith recorded in his diary on the eve of one trip abroad, "and made out my game list: 289 snipe, 63 woodcock, 48 quail, 5 pheasants, 4 pigeons, 2 hares, 6 rails, 12 plovers, 6 ducks, 2 teal, 10 bitterns, 5 hawks and owls, 7 various. In addition, for want of a dog: 129 snipe, 5 woodcock, 7 quail."

Gordon Smith became a collector of specimens and curios for the British Museum and a transcriber of Japanese folk tales.

MISSIONS AND MOUNTAINS

Meanwhile, the Meiji era attracted still another kind of foreigner with a different perspective on newly opening Japan: the Christian missionary.

In 1873, the same year Archibald Douglas arrived to assist in modernizing the Japanese navy, Alexander Shaw of Toronto was camping out at the Daisho-ji, or Great Tree Temple, in Tokyo's Mita district. Disillusioned with the Tsukiji foreign settlement, with its foreign-style houses and foreign-style people, he had quietly slipped away into "the real Japan." There, among the priests and the gongs and the *shōji* screens, he had the great fortune to be discovered by Fukuzawa Yukichi.

Recognizable today as the man on the 10,000-yen note, Fukuzawa embodied the Meiji spirit. As a young interpreter on the first official Japanese visits to America and Europe in the early 1860s, he soaked up everything from Western dress and table manners to military organization and systems of taxation. *Things Western (Seiyu Jijo)*, the 10-volume series he turned out between 1867 and 1870, was so influential that for a time all works about the West were popularly known as *Fukuzawa-bon*.

He was the originator of *Bunmei Kaika* ("Civilization and Enlightenment"), the catchphrase that became the new Meiji mantra. He was the founder of Keio Gijuku, the leading institution of Western learning and the forerunner of prestigious Keio University. His newspaper, *Jiji Shimpo*, was an important platform for reformist views. Born into a class that scorned commerce—his own father considered it abominable that his children should learn mathematics, the tool of merchants—he was also instrumental in persuading young samurai to turn tradition on its head and enter trade.

On the lookout for interesting young foreigners, Fukuzawa invited Shaw to join his household on the grounds of a magnificent former feudal estate overlooking Tokyo Bay to tutor his two elder sons and teach ethics at Keio. The years Shaw spent there, from 1874 to 1877, coincided with some of Fukuzawa's most important writing.

If Fukuzawa had come across Shaw a year earlier, he might not have extended such an invitation. The period immediately following the 1868 Restoration had been one of great turmoil and personal insecurity; an era of spies, conspirators and assassins, with no telling when a murderous blade might suddenly thrust up through the *tatami* mats. Openly espousing foreign ideas in the early 1870s could still be dangerous, and Fukuzawa had feared for his own life more than once. Nor did early Meiji-era interest in foreign things extend to foreign religion, which remained strictly prohibited. And Alexander Shaw was not only a graduate of the University of Toronto's Trinity College, but also a Christian missionary, a recent recruit into the British Society for the Propagation of the Gospel.

Fukuzawa Yukichi in 1860 as a young samurai. He became a leading Meiji-era modernizer. *Keio University, Fukuzawa Memorial Center for Modern Japanese Studies*

The ground shifted in 1872 after a high-level Japanese mission returned from abroad convinced that the unequal treaties would never be abolished until Christians were allowed to operate freely in Japan. The old notice boards banning Christianity came down, though officially it remained proscribed.

It was not much, but it was enough for the churches, to whom it seemed natural that Japan, as it took on the material trappings of Western civilization,

TOP Fukuzawa Yukichi (bottom right) and other members of the *Kanrin Maru*, which sailed to San Francisco in 1860. *Keio University, Fukuzawa Memorial Center for Modern Japanese Studies*

ABOVE Fukuzawa Yukichi (second left) with colleagues at Keio Gijuku, the forerunner of prestigious Keio University, in 1873, the year he and Alexander Shaw met. *Keio University, Fukuzawa Memorial Center for Modern Japanese Studies*

would also adopt the religion that went with it. Not only would Japan's conversion simply be a matter of time, but Japan would serve as a launching pad for the spread of Christianity throughout Asia.

To be fair, some early Japanese reformers thought along similar lines. Fukuzawa was not among them. An intensely Japanese modernizer, he was interested in adopting those aspects of Western civilization most useful for Japan while discarding the rest. To him, Shaw's Christianity was a possibly intriguing but largely irrelevant factor. Fukuzawa was interested in Shaw as a teacher, an Exhibit A for his curious Keio students—an example of an educated, morally upright, serious Western gentleman.

Such people were not easy to come by in the treaty ports. Deserters from the navy, stowaways from European taverns, bankrupt rogues from the open ports of China and discharged clerks from custom houses was how the well-known educator Nitobe Inazō once dismissed the ports' dominant population, expressing doubt there was even a single Christian among them. For Fukuzawa, the unexpected discovery of Shaw at the temple was a coup.

● ● ●

Meanwhile, the Meiji siren song also reached the Methodists. In the spring of 1873, Toronto's huge Metropolitan Methodist Church reverberated with hymns and prayers as the congregation wished George Cochran, their own minister, and Davidson McDonald, a young medical doctor, Godspeed on their mission to Japan.

There was nothing remarkable about the two men's decision to become missionaries. Churchgoing and religious revival meetings were the stuff of late-19th-century Canadian life. More curious was their choice of destination, as it is doubtful they had more than the vaguest idea of where Japan was and what it was about.

News at the time travelled slowly, typically by sailing ship to San Francisco and across the United States to Chicago and on to Toronto, where it occasionally showed up in the *Toronto Globe*, typically under the heading "China." One March 1873 snippet, however, would have made Cochran and McDonald sit up and take notice. "A special edict tolerating Christianity through Japan has been promulgated," it read, "and it is determined to throw the whole country open to foreigners."

By then Japan was also creeping into the collective Canadian consciousness for another reason. For if Canadians in the second half of the 19th century were susceptible to old-fashioned missionary fever, they were also increasingly susceptible to the gleam of newfangled steam engines and track. A resolution adopted by the Methodists in 1871 was a mind-bending muddle of railway enthusiasm and missionary zeal.

> (Resolved) that the opening and probable increase of Railway communications to the Pacific Coast, and the rapid progress of Railway construction in Japan itself, thereby bringing commercial relations, clearly indicate that this is the time and that the country, containing as it does forty millions of inhabitants, to which it is the duty of this society to send an Agent or Agents for the salvation of the destitute Japanese, a people most interesting in themselves, and having strong claims on our sympathy and efforts.

So it was that McDonald and Cochran set out for Japan with their dreams, their wives and, in Cochran's case, two young daughters.

• • •

Yokohama, as it turned out, was a place for some—but not for them. Once a quiet fishing village separated by a swamp from Japan's main north–south artery, the Tokaido, it had been a convenient place to stash prying for-eigners when the treaty ports opened. Now it was a wild, anything-goes, get-rich-quick boomtown of a thousand people, its streets swarming with pencil-sharp businessmen in search of a deal, rowdy sailors carousing tipsily from grog shop to grog shop, gaily dressed young women in kimonos and young ex-samurai looking for their first contact with a foreigner and some English lessons.

In Yokohama there were plenty of souls to be saved, foreign as well as Japanese, and many missionaries were content to remain there. Not so McDonald and Cochran, who immediately began scheming to get out of it.

McDonald had the first break when he received an offer to teach farther down the coast in Shizuoka. Famed for its tea and oranges, it was where the last shogun retired with 6,000 former samurai following the 1868 Restoration. Anxious to regain power and influence, the Tokugawa were also among those most determined to embrace Western education. Indeed, it was

Archibald Douglas's mentor Katsu Kaishū, the former Tokugawa retainer turned Meiji minister of the navy, who urged them to seek foreign assistance in establishing a school.

In the spring of 1874, McDonald set off on the two-day, hundred-mile journey over the mountains in a cavalcade reminiscent of a woodblock print. McDonald himself rode in front with his Japanese sponsor, Mr. Hitomi, on horseback, accompanied by a sword-bearing guard and two men in *jinricksha*. His wife followed behind kneeling in a *kago*, or enclosed sedan chair, which spared her the curiosity of onlookers but deprived her of seeing much of the beautiful scenery around Mount Fuji.

On arrival they set up housekeeping in a Buddhist temple, accompanied by a young prince of the Tokugawa family, moving later to a stone house built for them on the grounds of Shizuoka Castle. There the kindly, upstanding Dr. McDonald taught physics, chemistry, natural history and English, while Mrs. McDonald taught English, knitting and music. In the afternoon he saw patients; in the evenings, when not pressed into tending the sick and dispensing medicines, he studied Japanese.

Though not formally permitted to proselytize, in practice no one stopped him. Soon McDonald was conducting what were said to be the largest Christian meetings taking place anywhere in Japan at the time, drawing audiences of 500 or more, which he kept track of by counting the pairs of wooden *geta* at the door.

George Cochran also soon managed to escape Yokohama, thanks to an invitation from Nakamura Masanao (Keiu), a prominent Confucian scholar and one of the first Japanese intellectuals to convert to Christianity. A member of the Tokugawa entourage in Shizuoka, Nakamura was a professor of Chinese studies at Tokyo Imperial University and the translator of two books immensely popular at the time, *On Liberty* by John Stuart Mill and *Self-Help*, a small volume by the popular Scottish pundit Samuel Smiles. A member, like Fukuzawa, of a leading reformist intellectual group, the Meirokusha Six, Nakamura opened his own outstanding school of Western studies, the Dojinsha, in 1874. In 1875 he founded Tokyo Women's Normal Higher School, which became Ochanomizu University. Cochran and his family moved into a foreign-style house on Nakamura's property.

It must have been exhilarating: there, arrayed before him, were bright young men of the early Meiji era, anxious to learn all they could about Western civilization while picking up the new passport to success, the English

Davidson McDonald (front row centre) and George Cochran (front row far right), with Japanese and Canadian colleagues in 1889. *United Church of Canada Archives*

language. To his students Cochran would have seemed the perfect *sensei*, or revered teacher. Tall and serious, with a long beard and strong moral bent, he personified an ideal cross between a Christian educator and a Confucian sage.

• • •

It was a remarkably productive beginning. All three—Shaw, McDonald and Cochran—had been among the first missionaries to arrive following the 1868 Restoration. They had escaped the treaty ports. And they had linked up with some of the most influential personalities of early Meiji Japan.

Conversions, however, were few, never more than a few hundred thousand. Indeed, Christians in Japan never exceeded more than 1 percent of the population, and of that only one-third was Protestant. Numbers alone do not tell the whole story, for among those who did embrace Christianity were some influential Japanese politicians, educators and reformers. But the massive shift that many assumed was around the corner did not materialize.

VOL. XIV.—No. 13.　　MONTREAL, SATURDAY, OCTOBER 7, 1876.　　{ SINGLE COPIES, TEN CENTS.
{ $4 PER YEAR IN ADVANCE.

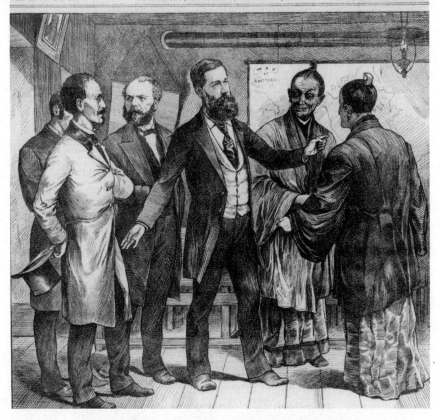

A visit by French and Japanese educators to Canada in 1876 made the cover of the *Canadian Illustrated News*—the Japanese visitors depicted more exotically than the Meiji-era gentlemen they undoubtedly were. *Library and Archives Canada, C-64605*

· Christian morality had some appeal to Confucian-trained former samurai like Nakamura, although his conversion proved short-lived. Foreign religion, however, was not like foreign things that could be adopted and let go of at will. Nor was Christian theology an easy fit in a society where spiritual values were rooted in the family, the community and the state. More ecumenical in their religious attitudes, many Japanese also viewed Christianity as an addition to indigenous religions, tending, as the saying goes, to "be born Shinto, marry Christian and die Buddhist."

At the same time, the novelty aspect of Christianity wore off, especially as the wave of more secular teachers, technicians and advisers swept into Japan in the late 1870s and '80s. Here was living proof that Japan could adopt the material side of Western culture without necessarily buying into its religion. Any prospect of large-scale conversion was ultimately doomed by the importation of the debate sparked by Huxley and Darwin over the theory of evolution. Indeed, if a popular taste could be discerned in the clash of ideas that ricocheted through the 1880s, it was for the doctrine of material progress and the natural evolution of nations reflected in famous late-19th-century philosopher Herbert Spencer's concept of "survival of the fittest" (*Yusho Reppai*, or "superior wins, inferior loses"), put into a Japanese context by the influential historian and journalist Tokutomi Sohō.

Few anticipated the extent to which Japan would naturally look to its own traditions as the rallying focus for modernization. When the long-awaited Japanese constitution finally made its debut in 1889, it was a German-influenced instrument that rested on the concepts of the emperor's divinity (*tennosai*) and the spirit of the nation (*kokutai*), which Prime Minister Itō rationalized as recognizing the role that religion played in Japanese society, similar to that played by Christianity in Europe and America.

Having set out to help change Japan, the three missionaries soon found themselves changing as they became swept up in the massive Meiji transformation machine.

McDonald left Shizuoka after a few years for New York to attend a famous institute for treatment of eye diseases, a significant problem at the time in Japan. Following his return he spent most of his life as a prominent Tokyo doctor. While he retained ties to the Methodists, when he eventually died there was surprise in the foreign community that the good doctor had ever been a missionary.

An increasingly frustrated George Cochran soon despaired of converting the intelligent but skeptical Dojinsha students. "The Japanese politeness to foreigners is only a mask," he ranted in one unhappy moment in 1877.

Under it there is a deep hatred to foreigners and their religion. There is spread abroad through England and America a most absurd and false idea of the civilization and progress of Japan which it will take some time to correct. The longer a man lives here, the more closely he comes to know the native character, the more thoroughly does he learn that they are false at the core, just as might be expected of a nation so long bound up in superstition and moral night.

By then ill as well as discouraged, Cochran returned to Canada in 1879. Like McDonald, however, he could not stay away. After a few years he was back, this time with a new focus on education as the Meiji authorities began looking to missionaries to help meet the growing need for English-speaking educators. Taking a leaf from Nakamura's book, Cochran opened the Canadian Methodists' own school in 1884. Located in Tokyo's Azabu district on the premises of a former brewery, the Tōyō Eiwa became one of the main preparatory institutions for young men hoping to get into Tokyo Imperial University or to study abroad.

Methodist missionary Daniel Norman (far right) and friends on a bicycle trip to the great Dai-Butsu in the ancient capital of Kamakura, south of Tokyo, in the 1890s.
United Church of Canada Archives, 2000.017P/2683N

Following the Japanese government's decision in 1889 to limit foreign religious teaching in schools for boys, the Tōyō Eiwa languished and finally closed. Undeterred, the Methodists plunged in further, joining in 1906 with some American colleagues to develop Kwansei Gakuin, a liberal arts and business college in Kobe.

The shift to education did not mean the end of the proselytizing spirit, which was personified by another Torontonian, the indefatigable Charles Eby, who joined McDonald and Cochran in 1876. He immediately set out for Yamanashi Prefecture, where curious crowds turned out to Buddhist temples to hear his "thunder, big guns, strong shot and heaviest artillery," as he variously described his fervent addresses in his journal.

Conditions, however, were trying, particularly from the standpoint of transportation, as rural Japan was still largely without roads. "Riding in *kangos* [sic] is not the easiest operation in the world," Eby observed. "You have to double yourself up like a jack-knife, and stow yourself in a clothes basket with the sides out, and then be jogged along suspended from a pole carried on the shoulders of two coolies. It is certainly an improvement on railriding but only one removed." He bought himself a horse.

Eby also soon found the intellectual debate raging in Tokyo more to his taste. Returning to the capital, he launched himself on the lecture circuit,

The main library at Kwansei Gakuin near Kobe, which became a prestigious university in 1932. *United Church of Canada Archives, 1999.0549/34N*

giving orations on history, philosophy, ethics and science designed to stave off the Darwinists. He also edited a newspaper, the *Chrysanthemum*, directed toward the Japanese intelligentsia. This was only the beginning. In 1884 he produced a pamphlet calling for a national Christian university that would rival Tokyo Imperial University—"the brain of Japan"—at a cost of $2 million, to be provided by foreign philanthropists and supported by a force of a hundred evangelists.

Back in Toronto, the church fathers began to worry; Brother Eby was getting out of hand. "I send you a copy of a pamphlet just received from Mr. Eby, from which you will see that he is at least a brother of very large ideas," one wrote to another.

> His plans may appear somewhat visionary, but after all, there is a splendid audacity about the brother which one cannot help admiring. Perhaps in this as in other matters the remark may hold good, that the arrow aimed at the clouds goes higher than if aimed at a bush. It is to be hoped, however, that this good brother will not go so high as to disappear altogether. His boundless enthusiasm is a grand thing in an evangelist, but a little ballast would be a great blessing just now.

Eby kept right on aiming. Returning to Canada he convinced 14 young men and women to go to Japan as part of his "Light Brigade." He also raised enough funds from Canadian and Japanese supporters to begin construction of a large building near Tokyo Imperial University.

A circular structure with turrets on top, the Central Tabernacle was vaguely reminiscent of something out of *Arabian Nights*. Church fathers feared it would become the architectural freak of Tokyo. It did not, but neither did it prove the fulfillment of Eby's dreams. As the Methodists became mired in the financial woes of paying for the tabernacle, Eby's star sank. In 1895 he left Japan and went to western Canada.

• • •

Meanwhile, Alexander Shaw embarked in quite a different direction. Like Cochran at the Dojinsha, he soon grew frustrated over his inability to make headway with the skeptical students at Keio—where, he once observed, "the most advanced opinions on all subjects are held, and in which Mr. Mill's and Mr. Spencer's writings are used as textbooks."

With the help of the British Legation, which made him an honorary chaplain, he obtained permission to live in nearby Shiba district on the southern edge of the city, the traditional gateway through which foreigners and foreign goods passed on their way to Tokyo.

There, in 1876, Shaw built St. Andrew's Church. In a country that preferred wood, he opted for brick gothic. Imported stained glass covered the windows, while the choir was dressed in surplices from France. Outward appearances, however, were deceiving. In Shiba, Shaw carved out a hybrid existence, gathering around him a group of adherents in paternal fashion, loosely modelled on a Japanese feudal household. He also adopted a Japanese son, Imai Toshimichi John, and began grooming him as his successor.

Where Protestantism tended to challenge Japanese society, Anglicanism was inclined to accept it more or less as it was. In Shiba, Shaw ministered to the British and Japanese anglophile elite in much the same way that the Church of England served English society. Where the Anglican prayer book referred to the queen, the Japanese translation substituted the emperor. Some leading Meiji-era personalities—Koizumi Shinzo, tutor to the crown prince and a future president of Keio; Ozaki Yukio, the future father of parliamentary government; Inamata Kozu, a leader of the Socialist Party—attended the church, as did Fukuzawa's daughters.

Fukuzawa himself was not a churchgoer. His view of Christianity, like his view of Western civilization generally, was essentially utilitarian. At times he railed against foreign missionaries, claiming they were spies. At others he advocated the adoption of Christianity, if only for the sake of appearances. A candid editorial in his newspaper in 1885 may come closest to reflecting his perspective.

> We cannot persuade Shintoists to change their views, but we can tell them that they should look at the ascendancy of Christianity in our country as an event in the natural order of things, and that for the sake of the country they should refrain from disturbances. We do not propose that a majority of our people should become Christians, a small proportion would be enough. All that is necessary is to accept the name of a Christian country.

Nor did Fukuzawa and Shaw see the world in the same light. An iconoclast by nature, Fukuzawa did not hesitate to strike down those aspects of Japanese tradition that he considered no longer served a useful purpose. At Keio he replaced the Confucian underpinnings of traditional samurai education in favour of an approach anchored in mathematics, logic and individualism. He also outlawed time-honoured traditions like formal gift-giving to teachers, as well as the student proclivity for scribbling on *shōji* screens. Shaw, in contrast, was an arch-conservative, a man descended from a well-placed Toronto family of colonial military background with an innate distaste for modern ideas, though he accepted the theory of evolution.

Despite their differences, however, the two remained friends. Shaw continued to teach at Keio well into the mid-1880s when English teaching was entrusted to other Trinity College graduates. It was probably also Fukuzawa who encouraged Shaw's abiding interest in the unequal treaties, which he felt interfered with the natural development of human relations. Like Henry Palmer, Shaw became an active proponent of their demise, even drawing up a petition favouring the Japanese position that was signed by all British missionaries in Tokyo.

It took courage to cut across the interests of the foreign merchants, and the symbolism was not lost. When Shaw left the country in 1894 he was given an impressive send-off. Fukuzawa Yukichi was there, as were the president of Tokyo Imperial University and a former governor of Tokyo. Following his death in 1902, his wife received a gift from the emperor of 1,000 yen, more than Shaw had made in a year.

• • •

Today Alexander Shaw is less known for his church than as the discoverer of Karuizawa, the mountain village that became Japan's premier mountain resort.

When he first came across it in the 1880s, Karuizawa was a small stopping point on the Nakasendo, the ancient road travelled by feudal lords through the mountains connecting Edo with the Japan Sea. Since fallen into decline, it was an idyllic spot beneath Mount Asama, a perfect retreat from the oppressive heat and humidity of a Tokyo summer. In Canadian fashion, Shaw built himself a summer cottage.

A few years later, Hatta Yujiro, a naval captain and future member of Japan's House of Representatives, was vacationing at a nearby hot spring. Shocked to find himself served beef one day, he learned on inquiry that it came from the other side of the mountain. Curious, he set off and soon found about 20 foreigners living in the woods.

Archdeacon Alexander Croft Shaw is best remembered today as the founder of Karuizawa, the resort in the Japan Alps where the present emperor courted the empress on the tennis court.

Courtesy of the late Mrs. Elizabeth Grandy, Shaw's granddaughter

Taken by the refreshing air as well as by the opportunity to converse with foreigners, Hatta joined them. Other upper-class Japanese followed. When the railway broke through Usui Pass in the mid-1890s, Karuizawa blossomed. The ultimate in casual international elegance, it was a lively place where foreign businessmen, diplomats and missionaries mixed with Japanese politicians, businessmen and writers—a microcosm of the kind of cosmopolitan Japan that Western and Japanese reformers dreamed of, without the vices of Yokohama.

What all of this cross-cultural communion meant to the participants themselves is impossible to say. Perspectives were certainly different. For Shaw and his contemporaries, mountains were places for recreation and socializing, a welcome respite from the inevitable stresses of living in another culture, a place to breathe different air. For Japanese, mountains were sacred places, the traditional home of the *kami*, the divine spirits of the Shinto religion.

All the same, it is difficult to imagine that as they roamed the lush mountain landscape around Karuizawa, dotted with temples and little shrines to Inari, the rice god, foreigners did not come to some appreciation of the Japanese sense of God (or gods) in nature. Increasingly, they and their Japanese friends also had something in common: a shared nostalgia for the loss of the natural landscape in the face of growing industrialization and urbanization. By the late 19th century the traditional Judeo-Christian view of nature as something to be feared and subdued was accompanied by a sense that it should be revered and, where possible, protected—although where the balance came out between the subduing and the preserving has remained a challenge.

Foreigners arriving in Japan were entranced by the richness of the landscape and the Japanese sense of living in harmony with nature, even if the latter frequently felt the improving hand of humankind. In their eyes Japan was a hitherto unseen garden filled with exotic flowers and foliage and exquisite vistas. The sentiments that drew them to the English Romantics like Wordsworth or Shelley, Thoreau's *Walden, or Life in the Woods* or the national parks movement would also have been understood by many Japanese, the more so because their own march to industrialization was so rapid.

Hatta, who headed the Karuizawa Residents' Association for many years, perhaps put it best. When asked toward the end of his life what Karuizawa meant to him, he wrote three Chinese characters: *Bet-ten-chi*, "a different heaven and earth"—a kind of paradise.

● ● ●

Beyond the warmth and congeniality of Karuizawa lay the long mountainous backbone of the Japanese interior, which drew growing numbers of missionaries from 1890 onward. In part the trend simply responded to dwindling demand for foreign teachers in the cities, coupled with the removal of restrictions on internal travel. Rural life also appealed to those who came from rural backgrounds themselves. But it was more than that. As time went on, some missionaries found themselves identifying less with the architects of Meiji reform than with those affected by its social and economic fallout.

Less a bottom-up revolution than a top-down change in oligarchies, the 1868 Meiji Restoration had the effect of concentrating wealth and power in the hands of a small Tokyo elite at the expense of millions of dispossessed samurai, peasants, craftsmen and merchants who continued to labour under high taxes and demanding landlords. Nor was the reformist spirit confined to cities. Discoveries of "people's constitutions" tucked away in old barns and buildings testify to the extent to which Meiji-era aspirations radiated beyond the capital. Awash in agricultural revolts, rural Japan in the 1880s saw the emergence of an incipient "People's Movement" aimed at securing a better deal for those at the lower end of the socio-economic ladder, frustrations that were later channelled into growing nationalism.

Still locked in tradition and instinctively suspicious of foreigners, rural Japan was not propitious territory for a missionary. Life was difficult, and the prospects for proselytizing more so. Nagano, a favourite of Canadian Methodists and Anglicans, was a poor and rugged region high in the Japan Alps—and the headquarters of Nichiren Buddhism. But it was a progressive area, one of the first to shift into silk cultivation and home to several prominent Japanese social and economic reformers.

Nagano also had a salubrious climate, something that could not be said of the far side of the Japan Alps near the Sea of Japan, where the cold Siberian winds swept down, plunging the region into rain and snow. This was *ura Nihon*, the back side of Japan, not a place where most Japanese could envisage themselves living. Some Canadians did. Percy and Ruth Powles, graduates of McGill University, arrived in 1916 and spent much of their lives as Anglican missionaries in Takada (now Jōetsu City), deep in the mountains where life was hard and snowdrifts could reach 15 feet high. They and their children lived in a Japanese house, ate Japanese food and spoke Japanese at home. Japanese callers sat on the floor while Westerners sat on chairs.

Another Canadian Anglican attracted to the interior was Heber Hamilton, a University of Toronto graduate who spent most of his life in the country's mountainous midsection stretching from Nagoya to Niigata

"Canadians crossing oceans" is the theme of this Japanese family crest, or *mon*, designed for a kimono presented to Percival and Ruth Powles in 1927 by the mayor of Takada. Three generations of the Powles family were associated with Japan.
Courtesy of the late John Powles, Michelle Brazeau and the Powles family.

A pilgrim band on Mount Ontake, one of Heber Hamilton's photographs in the influential book by Walter Weston that helped open the Japan Alps to mountaineering. *Walter Weston, Mountaineering and Exploration in the Japanese Alps, 1896, p. 273, Library and Archives Canada, NL-22295*

on the Japan Sea. He and his associates established a school for the blind in Gifu, as well as one of Japan's first mountain sanitoriums for the treatment of tuberculosis.

Hamilton was also drawn to the high mountain peaks, which in Meiji times were still largely untrodden territory except for a few religious pilgrims, bear hunters and "mountain folk." As with Switzerland, it was the British who opened up the Alps and made them famous. *Mountaineering and Exploration in the Japanese Alps*, a book by English cleric and mountain climber Walter Weston, caused a sensation in Japan and abroad when it was published in 1896. Hamilton accompanied Weston on his travels and took some of the photographs that made the mountains, and Weston, famous.

In the 1930s, Kenneth Kirkwood, one of Canada's first diplomats in Japan, came across Hamilton's tracks. Another Canadian attracted to the mountains, Kirkwood liked to roam the lofty peaks and remote valleys, where he wrote sentimental sonnets to the scenery. In an inn in Kamikochi, deep in mountain country, he was shown a logbook recording Weston and Hamilton as the region's first foreign visitors.

That evening Kirkwood shared a hut at the foot of Mount Yariga-tate, "Japan's Matterhorn," with Komanji Kanujo, the grandson of the Japanese guide who had conducted Weston and Hamilton over the mountains. Huddled in the hut around a hibachi, the air thick with woodsmoke and the wind and rain rattling outside, he and the Japanese climbers reminisced about the early days. Kirkwood commemorated the occasion in verse.

Sessho Hut

Storm of wind and rain has brought us here
In Sessho hut—close, underneath the peak
Of that stark mountain whose high crest we seek
Waiting for storm to cease and skies to clear.
Within the hut, in gloom and smarting smoke
We warm ourselves at charcoal fire and speak
Of mountain climbs, and while the dark coals reek,
Tell of how Weston first those rough trails broke;
And how with Hamilton he scaled these mountain heights;
And as stormbound we sit, thus ill-confined,
I think in isolation we may find
In Sessho hut some warmth of heart, and lights
Of mountains' fellowship. Though stormbound we,
Note here this friendship in adversity.

NO GEISHA

In Japanese, *no* means "our." And the young Canadian women who began pouring into Japan from the 1880s onward had nothing in common with the geisha stereotype, except perhaps their relative independence.

Straightlaced and stiff-collared, they were daughters of the prosperous middle classes of small-town Ontario and Atlantic Canada. Why they went to someplace halfway around the world about which they and their families knew practically nothing says much about the pull of the missionary movement at the time. But the call of God, if that was all it was, could presumably have been satisfied closer to home.

The decision to go all the way to Japan hints at something more: an interest in a wider world inspired by education, perhaps; most were graduates of recently established women's colleges and teacher-training schools. The new Canadian Pacific route to Japan and the lure of travel advertising probably played a role, as did the exotic view of Japan and Japanese womanhood. One young woman admitted she was inspired to go to Japan after seeing woodblock prints at the 1889 world's fair in Paris.

For some, the motivation may have been simple escape. Going to Japan at the time was highly unusual, but it was also one of the few ways a respectable woman could break free of the narrow life of the day, with its stifling social regimen and rigid domesticity. And for those whose future did not lie in marriage, it was an alternative to another destiny as that now-almost-forgotten family institution, the live-in maiden aunt.

• • •

Martha Cartmell arrived in Japan in 1882 accompanied by a coal-oil stove, several changes of clothing, a desk, cooking utensils and some books—along

Martha Cartmell founded a popular girls' school in Tokyo in 1884. *United Church of Canada Archives, 76.001P/929N*

with the blessings of the ladies' missionary society of Hamilton, Ontario, and a well-filled purse.

Cartmell was off to "the land of the geisha," the most powerful Japanese image in the foreign mind next to Mount Fuji. In her colourful kimono, lacquered hair and high wooden *geta*, the geisha (literally artist or "beauty person") was never understood very well by foreigners, but she personified everything enticing and ultimately unknowable about Japan. For men reared in the Victorian era, she was a positive sensation.

Japan was also the land of the geisha's polar opposite, the "Good Wife and Wise Mother." A reinvention of the traditional Confucian doctrine of the "three obediences"—to father in youth, husband after marriage and son in old age—the GWWM was the Meiji ideal and her role was to mould the next generation of Japanese men.

Like many of her contemporaries, Cartmell was inherently critical of the position of women in Japanese society generally, believing it to be the root cause of the country's social ills, notably widespread prostitution. "Japanese women," she bemoaned in a letter home soon after arrival, were "unwelcome at birth, untaught in childhood, enslaved when married, accursed as widows, and unlamented when they died"—thereby summing up much of the worst that foreigners could possibly say on the subject.

A point on which reform-minded foreigners and Japanese could agree, however, was that the future lay in raising the status of women through education. While some bold steps in this direction were taken in the early 1870s, progress was slow, much slower than with boys. Suddenly in the 1880s, female education took on new cachet. It was the era of the Rokumeikan, the large building near Hibiya Park that was Foreign Minister Inoue's monument to Western style and comportment. Young Japanese women whose families

Students and faculty of the Tōyō Eiwa Jo Gakkō in 1886. The school was the beginning of a long and productive Canadian involvement in the development of female education in Japan that came to encompass other schools, kindergartens, orphanages, training institutions and universities. *United Church of Canada Archives, 1999.054P/43*

hoped them to marry up-and-coming men and raise up-and-coming sons required exposure to Western education and social graces.

Seizing the moment, Cartmell decided to open her own school in 1884 with the assistance of three Japanese male benefactors who held formal title to the property. Located in Tokyo's Azabu district next to the Canadian Methodist–run school for boys, the Tōyō Eiwa Jo Gakkō offered education akin to an Ontario boarding school of the day, with additional classes in Japanese and Chinese. Before long it was the "snob school" of Tokyo, not least because it accepted only paying pupils, thereby ensuring both financial solvency and social status. Even after the empress opened her own school the following year, the Canadian-run institution remained popular. Ushiba Tazu, a high-school student there when the Westernization craze was at its peak, recalled the era this way:

> When I was a young girl it was the period of the Rokumeikan. I commuted to Tōyō Eiwa Girls School wearing Western-style dresses. My mother was very progressive, and in growing up I never wore the

shimada hair style. At school with me were . . . the mother of the present Mr Kido [Marquis Kido, the emperor's close adviser before the Second World War] and the daughter of Prince Itō. Japan at that time was similar to today—it was quite Westernized. Dr. Takaki used to tell us, "Kimonos for Japanese women are no good. You must eat about a pound of meat a day."

The daughter of a prominent Japanese businessman and politician, young Tazu went on to marry the son of a leading Japanese silk merchant in New York.

All the same, Cartmell seems an unlikely role model for young Japanese women. For one thing she was unmarried, a living example of the ability of women to survive and prosper on their own. In a world governed by the doctrine of the Good Wife and Wise Mother she was quite manifestly neither. Still, there was something about her that appealed. Perhaps the gulf between spartan Victorian and samurai-inspired values was not as great as might be supposed.

What ultimately made her most acceptable, however, was probably that she was safe. Japanese parents wanted a Western education for their daughters without them actually becoming Westernized. Daring upper-class Japanese wives might kick up their heels for their country at the Rokumeikan, but their daughters would not learn the steps to the waltz from the Methodists, for whom dancing, along with gambling and card playing, was strictly forbidden.

● ● ●

Part of that strange phenomenon, the 19th-century lady missionary, the women who followed Martha Cartmell to Japan also bore a striking resemblance to that even stranger phenomenon, the intrepid 19th-century lady traveller.

They were rough contemporaries of Isabella Bird, the English globetrotter par excellence celebrated for her spectacular travels off the beaten track. The rigours of the Japanese interior proved too much, however, even for her. Venturing into the little-trodden region north of Tokyo in 1877, she found it eternally damp, bug-infested and depressing. Ill-tempered horses stumbled, kicked and rocked like camels on roads that dwindled into bridle paths and slithered across log bridges and into quagmires. Villages gradually degenerated into collections of huts with impoverished inhabitants.

Subsisting on a diet of rice mush, old eggs, sago (an edible palm starch) and cucumbers, Bird's health deteriorated and she contracted a permanent wet chill. Feet and hands swelled horribly from horsefly bites and hornet stings. Inns that promised refuge instead reeked of sour sewage. Her privacy was shattered by holes poked through rice-paper walls by crowds of people trying to catch a glimpse of her—perhaps understandably, for she insisted on travelling with an inflatable rubber bath. At night she shivered in wet clothes, listening to rats gnaw her boots while trying to get some sleep amid the din of singing and carousing and visits from local policemen demanding to see her passport.

At the end of it all Bird admitted that, for the most part, the journey had left her just plain unnerved, conscious that beneath the apparent order of her surroundings was something raw, alien to her understanding. This was not the willow-pattern pretty Japan of the postcards, or even the modern Japan of the white-gloved railway stationmasters. It was late feudal Japan, still backward, poor and xenophobic. It was the *inaka*, the countryside, even further distant from Tokyo culturally than it was geographically, the equivalent in Canadian terms of the bush, the boondocks, the back of beyond.

Canadian women who ventured into similar territory in the mountainous regions beyond Tokyo reported similar experiences, though with rather fewer complaints; perhaps the Japanese interior sat better with those familiar with the rigours of early Canada than with someone from London. Hannah Lund set off in 1889 from Shizuoka to Yamanashi Prefecture northwest of Tokyo, travelling for four days by *basha*, or stagecoach, over bad roads made worse by mud and constant drizzle. From Kofu she and a Japanese associate made forays into the surrounding mountains. Any foreigner was a huge novelty; a foreign woman was a stellar attraction. Everywhere they went she drew crowds of the curious, anxious for a glimpse of her. Townspeople showed up 200-strong to hear her speak. At times the pressure was so great that she had to retreat to her hotel, where more crowds gathered. Drunken men peered into her room at night.

Like Bird, however, many found the Japanese environment inhospitable. Indeed, early foreigners generally seem to have been constantly plagued with mysterious ailments of one sort or another. One, known as "Japan head," was said to be brought on by too much language study in the evening, for which the cure was a period of extended rest in the resort village of Karuizawa.

In all likelihood some of this was a manifestation of culture shock, for Japan was not entirely what was expected. While they wrote home

Canada in Japan: Miss Hargraves and Miss Cunningham travelling by sled in the 1890s. *United Church of Canada Archives, 2000.01.17P/2715N*

enthusiastically at first about the beautiful scenery and charming people, it was not long before they realized they were not in the land of the travel brochures. One young woman reported finding only "degradation, poverty, misery and filth in equal degrees. It made me quite unwell."

Margaret Elizabeth Armstrong, who went to Toyama on the Japan Sea coast, found the place "permeated with subtle temptations . . . which never assail us in our native land. They are in the air, and they come to you with all the insidiousness of a serpent gliding through the fragrant blossoms. Don't imagine that temptations will not beset a missionary!" Just what her temptations were, she did not elaborate. But they could not have been too dreadful, as she remained there for the rest of her life.

There was certainly plenty about Japan at the time to shake up the sheltered and the prudish. One was nudity; many foreigners were disconcerted by their first sight of labourers and *jinricksha* runners, naked except for loincloths. More disturbing was the sight of men and women mingling together in public baths.

There was also sex in all its unavoidable manifestations, from concubinage to prostitution, as well as more accepting Japanese attitudes toward divorce and homosexuality. Unencumbered with the Garden of Eden and other elements of the Judeo-Christian tradition, Japanese tended to be more matter-of-fact and practical in such matters; sex might be an issue of taste or honour but rarely guilt or sin. How the women reacted to the tradition of parading enormous male and female fertility symbols through the streets during agricultural festivals can only be imagined; it was not something they wrote home about for the missionary newsletter.

For the most part, the women seem to have dealt with the disturbing aspects of Japanese society by retreating into the security of their own. Like Isabella Bird and her inflatable rubber bath, they carried their cultural baggage with them.

One of the most important items in this baggage was clothing. Photographs of early foreign women in Japan almost always show them in awkward, tight-fitting Western dress, in contrast to their counterparts in China and India. Indeed, their Japanese sponsors and colleagues would have expected nothing else. It is tempting to imagine that someone, somewhere, once in a while took off her hat, undid her collar, corset and high-buttoned boots, and eased into the comfort of a crisp *yukata* (cotton robe) or slipped naked into a steamy Japanese *onsen* (bath). If they did, this too is unrecorded.

They also seem to have been rather incurious about Japanese culture, at least in the beginning. For the most part they lived in Western-style accommodation, ate Western-style food, read Western books and generally carried on lives as similar as possible to those they had left behind. The little conventions and rituals of late-19th-century Canadian domestic life were meticulously maintained, even after these had begun to fade away at home. Spare time was for needlework and letter writing, and nothing resembling work, even opening mail, was done on Sunday.

The biggest challenge, especially for those in remote towns and villages, was loneliness. Deaconess Archer, an Anglican woman who lived deep in Japan's mountainous west coast, found herself the only single foreign woman in an area of 2 million people. Her only opportunity to mix with other foreigners was during her summer vacations in Karuizawa.

Not surprisingly, some left after a few years. More remarkable are the many who stayed. Of these, most remained single, if not by inclination then by lack of opportunity. Most male foreigners arrived in Japan already married or formed relationships with Japanese women. The prospects of a foreign

Mary Haru Chappell, shown teaching English to young men, also taught at Tsuda College and became a tutor to the empress in the 1960s. Her twin sister, Constance, taught at Tokyo Women's Christian College. *United Church of Canada Archives, 1989.054 P45N*

woman marrying a Japanese man, while not unknown, were slim. The novelist Tanizaki Junichiro summed up the situation aptly when he wrote that foreign females were best seen at a distance—to be looked at, even admired, but not touched.

It would be a mistake, however, to dismiss such women as pinched and drab spinsters, filling their days with selfless pursuits and endless good works. On the contrary, they give every indication of having been feisty, energetic individuals who got on remarkably well in Japan's male-oriented society. For the most part they seem to have been treated essentially as what they were: foreigners, different but only incidentally so from their male counterparts. And perversely, in Japan they found themselves with more opportunity than they would probably have enjoyed had they remained at home.

● ● ●

Agnes Wintemute Coates, who arrived in Japan in 1886, diverged from the classic female missionary model.

Her journey began conventionally enough. At loose ends following graduation from a ladies' college in St. Thomas, Ontario, she was urged to go to Japan by her local minister. She prepared by attending a Chautauqua, one of the travelling intellectual-cum-religious and entertainment fairs popular across North America at the time. Her arrival in Yokohama apparently left her nonplussed, according to her letter home.

> The majority were only half dressed, and very few indeed wore shoes or hats of any description; and when I saw a couple at a little distance who had left all their clothes at home I began to think I had reached a barbarous country . . . The most novel things in the way of clothing were the straw suits that many wore, consisting of a shirt and a long shoulder cape very much the shape of the fur capes our ladies wear at home in winter.

She soon acclimatized, especially after a surprise spotting of Mount Fuji on her usual Saturday morning walk.

> Intent on my study of Japanese and not thinking of the scenery as I walked along . . . I happened to look up and there straight in front of me was beautiful Mount Fuji, with its snow covered top gleaming in the morning sunlight. It was such a wonderful sight that I stood transfixed to the spot and could not take my eyes off it for some time.

After a brief teaching spell in Tokyo, she went to Kofu as principal of a new girls' school sponsored by a wealthy landowner. She also soon married a fellow Canadian Methodist missionary named Harper Coates. Together they moved to Hamamatsu farther down the coast, where she produced six children while sharing her husband's teaching duties, giving cooking and sewing classes and struggling to make ends meet on a missionary's salary.

Before long, however, she began veering off course. Perhaps it had to do with the transition from career to the less enviable role of missionary wife; while wives often did the same work as the single female missionary teachers, they rarely received the same recognition. Whatever the reason, photographs from 1900 onward rarely show her smiling.

Living in an area conducive to growing peanuts, she began experimenting by thinning peanut butter with water to produce a milk substitute that could be used in salad dressing as well as soups, gravies, nut loaves and other meat substitutes, even custards. A typical meal in the Coates's household consisted of bread and jam for breakfast, a "boiled salad" for lunch and peanuts in some form for dinner.

The relevance of her discovery became apparent after the price of rice skyrocketed around 1918. Bread suddenly became more popular, and peanut butter, some found, made it go down better. Coates took up the cause with gusto.

> I saw by my experience that with peanut butter for bread and peanut oil and peanut milk as a basis for cooking, there was the possibility of a foreign meal at from one-third or one-half the usual cost, and one that would suit ordinary Japanese better than if made with cow's butter and milk, as Japanese dislike both unless they have cultivated a taste for them . . . So I set my brains to work to see how many dishes could be prepared on this basis and cooked with the ordinary utensils in a Japanese kitchen and served in Japanese style, i.e. with bowls and chopsticks.

Before long she and one of her husband's associates, a fellow peanut aficionado named Takeuchi, went into peanut butter production using a customized rice-polishing mill. General Oe ordered 300 pounds and became a leading stockholder and director; he had recently invented a portable oven for baking bread and planned to introduce peanut butter into the rations of the army. The venture soon turned into a full-scale commercial business with 31 shareholders including landowners, a banker, a wholesale peanut dealer, two businessmen, a magazine editor, a retired naval officer, a watchmaker, a tailor, two doctors and a Japanese evangelist, as well as Coates herself.

What the ordinary soldier thought about this dietary innovation is unknown. The resident Canadian Methodist community was more vocal. One referred to Coates's stint as matron of the Canadian Academy—the popular international school started by the Methodists in Kobe in 1913—as the peanut butter era: "We had peanut butter on the table, peanut butter stew, peanut butter soup—peanut butter in all forms . . . it was all very tasty if a bit monotonous." In Coates's mind there was nothing strange about it. She was simply helping people by providing a needed product at a fair price—a simple case of Christianity in action.

As Coates's success as a nutritionist grew, her interest in mainstream Christianity declined and she became increasingly attracted to Asian religions. This was not unusual among intellectually minded missionaries; Harper Coates, who taught theology at Aoyama Gakuin College, was a respected

Buddhist scholar who co-wrote a well-known book on the life of Honen, the founder of the Pure Land Sect branch of Buddhism. When he died in 1934 he was given a Buddhist as well as a Christian service.

His wife's spiritual quest took another direction. During a visit to Vancouver in the early 1920s she became involved in the New Thought movement initiated by Phineas Parkhurst Quimby, a clockmaker from Maine with an attraction to transcendental metaphysics. She also dipped into the Theosophical Society of Mme. Blavatsky, which attempted to blend universal brotherhood with the study of religion and science and an interest in the occult.

By the time Coates returned to Japan in the mid-1920s, she had reinvented herself as an interpreter between East and West, a kind of self-styled *nakodo*, or marital go-between. Bolting from the Methodists, she began devoting herself to a full-time career as a nutritionist. She wrote a book explaining how to incorporate Western food into Japanese diets, with recipes ranging from strawberry shortcake to eggs tofu soufflé, as well as the ubiquitous peanut loaf. She taught nutrition at Ōmori in Japanese. The City of Nagoya asked her to set up a school lunch program and she was invited by the head of the

Agnes Wintemute Coates (centre) with her husband, Harper, their children and Japanese students, ca. 1900. *United Church of Canada Archives, 86.067P/7*

Imperial Government Institute for Nutrition to use its laboratory facilities. The Imperial Household even consulted her regarding the diet of the emperor's children.

As the fabric of the 1930s unravelled she became a committed advocate of Japan in its growing confrontation with China, barraging her former missionary colleagues with pamphlets, letters and books. Then, when the Pacific War came, she could not bring herself to leave her adopted country. During the early war years she continued to move about freely, and Japanese friends sent gifts of fresh fruit and eggs. As conditions worsened, however, life became increasingly difficult. She died in Tokyo shortly before the end of the war, of malnutrition.

• • •

Although Japanese appreciated foreigners who understood Japanese culture, they did not expect them to live in a traditional Japanese way, nor necessarily respect those who tried—especially when many Japanese were in the process of adopting attributes of Western life themselves.

The "pure Japanese style" in which foreigners tended to assume Japanese lived—a Zen-like existence of *shōji* screens, *tatami* and *koi* ponds—had always been partly a product of Western imagination. By the turn of the century the pattern of daily life for many Japanese had already given way to an eclectic blend of East and West, particularly among members of the upper classes, who found themselves with a foot in both worlds, the so-called double life of a modern Japanese.

This quickly became apparent to Florence Rothwell, who arrived in Kobe in 1918 in response to a Toronto newspaper advertisement for a teacher at the Canadian Academy, the popular Methodist-run school that catered to the increasing number of foreign children in Japan and the rest of the Far East. Invited to visit a young American friend engaged to teach English to the sons of one of Japan's leading industrialists, Baron Sumitomo, she was amazed to find herself in his home overlooking the Inland Sea. One of four properties owned by Sumitomo, the estate consisted of three attached dwellings: a large one for himself when he was in residence and smaller ones for the sons and the tutor. A nurse, other tutors and some 20 servants rounded out the household.

What impressed Rothwell most was a large William Morris–designed stained-glass window in the entranceway that depicted three maidens picking oranges. Other walls were hung with immense paintings, including one of Martin Luther and his disciples. Upstairs, the "crown prince's room" was furnished with rugs, inlaid floors, a grand piano and upholstered furniture. In the surrounding grounds the baron raised orange and lemon trees as well as chickens, ducks and lambs. There was also a huge Western-style flower garden and a pond with storks.

Soon afterward she was invited to take up such an arrangement with the family of one of the Sumitomo directors, a Mr. Suzuki, whose home took a more modest but similarly hybrid form. On arrival she was welcomed with a sumptuous afternoon tea complete with English china and silver, served in an uncluttered Japanese drawing room graced by an arrangement of irises, the *shōji* screens drawn back to show a tiny waterfall and fishpond with a stone lantern and arched bridge. Dinner that evening was steak, potatoes and peas.

Even by Japanese standards of politesse, the Suzuki family went to extraordinary lengths to make Rothwell comfortable. While they slept on *tatami*, she had a bed, a huge closet and a tiny Japanese-style dresser 18 inches high. Another room used for lessons was furnished with an upholstered chair and a table and chairs, as well as books and paintings, including two Rembrandts and a Whistler. The Western rooms were on the ground floor; the Japanese rooms, which included one with a gold Buddha and offerings, were upstairs.

Mr. Suzuki, who had attended Oxford, was convinced breakfasts were the most difficult feature of life in another culture and insisted she have oatmeal porridge, a boiled egg, toast, jam, cheese and tea every morning. In the evenings they all dined together Japanese-fashion on the floor around a large wooden table in the dining room. In her off-hours Rothwell joined in a round of teas with friends, trips to department stores and visits to Kyoto and to Baron Sumitomo's other residences. Sometimes she and members of the Suzuki family went mushroom hunting in the countryside.

For all the outward manifestations of Westernization, however, the Suzuki family remained profoundly Japanese. Rothwell's main pupil, the elder Suzuki son, was simultaneously studying at a nearby Buddhist monastery in preparation for Harvard. Mr. Suzuki's prize possession was his newly erected tea house in the garden, where he spent his spare time taking lessons in the tea ceremony.

One day the elder Suzuki shared with her some misgivings about the future. Like many Japanese of his age and station in life, he foresaw a time when the rest of the world would come to embrace Japanese culture. If, however, the United States chose to shut Japan out, he feared other countries would follow suit, leading to war.

• • •

In retrospect, images of womanhood on both sides of the Pacific have been heavily influenced by fiction.

Anyone puzzled today by the astonishing popularity in Japan of *Anne of Green Gables*, Lucy Maud Montgomery's famous novel published in 1908, need look no further than the Canadian-run Tōyō Eiwa Jo Gakkō, where the book's future translator, Muraoka Hanako, was a student. Like Anne, Muraoka was a lively little girl with a passion for literature and an aspiration for higher education who went on to become a writer and translator of children's books. On the eve of the Pacific War, she received a copy of the book as a parting gift from Loretta Shaw, a Canadian Anglican missionary friend in Osaka.

The connection was instant. In Anne's guardian, the crusty Marilla Cuthbert, Muraoka would have discerned her stern but well-intentioned Tōyō Eiwa teachers, with their schoolmarmy strictures and admonitions. In the book's bucolic Prince Edward Island setting, she probably recognized the wonderland her teachers talked about. And in Anne's imaginative and feisty spirit and love of literature, she may have seen something of herself. There was also, of course, the deliciousness of all that red hair, something only a country of uniformly black-haired little girls could fully appreciate.

To Muraoka the book also seemed less saccharine than the then-standard foreign novel for Japanese girls, Louisa May Alcott's *Little Women*. Instead it spoke to Japanese sensibilities: Anne's reverence for nature and "special places," her willingness to sacrifice for her family, her sincerity of heart. During the war Muraoka began translating it, rushing the manuscript into the garden wrapped in a large *furoshiki*, or cloth, whenever the air raids sounded. When the title posed a challenge, there being no Japanese equivalent of a gable, green or otherwise, her daughter Midori suggested *Akage no Anne*—literally, *Red-Haired Anne*.

Published in Japan in 1952, the book was an instant bestseller and has remained so ever since, running into countless editions and spawning films,

Anne of Green Gables look-alikes: Jane Cunningham, principal of the Shizuoka Eiwa Jo Gakkō, and pupils in the 1890s. *United Church of Canada Archives, 1999.054P/29N*

plays, cartoons, Anne fan clubs, an Anne theme park in Hokkaido and even Anne-style houses complete with gables and gingerbread. Thousands of Japanese make a pilgrimage to Prince Edward Island every year.

North American images of Japanese womanhood were influenced by the writings of Winnifred Eaton, a half-Chinese woman from Montreal who passed herself off as a Japanese noblewoman with the improbable name of Onoto Watanna—and got away with it. Dressing in quasi-Japanese style, the flamboyant Eaton produced highly romanticized, outrageously inaccurate and very commercially successful novels with names like *Miss Nume of Japan* and *The Heart of Hyacinth*. One, *A Japanese Nightingale*, sold 200,000 copies in 1901 and was made into a Broadway play and a silent film.

After living the literary life in New York, churning out, as she liked to say, "a book and a baby a year," Eaton eventually jettisoned her kimono and moved to Calgary to try ranching with her second husband. When life on the range palled, she decamped to Hollywood, where she became a screenwriter on such hits as *Shanghai Lady, Mississippi Gambler, Phantom of the Opera* and *Show Boat*. After screenwriting dried up in the 1930s, she returned to

Beguiled by "geisha": Vancouver mayor Louis Denison Taylor on a visit to Tokyo in 1929. *City of Vancouver Archives, S. Ichikawo Studio, CVA 1477-61*

Calgary, where her husband had made a success in the oil business. She persuaded him to give up his mistress, and lived comfortably there for the rest of her life.

HIGHWAY TO THE EAST

The sheer physical challenge of getting to Japan was overcome when the Canadian Pacific established its rail and ocean service to Asia in the mid-1880s.

In recent times the transcontinental railway has become a virtual metaphor for Canadian nation building, the price of British Columbia's participation in Confederation, the fulfillment of Canada's "National Dream," in the language of author Pierre Berton's historic volume. A railway across sparsely populated western Canada, however, was not economically viable on its own. From its inception the Canadian Pacific enterprise was also about the older "International Dream" of the so-called all-red route, a fast transportation route from Britain across North America to Asia.

No one understood this better than Canadian Pacific president George Stephen, who worried about the company's finances—which explains a glaring absence in the iconic photograph that commemorates the railway's completion: Stephen is not there. While others hammered, he was in London seeking the financial commitments required for a service that would take over where the railway left off for the journey across the Pacific.

Stephen came by his interest in Asia naturally. As a young man from Edinburgh he spent time early in life in the London home of James Morrison, a rags-to-riches English multi-millionaire who made an immense fortune in the international textile trade and spent much of it on Asian works of art. When Stephen became a highly successful banker and businessman in Montreal, he furnished his own home with similar enormous urns and vases. He also befriended a British military officer, Colonel Garnet Wolseley, who arrived in Montreal in the early 1860s fresh from the Opium Wars and fascinated Stephen with stories of China and newly opening Japan. This may help

TOP The last spike, completing the transcontinental railway at Craigellachie, British Columbia, on November 7, 1885, is driven by Donald Smith (Lord Strathcona), while chief engineer William Van Horne, company director Sandford Fleming, and others look on. *Canadian Pacific Archives, NS1960A*

LEFT Missing from the famous photograph: George Stephen, president of Canadian Pacific, ca. 1900. *Canadian Pacific Archives, NS 30245*

explain why the cool, shadowy Stephen agreed to take on the monumental job of president of Canadian Pacific when the post was offered to him in 1881, a decision that caused some of his contemporaries to think he had taken leave of his senses.

By then the idea of a trans-Pacific service had already taken root. Indeed, in 1879 Prime Minister John A. Macdonald received an unexpected feeler from the new Mitsubishi Company raising the possibility of a jointly sponsored shipping enterprise. Considering the idea premature until the railway was closer to completion, Macdonald drew it to Stephen's attention in an 1884 letter.

> I think however now that it would be well for you to consider the matter. Any subsidy granted by the Dominion government would be principally for the sake of encouraging an Asiatic trade for the C.P.R. and it would be well that your railway should have some control over the line. I think, therefore, the proper plan would be for the establishment of a line to be under the joint control of the Mitsu Bishi Company of Japan and your railway. The Dominion government would encourage such a joint line by a reasonable subsidy for carrying the mails to Hong Kong and Yokohama.

This intriguing prospect never got off the ground, and in any case Mitsubishi's interest was soon taken elsewhere as it merged its shipping interests in the mid-1880s with those of its main rival, Mitsui, to create the huge Japanese shipping conglomerate Nippon Yusen Kabushiki Kaisha (NYK), which became a major trans-Pacific line. The vision of a trans-Pacific service, however, was firmly in Stephen's mind. "The Canadian Pacific," he wrote to Macdonald in September 1885, "is not completed until we have an ocean connection with Japan and China." Stephen also had a vision of his own. Concerned about the new railways popping up across the United States, which already had a foothold in Asia, he was convinced that Canadian Pacific could not compete successfully without its own ships.

For a few years the company made do with vessels leased from the Cunard Line. But by the early 1890s sufficient financial commitments had been squeezed to launch the company's own fleet of *White Empresses*. Named for their white hulls and the three leading empresses of the day—those of India (Queen Victoria), Japan (Empress Haruko, later Shôken) and China (Empress Dowager Tz'u-hsi)—they were the sleekest, fastest, most elegant ships on the Pacific for decades.

Stephen was raised to the peerage in 1891 by Queen Victoria, who named him the first Baron Mount Stephen, after a peak named in his honour in Kicking Horse Pass. Donald Smith, who famously drove the last spike, became Lord Strathcona a few years later.

• • •

It was the tales that Marco Polo allegedly brought back from far Cathay in the 1200s that first fixed Japan in the Western mind. His claims of strange islands east were gleaned from the court of Kublai Khan, whose attempts to invade Japan twice during the 13th century are said to have been turned back by divine winds, or *kamikaze*.

World geography was then turned upside down two centuries later, when Christopher Columbus set out to prove that Asia could be reached by sailing west instead of east. In the process, Japan's relative position on the world map changed. No longer a splatter of remote islands on the far side of China, it became the first place ships could expect to reach when they sailed across the Pacific. Indeed, it is said Columbus initially mistook Haiti for Marco Polo's fabled "Zipangu."

Canada's early history was part of that elusive western search for Asia. John Cabot allegedly arrived on the Atlantic coast in 1497 carrying a map showing Europe and Asia joined at the top, thinking he had arrived on the first stop on a trip to Zipangu. Jacques Cartier sailed up the grand waters of the St. Lawrence River in 1534 convinced he had found the passage to the Orient.

A hundred years later the idea that the rivers and lakes of Canada were the gateway to Asia remained strong. Sieur de La Salle named his settlement on the St. Lawrence "La Chine" (Lachine). It was also common belief among the first settlers in New France that China could eventually be reached by travelling overland from Montreal. One young adventurer, Jean Nicollet, spent a decade trekking through the wilds with a colourful Chinese damask robe carefully packed in his knapsack to ensure he would be properly attired to meet the mandarins of Cathay.

Inevitably, expectations of a route to Asia were dashed on the hard reality of an almost impenetrable wall of endless rivers, rock and muskeg. And codfish and beaver pelts, however valuable, did little to quell the appetite for the supposed riches of the Orient. The reality was that North America stood in the way of where Europe wanted to go. And what could not be got through must be got around.

For 300 years brave men like Davis, Hudson and Frobisher beat themselves to death with the obsession of a route to the Pacific through the Arctic—

"The New North-West Passage," a cartoon in the October 15, 1887, edition of the British satirical magazine *Punch* showing the Canadian Pacific on its way to "Zipangu" had the caption, "Britannia: Now from my western cliffs that front the deep, to where the warm Pacific waters sweep around Cathay and old Zipangu's shore, my course is clear. What can I wish for more?" *Library and Archives Canada, C-22248*

TOP Sailing ships and freight cars meeting in Vancouver Harbour, ca. 1890. *BC Archives, A-169*

ABOVE The *Empress of Japan* in Victoria Harbour in 1901. *Vancouver Maritime Museum, W.K. Lamb collection, LM2006.1000.470*

only to be cruelly hoaxed by Hudson Bay and defeated again and again by icebergs, starvation and unbearable cold—while Cook, Vancouver, Quadra and others probed to no avail from the Pacific end. In the mid-1800s the dream of the Northwest Passage was still alive in the expedition of John Franklin, until its grisly demise.

By then, however, the global gears had shifted again, this time as a result of the invention of the steam engine. What could not be got around could perhaps be got through after all. And geography, for a change, played to Canadian advantage; the distance to Japan was shorter via a land bridge across Canada than via San Francisco.

• • •

In the summer of 1886, less than a year after the last spike was hammered in, William Van Horne sat on the edge of the Pacific Ocean watching the *W.B. Flint* sail in from Yokohama. For him it was a moment of triumph: what the early explorers had dreamed of and risked so much to do was accomplished; the shortest route from Europe to Asia was opening up.

An American turned ardent Canadian, the expansive Van Horne was a perfect counterpoint to the canny, Scots-reared Stephen. As the railway's chief engineer, Van Horne had huffed and chuffed his way across the continent for four long years, dragging track through interminable lakes and rocks and trees, across endless stretches of prairie and up impossible mountain grades, prodding exhausted railway workers and dodging hungry creditors. Now the company faced the formidable task of making the railway pay. Part of the answer lay in populating the Canadian west through immigration, another in British subsidies for carrying mail. But these were not enough.

Van Horne drew up a careful memorandum on the need to cater to the growing North American fancy for tea, silk and other Asian luxuries. That left passengers. Taking charge of advertising himself, he set about enticing the well-to-do of Boston, Montreal and London to climb aboard. Boldly declaring "if we can't export the scenery, we'll import the tourists," he seized on the splendid Rocky Mountain terrain that the trains passed through and began building a string of luxury hotels modelled after European châteaux. Artists and photographers were commissioned to render the mountain landscape in the most appealing way possible. One day he hit the jackpot in the form of a sulphurous hole in the ground along the railway line, subsequently turning it into a million-dollar tourist attraction he named Banff after George Stephen's birthplace in Scotland.

Mountain scenery alone, however, would not get passengers across the ocean. For inspiration Van Horne drew on the centuries-old lure of the Orient. Instead of urging prospective travellers to "go west," the direction they would actually head in, Canadian Pacific's 1887 advertising brochure urged them to take the "New Highway to the East"—that is, the Far East. Two sleeping cars were named "the Yokohama" and "the Honolulu."

The draw was partly efficient transportation; but it was also the lure of the exotic. A decade earlier Japan had been a destination for a handful of adventurous globetrotters armed with trunks and hat boxes, cameras and deck chairs, guns and picnic hampers, in search of new thrills on Isabella Bird's unbeaten track. Now it starred in an exciting new boom in around-the-globe travel. The world, or at least the chic and well-heeled part of it, was beating a path to Japan's door.

In 1891 Canadian Pacific published *Westward to the Far East: A Guide to the Principal Cities of China and Japan*. Prepared by American travel writer Eliza Ruhamah Scidmore and reissued several times from 1891 to 1905, the guidebook was an ode to Japan.

Scidmore took her cue from the popular dictum coined by British diplomat and historian Basil Chamberlain to the effect that old Japan was like an oyster—to open it was to kill it. Once opened, the oyster also had to be ingested quickly before it spoiled from exposure to modern air. "Each year is Europeanizing and changing Japan and the sooner the tourist goes the more Japanese will he find those enchanting islands."

> Fortunately for us, Japan was held in reserve for this century and this generation, and this exquisite country—different in itself from the rest of the world and all this side of the planet, as quaint and unique, as beautiful and finely finished as one of its own *netsukes* or minute works of art—delights the most jaded traveler and charms everyone who visits it.

If the flood of treacly travelogues produced in the 1890s is any indication, it was also this Japan of the travel brochures that early visitors saw, or thought they saw. The new, modernizing, industrializing Japan, the one with which Japanese themselves wanted to impress foreigners, went largely unremarked.

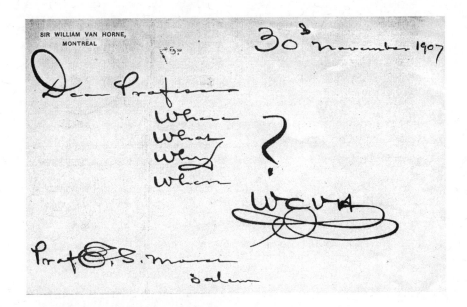

ABOVE Note from William Van Horne to his friend Edward Sylvester Morse, the originator of "the Japan craze."
Whyte Museum of the Canadian Rockies, Van Horne collection

LEFT William Van Horne, the driving force behind completion of the Canadian Pacific railway and George Stephen's successor as president of Canadian Pacific in 1888, was a renowned collector of Japanese ceramics.
Library and Archives Canada, PA-182603

Instead it was the exquisitely beautiful, profoundly curious, quaint "old Japan" that appealed to Western sensibilities.

It is possible, too, that the jolt of Asian adrenalin that many travellers experienced on arrival had something to do with the Canadian Pacific experience itself. Boxed up for days on a railcar with the vast scenery, followed by more days on ship with little to look at but a rolling sea, passengers suddenly found themselves thrust into Japan where everything—from the first sight of

Mount Fuji to the first glimpses of *shōji* screens and *torii* gates—was instantly dear and wee and delightful, just as the travel brochures promised. "Japan is a dream of Paradise, beautiful from the first green island off the coast to the last picturesque hilltop. The houses seem toys, their inhabitants dolls, whose manner is clean, pretty, artistic and distinctive."

The ultimate in turn-of-the-century travel was to go to Japan—and shop like mad. And Japan, eager for foreign exchange, happily obliged. Yokohama, Tokyo and Kyoto provided everything a foreign visitor could wish for, from European-style hotels to antique and curio shops, porcelain factory outlets, silk and textile stores and photographic studios. Mrs. Howard Vincent, an Englishwoman who travelled from Newfoundland to Japan via the Canadian Pacific in the early 1890s, summed it up this way:

> You never fully know the joy of buying until you buy in Japan. Life condenses into one long desire, keener and more intense than any want you ever had before—the desire of paying and possessing . . . And as to the ordinary individual, without the guidance of superior aims, time is no more for him, nor things temporal; he is lost in contemplation of the ancient and the beautiful in the art of Nippon.

It was the textiles, however, that spoke to her most. "Oh! they are things to make your covetousness strong, your heart ache, unless your purse is full and deep. Everything you see in Japan is art."

• • •

Or so it seemed. Indeed, it is something of a paradox that at the very point in history when Japan was in the throes of Westernization, the Western world was busily falling in love with the traditional arts of Japan. From the moment that European and North American audiences caught their first sensational glimpse of the Japanese exhibit at the great international exhibition in London in 1862, they were gripped by "the Japan craze," or "Japonisme."

In part it was the intrinsic appeal that exquisitely handcrafted goods held for people in the machine age. It also had to do with the refreshing impact of a lighter Japanese aesthetic on jaded palates. Most certainly it involved a skilful collaboration between Western and Japanese art critics and entrepreneurs, who actively prepared, packaged and served up traditional Japan to eager foreign audiences.

Missie Hattie Atwater in a costume decorated with fans at the Montreal Winter Carnival, ca. 1869–70. *McCord Museum of Canadian History, William Notman and Son photograph, 1-43635.1*

Whatever it was, the phenomenon revolutionized Western art and aesthetics, contributing to the rise of Impressionism, the Aesthetic movement and art nouveau, and influencing popular taste in design and home décor. Cherry blossoms and flying cranes landed on everything from teacups to wallpaper, while audiences flocked to a caricature Japan served up as the exotic setting for Gilbert and Sullivan's otherwise-English comic operetta, *The Mikado*.

From London, Paris, New York and, most particularly, Boston, the Japan craze easily found its way to Montreal. Van Horne, a cosmopolitan with ties to

W.R. Miller, a stockbroker, dressed for a role in Gilbert and Sullivan's *The Mikado*, which opened in Montreal in 1886. *McCord Museum of Canadian History, William Notman and Son photograph, 11-79811.1*

the US eastern seaboard, quickly succumbed. While working on the railway he began assembling an impressive collection of Japanese pottery and porcelains.

Van Horne came to his collecting, oddly enough, via paleontology. As a boy growing up in Illinois, he was intrigued by the fossils found embedded in railway embankments. It was a passion he shared with zoologist Edward Sylvester Morse, who was bowled over by the Japanese exhibit at the 1876 world's fair in Philadelphia. When Van Horne went off to build railways in Canada, Morse left to chase brachiopods in Japan, where he quickly made a name for himself as the discoverer of the Ōmori shell mounds, a heap of shells he spotted along a railway cut on the new line from Yokohama to Tokyo. Soon he was teaching archaeology at Tokyo Imperial University, one of the secular professors who bedevilled the missionaries with lectures on Darwin and evolution.

From a fascination with fossils, Morse graduated to ceramics, particularly the simple, subtle pieces coming out of family-run kilns with rough surfaces, crackle glazes and accidental lumps and indentations. He began to classify these, too, in scientific fashion. His collections made a huge impression on late-19th-century America, as did his writings—*Japan Day by Day, Japanese Homes and Their Surroundings, Latrines of the East*—which advanced the increasingly popular view that not only could Japan learn much from the West, but the West could learn much from Japan.

With Morse's help, Van Horne acquired pottery and porcelains through auction houses and dealers in New York and London. He was a collector in the great Victorian tradition, in which vast quantities of exotica were assembled with scientific precision and stuffed into large mausoleum-like houses and museums. Every tea jar, sake cup, bowl and vase was duly recorded in his notebook, sometimes with an accompanying sketch, with details as to its provenance, how it had been acquired and its estimated value. He was known to love the form, the colouring and the glazing of pieces wrought by master craftsmen, gazing at them for hours. A knowledgable collector, he is also said to have been able to correctly identify, while blindfolded, 70 percent of the samples put before him by a dealer, including the names of artists long since dead and kilns no longer in existence.

To house his collections, Van Horne expanded his home on Montreal's Sherbrooke Street—a three-storey, 52-room baronial mansion, "big and bulgy like myself," as he was wont to say. The Japanese ceramics were in his study, which also housed his collections of model ships, paintings and other works of art. There, he liked to entertain his friends and business associates after dinner. "Undoubtedly Sir William was a splendid talker," wrote an observer of a typical Van Horne evening.

His mind was capacious, the range of his interests wide, his self-confidence untouched. Much of the talk might be about art. But it was likely to be followed, or interspersed, with his opinions on an astonishing range of topics: the ideal planning of cities; cattle breeding; bacon curing; protective tariffs; the theory of evolution; the perfectibility of man; geology; the future of Asia. Again and again some story would be introduced from his railroading experiences—some tale about the struggles and crises in the building of the C.P.R.

● ● ●

Surprisingly enough, Van Horne never hopped aboard his own "Highway to the East." It was not for lack of interest or want of invitations, as he had plenty of both. When he stepped down as president of Canadian Pacific in 1899, he began making plans. But somehow, he never quite got around to them. Possibly it was because he was at heart a railway builder, and Japan by the turn of the century was already grid-ironed with track. He accepted, instead, an offer to build railways in Cuba, where a brand of Havana cigars was named after him, his likeness placed on the label.

But while he never got to Japan himself, Van Horne was responsible for sending there the most famous Japanophile of them all, the eccentric Greek American writer Lafcadio Hearn. When Van Horne discovered him, Hearn had just been to the 1885 international exposition in New Orleans, where his first glimpse of Mount Fuji on a screen is said to have imbued him with a burning desire to see the real thing. Hoping to publish Hearn's writings, *Harper's Bazar* approached Van Horne for assistance in sending him to Japan. Van Horne obliged, providing Hearn with passage and $250 on the understanding he would write about the journey.

Published in 1890, *A Winter Journey to Japan* started out in Montreal, "a city of ice and sleighs as picturesque as old St. Petersburg," and crossed the prairies, where "the world is a bare white disc rounding to an unbroken skyline and a limitless sea," before reaching the Rocky Mountains, "where the most colossal scene of the almighty panorama begins to unfold itself." The voyage across the Pacific, by comparison, was dull, full of grey days without incident or colour, one much like the other. Suddenly there was the greatly anticipated first sight of Mount Fuji.

Then with a delicious shock of surprise I see something for which I had been looking—far exceeding all anticipation—but so ghostly, so dream white against the morning blue, that I did not observe it at first glance; an exquisite snowy cone towering above all other visible things—Fujiyama! . . . Its base, the same tint as the distances, I cannot see—only the perfect crown, seeming to land in the sky like a delicate film—a phantom."

Image piled upon image; the piece was classic, if rather florid, Hearn. Van Horne pronounced himself greatly pleased. "If you know where to reach Lafcadio Hearn," he cabled his passenger agent, "I will be glad if you will tell him that I think his article in the November *Harper's*, 'A Winter's Journey to Japan,' is one of the most charming things I have ever read." By then Hearn was already off busily falling in love, quite literally, with Japan. He accepted a teaching position in Matsue on the far Japan Sea coast close to Izumo, one of Japan's most important shrines, married a Japanese woman and changed his name to Koizumi Yakumo. It was not so much Japan itself that Hearn fell in love with, however, as his own breathtaking sense of first discovery.

There is some charm unutterable in the morning air, cool with the coolness of Japanese spring and wind-waves from the snowy cone of Fuji . . . The sun is only pleasantly warm; the *jinricksha*, or *kuruma*, is the most cosy little vehicle imaginable, and the street-vistas as seen above the dancing white mushroom-shaped hat of my sandaled runner, have an allurement of which I fancy that I could never grow weary . . . Elfish everything seems, for everything as well as everybody is small, and queer, and mysterious; the houses under their blue roofs, the little shop-fronts hung with blue and the smiling little people in their blue costumes.

Ultimately, Hearn's writings, which influenced Western images of Japan for generations, were about a Japan largely of his imagination. In his eyes Japan was a kind of gossamer fairyland, a fantasy world of local beliefs and rituals, ghost stories, old tales and legends. People, animals, silkworms, cicadas, butterflies, ants and grasshoppers were all unique and charming and infinitely fascinating. It was all real—and at the same time, it wasn't. Like Morse and other early romanticizers of Japan, Hearn idealized everything traditionally Japanese and scorned anything to do with "civilization." What he did not want to see he stripped away mentally and blotted out of the picture. Old Japan was beautiful; new Japan was ugly, the "dead oyster" of Chamberlain's famous dictum.

In particular, he conceived an intense distaste for Tokyo, the booming, bustling capital of rapidly modernizing Japan.

> In this Tokyo, this detestable Tokyo there are no Japanese impressions to be had except at rare intervals . . . Immense silences—green and romantic—alternate with quarters of turmoil and factories and railroad stations . . . Miles of telegraph poles looking at a distance like enormous fine-tooth combs, make a horrid impression. Miles of water-pipes—miles and miles and miles of them—interrupt traffic of the principal streets: they have been trying to put them underground for seven years . . . Streets melt under rain, water -pipes sink, water pipe holes . . . swallow up playful children; frogs sing amazing songs in the street. To think of art or time or eternity in the dead waste and muddle of this mess is difficult.

Similar objections might, of course, have been levelled at the disorderly towns and cities then sprouting up across North America. Hearn, however, had little interest in identifying similarities. What he was really about, what lay behind all the butterflies and ghosts and legends, was difference.

Most foreigners already thought of Japan as an upside-down place, a topsy-turvydom. Japanese spoke backward, read backward, turned keys backward, even threaded needles backward; what should be on the right, it seemed, was always on the left. Hearn's Japan was more different still. It was not just another place but another planet, a lotus land where, as he once pointed out, "they really do eat lotuses." Unquestionably, Japan was foreign. But it was not as strange as Hearn and other purveyors of the exotic on both sides of the Pacific made it out to be.

Fundamentally a tortured soul, Hearn left Tokyo Imperial University in 1902 and decided to leave Japan for good. Again Van Horne came to the rescue, offering return passage to Montreal. Hearn was grateful but opted to remain in Japan, where he died a year or so later.

• • •

Wealthy businessmen art connoisseurs like Van Horne played a catalytic role in the early development of Canadian museums and galleries.

When Van Horne's old mansion on Sherbrooke Street came down in 1969 in the course of Montreal's own modernization mania, some of his ceramics became part of a splendid Asian art collection in the Montreal Museum of Fine Arts, as did a collection belonging to Montreal department store magnate Cleveland Morgan, who founded the museum's decorative arts department.

In Toronto, one of North America's foremost collectors of *ukioy-e* prints—the colourful woodblock depictions of kabuki actors, geisha and other denizens of the "Floating World" that so fascinated artists like Whistler and Monet—was Edmund Walker, the president of the Canadian Bank of Commerce from 1907 to 1924 and the first chairman of the Royal Ontario Museum. One of the best-known members of the Canadian business community, he also served as Japan's honorary consul general in Toronto.

Edmund Walker, president of the Canadian Bank of Commerce and chairman of the Royal Ontario Museum, with Mr. Yamashita, a Japanese industrialist, in Japan in 1919. *Canadian Imperial Bank of Commerce Corporate Archives*

In 1919 Walker travelled to Japan, Korea, China and Manchuria to explore prospects for expanding his bank's business, hoping at the same time to add to his print collection. His time in Japan—"one long dream"—more than measured up to his print-inspired expectations. When it came to prints themselves, however, he was doomed to disappointment; things he had imagined obtainable were virtually impossible to find. He was also jolted to hear that architect Frank Lloyd Wright, who was in Tokyo at the time designing the Imperial Hotel, had been taken in by a dubious scheme to provide thousands of revamped prints and facsimiles for the US market. Walker, whose early banking career made him an expert at detecting counterfeit currency, feared Wright was a victim of cleverly planned frauds.

Whatever the merits of the well-known Wright case, it spoke to the dwindling supply of genuine Japanese artworks still available. By the 1920s the collecting dynamic had shifted into reverse, as a generation of newly affluent Japanese began repatriating what their Meiji forebears had allowed to leave the country in the rush to modernity. Genuine collector's items were scarce and commanded extravagant prices. By the 1930s, prints purchased in London years before for pennies were reselling for thousands of dollars.

Walker's collaborator and travelling companion on this and other excursions was Kurata Bailey Takatsuma, a Toronto scientist who worked at the Royal Ontario Museum. Kurata's expertise was spiders and fish, Walker's was fossils and dragonflies, and they shared a fascination with woodblock prints and the future of Asia.

The most comprehensive collection of Japanese art in Canada, which resides in the Art Gallery of Greater Victoria, also owes its origins to a businessman: Fred Pollard, a successful raw-silk merchant in Yokohama who retired to Victoria in 1923. After Pollard's death, his wife Isabel decided to acquire an impressive collection of Japanese art and donate it to the gallery in his memory. Assembled largely through San Francisco with the expert assistance of Mori Toru, former chairman of the art history department of the University of Osaka, and Nakanishi Bunzo, a prominent art dealer-connoisseur-collector in Kyoto, the Pollard collection became the foundation of the gallery's extensive holdings of Japanese art, which expanded over the years with the addition of other significant collections.

● ● ●

When all was said and done, the new "Highway to the East" involved more than getting trains across the continent and ships across the ocean. It also went beyond the romance of new travel, tastes and ideas, or even the fascination of collecting.

It was about seizing exciting opportunities for new commerce across the Pacific, as well as looking at the world differently, in what would soon be the dawn of a new century.

PART 2

GROWING (1900–30)

MYTHS AND MARKETS

> I have been considering for some time what can be done to plant in the stomach of the Orient an increasing desire for Canadian food . . . It is unnecessary to point out what it would mean for the farmers and railways of Canada if even a percentage of the people of Japan 45,000,000, or of Korea 20,000,000 were inoculated with a taste for Canadian food. As you are aware the scientists of Japan have concluded that a diet of bread is preferred to rice, and it would appear to be only a question of education and of time before the Japanese will conform their practices to the teaching of their scientific experts.

These extraordinary words were penned in 1906 by Canada's Governor General, Earl Grey, and sent to the presidents of the country's three railways.

Grey had just fallen and fallen hard for what has been called the "myth of the Japan market." In much the same way that 19th-century Yankee traders and British trading houses viewed China as a market of millions clamouring for manufactures, Canadians in the early 20th century convinced themselves that Japan represented an almost limitless outlet for the resource output of the newly opening Canadian west and a gateway to Asia.

Before putting pen to paper, Grey had consulted Nose Tatsugoro, Japan's able consul general in Ottawa. An internationally minded man who no doubt ate bread himself, Nose affirmed that giving up rice for the convenience of Western food was only a matter of time. Not only did rice involve cooking, which meant time and trouble as well as expense; it also required the addition of fish or some other food to make it palatable. "On the other hand," Nose affirmed, "a loaf of bread baked from the hard wheat flour, which is only produced in the Northwest, a tin of butter and a Canadian cheese, can be left

Chief Trader Archibald McDonald Descending the Fraser, 1828 by Adam Sheriff Scott
(ca. 1942) is the subject of a popular Hudson's Bay Company calendar.
Hudson's Bay Company Archives, Archives of Manitoba, HBCA P-408

INSET Archibald McDonald was the father of Ranald MacDonald, who smuggled
himself into Japan in 1848. Daguerreotype portrait, 1852. *Library and Archives Canada,
Jean Murray Cole collection, PA-143286*

ABOVE A map of Kanagawa harbour by Ichigyokusai in 1859, the year the sleepy fishing village across the bay opened to foreigners as the new treaty port of Yokohama. Vancouver and Yokohama are sister cities. *UBC Library, Rare Books and Special Collections, George Beans collection, Tokugawa maps, 1859.5*

RIGHT *Yokohama Road*, a woodblock print by Hiroshige III, Utagawa ca. 1875 features new modes of transportation: ships, a train and the recently invented jinricksha, as well as a Western figure on horseback. *Art Gallery of Greater Victoria, gift of Ralph and Jean Greenhill, AGGV 1996.041.011*

ABOVE The last shogun, Tokugawa Yoshinobu (1817–1913), painted this hanging scroll, *Mount Fuji*. He gave it to a chief retainer, Muramatsu, whose son presented it to Canadian Methodist missionary Eber Crummy in 1896. *Art Gallery of Greater Victoria, gift of Margaret Crummy in memory of her father, AGGV 1977.235.001*

LEFT *Imperial Lineage*, a woodblock print by Chikanobu Toyohara in 1878, illustrates the imperial line of descent from the first emperor, Jimmu Tenno (top middle with bow and arrows) to the Emperor Meiji (bottom left in Western uniform) and Empress Haruko. The Emperor Meiji replaced Tokugawa Yoshinobu in the 1868 Restoration. *Art Gallery of Greater Victoria, gift of Lund's Auctioneers and Appraisers, AGGV 2004.035.001*

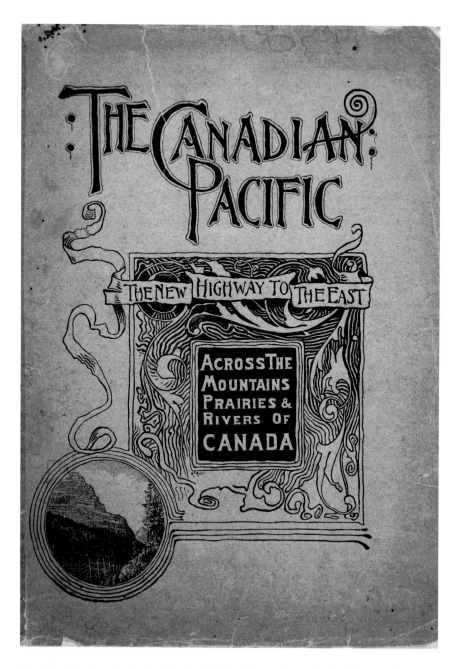

"The New Highway to the East" —the Far East, that is. Canadian Pacific issued this brochure in 1887, two years after completion of the transcontinental railway.
Canadian Pacific Archives, A.18110

A painted glass window from the dining saloon of the *Empress of Japan*, launched in 1891, shows the railway entering a tunnel near Field, British Columbia, with Mount Stephen in the background. *Vancouver Maritime Museum, J.A. Claridge collection, LM 2006.1000.404*

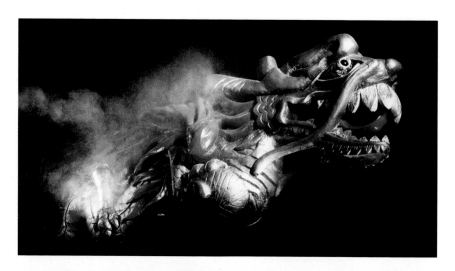

TOP This imposing carved dragon figurehead complemented the elegant and sweeping lines of the *Empress of Japan*. The original is in the Vancouver Maritime Museum; a replica is in Vancouver's Stanley Park. *Vancouver Maritime Museum collection*

ABOVE The legendary William Van Horne, chief builder of the Canadian Pacific, was also a well-known collector of Japanese ceramics. This Imari-ware porcelain ewer of the Edo period (1615–1868) is from his collection. *Montreal Museum of Fine Arts, Adaline Van Horne bequest, 944.Ee.19*

Edmund Walker, president of the Canadian Bank of Commerce (1907–24) and first chairman of the Royal Ontario Museum, collected woodblock prints like this one, *Two Boys with a Fishing Rod and a Small Turtle*, by Katsushika Hokusai, ca. early 1780s.
Royal Ontario Museum, Sir Edmund Walker collection, 926.18.609

A travel brochure from 1900 advertises connections to various Asian destinations, part of Canadian Pacific's around-the-world service. *UBC Library, Rare Books and Special Collections, Chung collection, box 224-20*

on the householder's doorstep and provide him with the chief article of his diet without calling from him for any further domestic trouble than that of opening his front door."

As for what should be done, Nose advised that bakeries be set up in major Japanese cities featuring bread-making demonstrations and accompanied by tea rooms serving Canadian bread, butter, jams and jellies, as well as samples of flour, biscuits, butter, cheese, ham, bacon, canned meats and vegetables. As advertising, free fans should be given to customers in mid-summer and free towels at Christmastime. In his letter to the railway executives, Grey elaborated further on Nose's suggestions.

> Attached to this tea room there should be a delivery wagon, painted bright red with gold maple leaf on the box, and also with large Japanese letters *Kanada Pan* (Canadian bread) and that the driver, dressed in a red suit, with a maple leaf in white as the crest, should carry a flag with a white maple leaf, and in Japanese letters *Kanada Pan* on red ground, and that he should go through the streets carrying a call bell and crying out "*Kanada Pan Kanada Pan tokuto no* (superior quality) *Kanada Pan.*"

Grey's letter concluded with a request for a modest guarantee of $50,000 from the railways, or the addressees themselves, to see the enterprise underway. While their responses are unrecorded, the proposal was presumably too imaginative even for traffic-hungry railway executives. There is, alas, no reason to believe that little red-painted wagons with gold maple leaves and red-suited drivers ever plied the streets of Tokyo and Osaka.

● ● ●

Grey was ambitious, but he was on the right track. When he wrote his letter, Canada's trade with Japan was still dominated by imports.

Indeed, when William Van Horne sat at the edge of the Pacific 20 years earlier, watching the *W.B. Flint* roll in from Yokohama, it was the old lure of Asian luxuries that danced before his eyes and the prospect of bringing them to eager customers in North America and Britain. Specifically, he was thinking about the ship's cargo of over a million pounds of tea, destined for central Canada, Chicago and New York. Soon, he grandly predicted, Canadian Pacific would control the tea trade for all points in North America east of the Rocky Mountains.

Van Horne knew of what he spoke. Ever since the great tea enthusiasm swept Europe in the 1600s, the Western world had imported it in enormous quantities. Tea was fashionable. Tea was good for health. Sold in an infinite number of varieties and blends, it gave rise to an entire industry of professional tea merchants and tea tasters in a phenomenon reminiscent of the modern wine industry.

Canadian tea tastes echoed British preferences for Chinese, Indian and Ceylon blends. James Bissett, a Hudson's Bay manager from Montreal who went on a buying trip to the Far East in the 1880s, was an exemplar of Canadian tea tastes: his principal destinations were China and Hong Kong, where he purchased great quantities of Chinese tea, as well as ginger, pepper, nutmeg and other items of the consumer trade. In Japan he spent most of his time sightseeing, socializing with the business elite and acquiring curios. Tucked into his shipment home, however, were 39 cases of Japanese green tea.

A late entrant to the international tea trade sweepstakes, Japanese tea was a product of the cash-strapped Meiji government's desperate need for foreign exchange. In Shizuoka former Tokugawa samurai capitalized on their location and turned to tea cultivation. The first recorded Canadian import from Japan was a shipment of tea that arrived in Quebec in 1870. During the 1880s, value of shipments rose tenfold, from less than $100,000 to close to $1 million, as Canada experienced a flurry of enthusiasm for Japanese green tea.

Tea was also something that Japanese and foreigners had in common, though from very different perspectives. One of the things that intrigued early visitors most about Japan was the *chanoyu*, or tea ceremony, the Zen-inspired spiritual art form that was a stark contrast to the various Victorian tea rituals—afternoon teas, high teas, cream teas, drawing room tea parties, garden teas and tea dances—each with its accompanying silver and saucered tea-time paraphernalia.

Tea, it turned out, also tasted best in cups of Asian inspiration, as the great chinaware companies like Royal Worcester and Royal Crown Derby merrily mixed Chinese, Japanese and European designs to meet consumer tastes. Toward the end of the 1800s a new vogue arose for direct imports of Japanese "china," as Japanese companies began supplying inexpensive wares to Western markets, challenging the predominantly British crockery trade. In the 1880s it was possible to buy a Japanese "five o'clock tea service" in Montreal for a dollar.

Unloading bales of raw silk in the port of Vancouver in 1931. *Vancouver Public Library, Leonard Frank collection, 16656*

• • •

Tea was soon joined by another prize: silk. Originally a cottage industry for rice farmers looking to earn extra cash, silk came into its own after the 1868 Meiji Restoration when Japan leaped into foreign trade.

Promoted by Fukuzawa Yukichi and other ardent modernizers, silk making rocketed to national prominence virtually overnight as large tracts of land were turned over to the cultivation of mulberry trees. The empress herself set an example by turning over part of the Detached Palace for the tending of silkworms and cocoons by some of the princesses. Former samurai, who a generation earlier would have regarded entering into commerce as unthinkable, eagerly transformed themselves into silk merchants. Nothing, it was said, could match the sound of thousands of silkworms in the rafters of Japanese farmhouses, munching their way through the night.

In a few years Japan replaced China as the world's leading silk producer, and Yokohama became the world's largest silk port. The new Silk Road lay eastward across the Pacific and on to the mills of the US eastern seaboard, where it fed the voracious appetite for luxury goods among the moneyed class of rapidly industrializing America.

Raw silk being perishable, the cost of insurance was enormous and prices erratic. Profits went to those who could transport it quickly and safely; days, hours, minutes counted. Arriving in Vancouver in burlap sacking crisscrossed with ties, the fragile bales were transferred onto specially fitted, sealed railway cars and whisked eastward at breakneck speed, vigilant stationmasters at the ready, up perilous mountain inclines, across the vast prairies and the rocks and lakes of northern Ontario before slipping into the United States—all in the interests of providing consumers with silk stockings and fashionable draperies. A train carrying future King George VI was once memorably shunted to a siding to make way for "a Silk."

With its fast ocean and railway system, Canadian Pacific had a commanding hand in the game. The entire journey could be accomplished in as little as 12 days, sometimes less—about 8 from Yokohama to Vancouver and another 4 across the continent. Canadian National Railway joined the fray in the mid-1920s, establishing offices in Japan and China, although it was not as successful when it came to silk as Canadian Pacific.

The Canadian route was integral to the business; at its peak about one-third of trans-Pacific raw-silk traffic passed through Canada, and Vancouver was the busiest silk port on the Pacific coast next to Seattle. Most histories, however, give little sense that Canada was involved at all. Essentially a Japan–US enterprise, the silk trade was carried out largely between Yokohama and importers in New York, home of the National Silk Exchange.

Then, as suddenly as they had appeared, the trains were gone, driven out of business by the arrival of synthetics, competition from the Panama Canal, and ultimately the Great Depression. The last silk train crossed Canada in 1939.

Today the phantom-like trains hooting their way across the country are at most a faint memory. What linger instead are recollections of *mikan*, or oranges, which made their first appearance in 1891. Each winter, when Canadians had long since had their last glimpse of fresh fruit, wooden boxes were loaded onto trains in Vancouver and dropped off along the railway heading east. Nothing heralded Christmas for a Canadian child like the magic of a Japanese orange, just the right size to tuck into the toe of a Christmas stocking.

• • •

The natural affinity of Canada's abundant natural resources for the Japanese market was first recognized by Japanese immigrants who trickled into the

Pacific coast of North America from the late 1870s onward, when the Meiji government relaxed restrictions on external travel. By the early 1890s small amounts of salmon, herring, wheat, lumber and coal were heading westward across the Pacific.

In 1897 Itō Hirobumi, Japan's well-known Meiji-era statesman and prime minister, crossed Canada on his way home from attending Queen Victoria's diamond jubilee in London. He was impressed with what he saw. In Vancouver he urged Canadians to take exporting to Japan seriously, pointing to prospects for a large and profitable trade in farm and dairy products as well as lumber. Nor, according to a report in the *Vancouver Daily World*, did Itō mince words.

> Count Itō, the premier, asserts that Canada could establish an extensive trade with the country in the products of the farm and dairy . . . It is only due to the carelessness of Canadians that the market has not been worked long ago. Lumber is very scarce and there should be a market for Canadian wood there also . . . The discouragement of foreign trade by the United States through very high duties . . . must militate against our neighbours and, if followed up by Canadians benefit them. Last year the United States sent $7,688,000 worth of goods to Japan.

What looked to Itō like inattention had much to do with the relative newness of the Canadian economy itself. The export pattern at the time was also still very much a colonial one, oriented eastward to Britain and the Empire. With the dawn of the 20th century, however, Canada experienced its first real burst of economic prosperity, spawning vast growth in construction, food processing, textiles, iron and steel and other industries. Toronto boomed, Montreal soared and Winnipeg thought it was set to become the Chicago of the north. Vancouver, little more than a clearing on the waterfront a decade earlier, was transforming itself into a major port on the Pacific.

In this growing mood of economic optimism, the Canadian government leaped at the opportunity to participate in a major industrial exhibition in Osaka in 1903. Designed to showcase Japan's growing industrial strength, the exhibition provided Canada with an opportunity to do some showing off of its own. Indeed, so large and so elaborate was the Canadian exhibit that a special building had to be erected to accommodate it.

Itō Hirobumi (centre), Japan's well-known Meiji-era statesman, exhorted Canadians to export to Japan when he crossed Canada by train in 1897. *Library and Archives Canada, Sir William Cornelius Van Horne collection, PA-206846*

Canadian products featured at the 1903 Osaka exhibition

Apples and fruits preserved in antiseptic fluid

Canned vegetables, soups, meats, fish, condensed milk and cream

Whiskey, butter, cheese, hams, bacon, honey, boxes of biscuits, maple sugar and maple syrup

Spruce, poplar and balsam fir

Sash and doors, wood pulp, printing and other paper

Furniture for houses, offices and schools

Metal ceiling and roofing, hardware (nuts, bolts, screws, wire, chain and loops of cord)

Cooking ranges, kitchen utensils and oil stoves

Bicycles

Cold-storage chamber topped with a huge crown made of Canadian grains and grasses

Models of a Canadian Pacific sleeping car and the *Empress of Japan*

A bakery with Canadian equipment and ovens

A piano

Inside the exhibit was a cornucopia, a veritable Victorian picnic basket, of all that Canada's thriving economy of the day produced. The pièce de résistance was the bakery. Several times a day, a cook demonstrated breadmaking with Canadian flour and equipment as hundreds of Japanese spectators, most of whom had never seen bread, let alone watched it rise and come out of the oven, looked on in fascination. The results were eagerly sampled and bread became a popular item on the menus of Osaka restaurants.

The objective of the exercise was not simply to showcase bread. It was to demonstrate the advantages of Canadian hard-wheat flour over the less expensive but lower quality American winter-wheat flour that Japan had been importing. According to the official Canadian report, the Canadian flour produced "large loaves with a rich nutty flavour," while American flour produced a "small, dry, hard loaf of little or no flavour which dried up and became brittle after two days."

The approximately 4 million visitors who toured the pavilion declared themselves most impressed. Local newspapers dubbed it the sensation of the exhibition and awarded a silver medal. The Canadian exhibit also received the honour of a special visit by the emperor and empress as well as by the crown prince and princess and members of the Imperial Household, one of whom purchased the piano. Itō Hirobumi also visited and gave rave reviews.

● ● ●

To manage its exhibit, the Canadian government turned to a rising Vancouver Japanese: entrepreneur Tamura Shinkichi.

Originally from Kumamoto on the southern island of Kyushū, Tamura came from a samurai family who felt the pinch following the Meiji Restoration. Apprenticed at 13 to a textile shop in Osaka with links to Kobe, he became acquainted with a missionary who helped him go to Canada to recoup the family fortune.

In 1888, 25-year-old Tamura arrived in Victoria, where he began working for a sulphur-producing firm that posted him back to Japan as its purchasing agent in Hokkaido. When the business went bankrupt in 1891, he returned to Canada, this time to rising Vancouver, then not much more than a collection of muddy streets and wooden sidewalks.

Capitalizing on growing demand for Japanese goods, he established Tamura Shokai (Tamura Trading Company), which became a prosperous business importing everything from small Japanese consumer goods to rice,

Tamura Shinkichi was a successful Vancouver entrepreneur who pioneered development of trade between Canada and Japan. *Courtesy of Arthur Hara and the Tamura family*

silk, soybeans, edible oils and oranges. Then, faced with growing competition from other Japanese importers, he decided to expand into exporting.

After noticing salmon drying on the banks of the Fraser River, he began salting them for export to Japan. An early attempt to reduce costs by cutting off heads and tails provided a valuable lesson in meeting consumer expectations; Japanese housewives wanted the whole fish and the shipment ended up as fertilizer. Another shipment sank, but with happier results. Tamura realized a $150,000 insurance bonanza, which allowed him to expand his business. For him, the Osaka exhibition could not have come at a better time.

On his return to Vancouver Tamura pioneered the first major shipment of Canadian wheat and flour to Japan. In the years that followed he grew even more prosperous. Tamura Shokai became a leading company in Canada–Japan

TOP The gentlemen of Tamura Shokai, a leading company in Canada–Japan trade that continued in Vancouver until the Pacific War and in Japan until the 1980s. *Courtesy of Arthur Hara and the Tamura family*

ABOVE The Tamura Building at the corner of Powell Street and Dunlevy Avenue is now a Vancouver historic landmark. *Japanese Canadian National Museum, 95/102.1.001*

trade, with branches in Kobe, Osaka, Tokyo, Yokohama and Seattle. An affil-iated Tamura enterprise, Nikka Chochiku K.K. (Japan–Canada Trust Savings Company), handled earnings of Japanese immigrants and managed financial transfers back to Japan. Two of the largest businesses in Vancouver's thriving Little Tokyo, they were located on the ground floor of the Tamura Building, which also housed the New World Hotel. A successful businessman who believed in giving back, Tamura also founded an organization to assist and teach English to newly arriving Japanese immigrants, and was a co-founder of the Japanese Methodist (later United) Church.

Unlike many Japanese who came to Canada, Tamura did not remain. After crossing back and forth across the Pacific many times, he eventually left his Canadian businesses to be carried on by family members and returned to Japan, where he became president of the powerful Kobe Chamber of Commerce as well as a member of Japan's House of Representatives and the House of Peers. As Baron Tamura he was a well-known figure on Tokyo's international scene during the 1920s. Edmund Walker, the president of the Canadian Bank of Commerce, considered Tamura the real pioneer in establishing business relations between Canada and Japan, and visited him when he went to Japan in 1919.

Tamura also left another legacy. Prominent Vancouver businessman and philanthropist Arthur Shigeru Hara, whose father came to Canada to work for Tamura, became the first Canadian chairman of Mitsubishi Canada and a major force in building connections across the Pacific.

• • •

The assumption in Grey's 1906 letter that Japanese were about to give up rice for bread was, of course, a fantastic one, born of little more than watching curious exhibition goers clamour for samples at the 1903 Osaka exhibition. But he was not alone.

Sydney Fisher, the federal agriculture minister, had returned from Osaka elated about prospects. "The use of bread is becoming more common every year among the Japanese," he reported. "This demonstration [at Osaka] of the superiority and relative economy of Canadian hard wheat flour has laid the foundation of what will, in a few years, become an enormous trade, not only with Japan, but throughout the far east generally."

The conversions of Grey and Fisher were modest, however, compared with that of Canada's prime minister of the day, Wilfrid Laurier. Fresh from his memorable prediction that "the 20th century belongs to Canada," Laurier was consumed by the opening of the vast Canadian Northwest. In particular, he viewed Japan through the lens of the wheat boom, as an avalanche of European immigration transformed the prairie landscape into instant farms and towns, and wheat production skyrocketed into millions of bushels.

Laurier drew a parallel with tea. In the same way that Europeans and North Americans had become enthusiastic tea drinkers, he reasoned, Japanese were destined to become enthusiastic bread eaters and spread this custom throughout Asia. As he rallied Canadians to his vision, the size of the potential Japanese market multiplied exponentially. "We would be blind to the times, if we failed to realize that there is a market of four or five hundred millions in the Orient. I want Canadian merchants to bear wheat and flour into that 400,000,000 market." This grand optimism rested on real Canadian exports to Japan of only a few hundred thousand dollars at the time. It was pure faith, akin to the blinding confidence of early missionaries who assumed that a modernizing Japan would naturally embrace Christianity.

Laurier's vision also involved more railroads. As he waxed enthusiastic about the tea of the Orient, he put his government's weight behind a second round of national transportation infrastructure building. The rationale was partly political; in Liberal eyes the Canadian Pacific Railway had been a Conservative venture, the godchild of Sir John A. Macdonald. There were also grumbles about Canadian Pacific's virtual transportation monopoly. At the same time, the prospect of a huge trans-Pacific trade was a compelling incentive.

Laurier's soulmate in the enterprise was Charles Melville Hays, president of the recently formed Grand Trunk Pacific Railway, which was designed to compete with Canadian Pacific by following a more northerly route, the shortest distance to Japan. Another railway magnate in the manner of William Van Horne but without quite the same panache, Hays was a blunt, vigorous American with a similar taste for grand enterprise. It was he who personally chose the new railway's terminus: a patch of beautiful, perennially damp rainforest near the mouth of the Skeena River, 500 miles north of Vancouver, which became the town of Prince Rupert. In recognition of his efforts he received the Order of the Rising Sun (Third Class) from Prince Fushimi, the emperor's cousin, when the prince visited Canada in 1907.

With the Grand Trunk Pacific, Canada's future tilted resolutely, if precariously, westward. Soon, however, the two principal architects were both

ABOVE Prince Rupert under construction, ca. 1906. "To this new port will come the ships of the Seven Seas. Ships of the East, laden with silk and rice, will soon be riding at anchor in this splendid harbour, to sail away laden with lumber; ships from the shores of far off continents trading through the new and picturesque port of Prince Rupert." *Canadian National Railway, Library and Archives Canada, C 46484; quote: Grand Trunk Pacific Railway brochure, 1912*

RIGHT Sir Wilfrid Laurier, shown en route to Prince Rupert, BC, in 1911, predicted Canadian wheat would become "the tea of the Orient." *Library and Archives Canada, C-090929*

gone—Laurier when he was defeated at the polls in 1911, and Hays when he died a year later while returning from London aboard the ill-fated *Titanic*.

Even the redoubtable Hays, however, probably could not have saved the Grand Trunk Pacific. By the time the railway was completed in 1914, Canadians had awakened to the fact that they now had more than one transcontinental line partially dependent on future trade across the Pacific. Traffic could not grow fast enough, nor was there a sufficient population base

Selling grain in the 1920s: Alberta agriculture leader Henry Wise Wood (centre with crossed legs), president of the Canadian Federation of Agriculture, in Japan in 1922, when Canadian exports to Japan exceeded imports for the first time, led by growing shipments of wheat. *Glenbow Archives, GBNA-3986-1*

in western Canada, to save the new line from being nationalized in 1919 or the port of Prince Rupert from languishing for decades.

By then, however, the vision of exporting to Japan was entrenched. And in the end Japan did become a huge market for Canadian wheat and other resources, although the future did not play out quite the way Grey and Laurier foresaw. Ultimately, as with Tamura's fish, success rested less on transforming Japanese tastes than in adapting to them. One of the most enduring Canadian exports to Japan turned out to be buckwheat, used for soba noodles. Even more valuable than the grain itself were the husks, used for stuffing Japanese pillows.

● ● ●

W.T.R. Preston was a controversial figure even before he arrived in Japan. A thorough-going political partisan, he had been an immigration specialist in London where he carried on a running feud with Lord Strathcona, by then Canada's high commissioner to Great Britain. However, as one of Laurier's contemporaries noted, "whatever his faults may be, he is a pusher and a kicker of approved quality." In 1906 Preston was removed from London and appointed Canada's trade representative to Japan, where true to form he soon pushed and kicked his way into fresh controversy.

Preston's issue was with the foreign commercial agents who still controlled much of Japan's trade. Japanese business got around them by relying on their own huge financial and industrial conglomerates, or *zaibatsus*, notably Mitsui, Mitsubishi and Sumitomo, which sourced their needs abroad. Foreign companies exporting to Japan typically went through the British and American trading houses in Yokohama and Kobe.

Specifically, Preston butted heads with one American agent over a shipment of allegedly overripe MacLaren's cheese received through a San Francisco exporter. Whether something really was wrong with the cheese, or American noses simply failed to recognize the merits of a fine Canadian cheddar, was not the problem. What mattered was that the agent refused to import it, which infuriated Preston both on principle and as a devotee himself of MacLaren's.

As Canada's first Japan-related trade dispute it was an unusual choice, for of the many foreign introductions for which the Japanese public had developed a taste, cheese was not one. The cheese, however, was symbolic of something more fundamental. In a speech to a large trade congress, Preston spoke to the incident as an example of why Canada and Japan needed "direct trade"— that is, trade outside the channels of the foreign agents. For this challenge to vested interests, he was virulently attacked in Japan's English-language press, which suggested he would do better to turn his ire in the direction of the "dishonest practices" of Japanese.

In response, the pugnacious Preston upped the ante, suggesting that in his experience Japanese merchants were just as fair, if not more so, than the foreign agents, who were mainly interested in preserving their own position. The feud dragged on for months until one of Preston's detractors in Canada forwarded some earlier press clippings critical of him to a Kobe newspaper, which printed them. Preston sued the owner in Japanese court and won 7,000 yen in damages and the right to an apology.

The foreign commercial agents then prevailed upon the British ambassador to persuade Preston to forego any further references to direct trade between Canada and Japan. This touched another nerve, and Preston informed the ambassador that he took his instructions from Ottawa, not London.

Meanwhile, Japanese enjoyed the spectacle of the Canadian upstart taking on the foreign agents, whom they had long regarded as parasitic middlemen.

It was all great sport, and the Japanese press was lavish in its praise of the court's decision. Preston, never short on ego, revelled in his newfound notoriety. A carriage was sent to bring him to a luncheon with the governor of Osaka, and he was singled out for attention by the foreign minister at a banquet on the occasion of the emperor's birthday.

Whatever the affair said about trade, it left Preston with a strong empathy for Japanese people. It is widely recognized, he wrote afterward, "that the Japanese are as honest, upright and honourable as any nation in the world, and a deal sight more honest, upright and honourable than many of the western commission merchants who shamefully libelled them for their own ends. The East has been very patient with the arrogance and presumption of Westerners."

He was also critical of foreigners who formed liaisons with Japanese women and later abandoned them to look after themselves and their children. "Loti's sad little story of *Madame Chrysanthème* (later *Madame Butterfly)* is more romance than tragedy. The grim reality is that the Westerner in the East who forgets or ignores his obligations to his own race and its standards of morality, is sowing dragon's teeth." Refreshing as this kind of commentary was, it did nothing to endear Preston to the resident foreign community.

In 1909 he left Japan and went back to feuding with Lord Strathcona. Before departing he received an unexpected invitation from Itō Hirobumi to visit him in his home in Ōmori. Preston was greatly moved.

> In the wondrous palace of Prince Itō were examples of beauty and exquisite workmanship such as I had never seen . . . To see a Japanese gentleman take out his treasures from the closed cabinet in which they are kept, to show to a visitor, is to have an example of how gracious an art may be made of possession.

He was even more impressed with Itō himself.

> He had had an immense experience of men and affairs, dating from the time, nearly 40 years before, when as an adventurous boy he had run away from home and shipped to London in a windjammer. Yet he was anything but a mere soldier of fortune. Of a set and iron purpose he had gathered knowledge in many parts of the world,

determined to come home with his sheaves, and place all that he had learned, and himself, at the service of his country and his Emperor.

Itō also talked of Korea, where he had recently served as resident general after stepping down as prime minister.

> He drew me to a window looking out on the garden and showed me some little boys happily at play. Pointing to one, he said "You see that lad? He is the Crown Prince of Korea, and has been sent here to be educated. The dearest wish and greatest ambition of my life is to see him secure upon the throne of Korea in friendly alliance with our Emperor."

A few weeks later Itō was assassinated on a railway platform in Manchuria by a Korean nationalist, and Korea was soon fully annexed by Japan. His vision—shared by Laurier's government—of vast new trans-Pacific trade between Canada and Japan endured, although it would not be fully realized until the 1920s.

KING'S JAPAN

William Lyon Mackenzie King, whose government was responsible for the egregious treatment of Japanese Canadians during the Pacific War, may seem an unlikely entry in this book. But King was a complex man of more than one persona. And there was another King with an earlier experience of Japan—one that influenced Canada's assumption of its place on the world stage after he became prime minister in 1921.

King's introduction to Japan began with what came to be known as the Vancouver Riot. On September 7, 1907, a mob of labour activists protesting Asian immigration set out for Vancouver's Chinatown and Little Tokyo, where they were turned back by a combination of banzai-shouting Japanese and the local constabulary. As riots go it was modest: some broken windows, ransacked stores and a few injuries, none fatal. For the most part it seems to have been a classic case of mob mentality, the crowd more wantonly destructive than anything else.

Nonetheless, the event was a shock. In Ottawa, Prime Minister Laurier, busily breathing life into his vision of a vast new trade across the Pacific, was appalled and immediately telegraphed Canada's apologies to the Japanese government and the emperor. Laurier also faced a dilemma. Beneath the surface lay growing antipathy to Asian immigration. At the same time, Canada had recently adhered to the 1894 Anglo–Japanese Treaty of Commerce and Navigation, which gave Japanese the same liberty as British subjects to enter, travel or reside in the country.

Any attempt to unilaterally impose immigration restrictions would certainly be taken badly by Japan. Instead, Laurier dispatched Labour Minister Rodolphe Lemieux to Tokyo for the delicate task of negotiating what became known as the Gentlemen's Agreement of 1908, under which Japan undertook

TOP 130 Powell Street, a building damaged during the Vancouver Riot of 1907. The photograph was taken to substantiate a damage claim of $139. *Library and Archives Canada, William Lyon Mackenzie King collection, C-14118*

ABOVE Labour Minister Rodolphe Lemieux, his wife (centre) and others in Tokyo in 1908 during negotiation of the "Gentlemen's Agreement" on immigration. *Library and Archives Canada, Rodolphe Lemieux collection, PA-202771*

to restrict immigration voluntarily. Meanwhile, the young deputy minister of labour, William Lyon Mackenzie King, went to Vancouver to investigate the causes of the riot, settle the modest claims for compensation and calm the troubled local waters.

• • •

Immigration was the flip side of the Japan craze. While the well-to-do of eastern North America toyed with the make-believe Japan of the teacups and travel brochures, real Japanese were arriving on their western doorstep. The ships that brought tea, silk and oranges also brought people.

Part of the broad ethnic mix that populated early British Columbia, Japanese immigrants initially attracted little attention, and when they did the tone was often positive. One turn-of-the-century Vancouver newspaper article praised Japanese as the kind of intelligent, enterprising, self-reliant immigrants Canada needed. The mood changed, however, after 1900 when they gained a prominent position in the fishery. Soon Japanese, together with the larger Chinese immigrant community, were caught in a groundswell of anti-Asian sentiment that washed up and down the Pacific coast of North America.

For a country reliant on immigration, Canada could be remarkably unwelcoming. Even British newcomers encountered the "no Englishmen need apply" caveat attached to prairie job advertisements. Asian immigrants, however, undoubtedly had the hardest time of it; the same qualities that made them "exotic" also made them, in the race-permeated thinking of the day, "unassimilable."

While the context was racial, the flashpoint was labour competition. Asian immigrants were willing to work for less, which made them a boon to employers but a challenge to workers, for whom they could mean the difference between having a job or not in British Columbia's volatile labour market.

A series of unrelated events in 1907 also inspired fear in an uneasy public mind. The number of Japanese arrivals shot up that year from about 1,000 annually to close to 8,000. Provincial election game-playing that spring uncovered an alleged railway plot to import 50,000 Japanese. In June a steamer arrived from Hawaii with over 1,000 Japanese on board. In July the Vancouver Trades and Labour Council formed an Asiatic Exclusion League.

The simmering stew boiled over later that summer when the federally appointed lieutenant governor, James Dunsmuir, refused a provincial attempt to ban Asian immigration. Also the largest employer of Asian labour in the province, Dunsmuir apparently had plans to hire up to 500 Japanese workers for his coal and railway interests on Vancouver Island. When this became known there were howls of protest and Dunsmuir was hanged in effigy, sparking the riot.

• • •

King's visit to Vancouver had an unanticipated side effect. Soon afterward he was invited to visit US President Theodore Roosevelt at the White House.

Japan was much on Roosevelt's mind at the time. By the turn of the century, American expansion westward across the continent was virtually complete, and the reach of Manifest Destiny had already stretched beyond continental North America to Hawaii and the Philippines. The power equation in the Pacific had also shifted dramatically as a result of Japan's unexpected victory in the 1904–05 Russo–Japanese War, which catapulted it into the major power leagues for the first time. Roosevelt was reportedly blown away by Japan's victory, declaring it the greatest phenomenon the world had seen, unmatched even by the Battle of Trafalgar.

In Canada, linked to Japan militarily by virtue of the 1902 Anglo–Japanese Alliance, the reaction was euphoric. Newspapers congratulated "gallant little Japan" on daring to take on the Russian bear and winning. Vancouver schoolchildren cheered the victory and bars handed out free drinks to Japanese Canadians. In Saskatchewan, where Ukrainian anti-Czarist sentiment ran high, a town was named Togo for Admiral Tōgō, the hero of the decisive battle of Tsushima. Another along the same railway line was named Kuroki after a general and a third was called Mikado, while one in British Columbia's Okanagan Valley was named in honour of another war hero, Prince Oyama.

In the United States, in contrast, realization that the two countries now faced each other across the Pacific as potential rivals bred new uneasiness. Increasingly the old sympathetic, rather paternal view of quaint, aspiring Japan would give way to the unflattering image of a clever, devious Japan that later came to be reflected in cartoon strips and the movies.

No one understood the changed dynamic better than Roosevelt, who personally mediated the Russo–Japanese War's drawn-out settlement in Portsmouth, New Hampshire. In early 1907 Roosevelt also found himself in a minor war scare fomented by rumours in European capitals. The Kaiser, in particular, was anxious to undermine the British alliance with Japan; it was he who coined the term "Yellow Peril," which inspired an Asian-looking cartoon figure riding a dragon laying waste to the cities of Europe. From German sources, Roosevelt received fantastic accounts of 10,000 Japanese disguised as coffee plantation workers in Mexico who drilled secretly at night in a plot to seize construction of the Panama Canal.

At the same time, Roosevelt was under pressure to restrict Japanese immigration, especially following the disastrous 1906 earthquake in San Francisco, which some locals, incredibly, blamed on Japanese. Roosevelt fretted not so much because he thought Japan harboured aggressive intentions, but because the hotheads on the west coast, as he called them, might provoke Japan and draw an unprepared United States into war. "The San Francisco mob bids fair if not to embroil us with Japan," he wrote, "at any rate to arouse in Japan a feeling of rankling anger toward us that may in time bear evil result, and the Japanese Jingoes are in their turn about as bad as ours."

Ultimately, however, Roosevelt viewed the Pacific as he viewed much else—through his passion for the navy. And the war talk, so long as it remained only talk, suited his purposes by rousing support in Congress for a more ambitious battleship program. He kept speaking of conciliation while waving the big stick of the American fleet, which sailed into Tokyo Bay in 1907, a visible reminder of Perry's arrival over 50 years earlier.

What nagged Roosevelt was Britain's place in the evolving Pacific equation. In the event of war the United States would face not only Japan, but a Japan allied with Britain, one wary of American aspirations in the region. Hence his interest in young Mr. King, who visited Roosevelt in Washington three times in early 1908.

The respective Canadian and American accounts of these meetings are quite different. In King's version it was Roosevelt who was deeply concerned about events on the Pacific coast, and Roosevelt who proposed that King go to London to enlist British cooperation in some kind of Anglo-American entente limiting Asian immigration: "I will speak to you frankly, Mr. King . . . if you were going to England I would give you some messages to take to Sir Edward Grey" (the British foreign secretary). In the US account it is the other way around; it is King who alarmed Roosevelt and proposed the London *démarche*.

King among the mandarins: William Lyon Mackenzie King (second row centre) with fellow participants at a meeting of the International Opium Commission in Shanghai in 1909. *Library and Archives Canada, C-055526*

Perhaps each simply heard what he wanted to hear. In any event the prospect of Canada being pulled into the US agenda was repugnant to Laurier when he heard of it. Personally distrustful of Americans, he was particularly suspicious of Roosevelt, believing his anxieties reflected little more than interest in a large naval appropriation. In Laurier's opinion, Roosevelt's talk was all flam.

The prime minister was next amazed to receive a letter from Roosevelt characterizing the London initiative as a Canadian idea that the US government would be pleased to support. To Laurier it all smacked of some smart Yankee trick. By then, however, he was boxed in. He could hardly refuse to have King go, nor could Canada appear to be playing errand boy to the US president. So a pretext was manufactured for King to go to London, where he cut his diplomatic teeth persuading a skeptical British government of the sensitivity of the immigration situation on the Pacific coast.

● ● ●

In 1909 King himself made a little-known visit to Japan, precipitated by an invitation to participate in an international meeting in Shanghai on controlling the opium trade. As it happened, he knew a little about opium. While assessing losses in Vancouver he had been surprised to receive two claims from local Chinese opium manufacturers. He had also visited a few opium dens and factories, witnessed sales over the counter and purchased a pouch.

By the time King arrived in Japan he bore the imprint of his China experience. As reported in his 900-page trip diary, he had found the country and its people fascinating, and had gotten on especially well with the senior Chinese Foreign Ministry official, the Yale-educated Liang Tun Yen. He had also been thoroughly exposed to unflattering Chinese views of Japan. Departing Shanghai via Tientsin and Mukden, he was astonished by the extent of Japan's presence; its soldiers seemed to be everywhere, in barracks beside the railway stations, even in his hotel where he was met by the incongruous sound of Japanese officers singing the American Civil War song "Marching through Georgia."

Imagine, then, King's surprise when he arrived in Shimonoseki and discovered not Japan the military machine but Japan the exquisite, Japan the charming, Japan the delightful. Travelling north he marvelled like any tourist over the landscape, exclaiming over endless vistas of meandering tea terraces and mountains sliding into the sea, contrasting them favourably to the greyish-brown sand plains of China. To him the whole country seemed like one beautiful garden in spring.

His timing, which coincided with cherry blossom season, was pure serendipity. In Kyoto he was fascinated by the subtleties of the tea ceremony and entranced by graceful young women in brightly coloured kimonos weaving their way through cherry blossom dances. In Tokyo he delighted in the celebrating crowds.

> It appears that for two weeks in the year the laws are suspended, provided behaviour does not become improper and the Japanese are allowed to dress up in fancy costumes and have a holiday time beneath the rows of trees in blossom . . . We passed thousands of people all holidaying, some of them on the water in barges prettily decorated and others enjoying little side-shows which were doing quite a business.

Much about Japan appealed to King's idiosyncrasies. He exercised his penchant for doodads by shopping for kimonos, ivory and other souvenirs for friends and family. He attended an elegant garden party, the men in frock coats and silk hats and the women in kimonos. He took tea with a Mrs. Shimizu; and became enthusiastic about Japanese housing, speculating on its suitability for country cottages, possibly with his own recently acquired retreat at Kingsmere in mind. He also went to dinner at the Maple Club, where he was attended by what he called "geisha girls," whose fortunes he told from their palms.

He even managed to gratify one of the more ambiguous aspects of his persona, his proclivity for rescuing fallen women, with a visit to a must-see on Tokyo's tourist itinerary: the infamous Yoshiwara, the licensed pleasure quarter where the main business was prostitution. He reported the experience as deeply discomfiting, without exception the strangest sight, the weirdest and most unnatural he had ever seen.

> Here were rows of buildings, the front of which were barred like cages and seated within behind the caged bars were rows of women, each group dressed in a costume of like colour. We were told that these women numbered some 4,000 in this quarter. I don't know if anywhere in the world such an extraordinary sight is to be seen. It is a strange commentary on human life and present day civilization.

● ● ●

Somehow in the midst of this, King the smitten tourist found time to play King the budding statesman. Over dinner one evening he pursued his main objective, immigration, with the foreign minister, Count Komura Jutarō, who tried to reassure him that Japan's strategic interests lay in Asia—specifically Korea and Manchuria—not North America.

King, who was still a little uneasy about what may have actually gone on in Vancouver, came away relieved. He was also personally taken with Komura, a fellow Harvard graduate and former Japanese ambassador to London and Washington. He felt Japan could be trusted to live up to the spirit of the Gentlemen's Agreement, provided Japan's dignity did not suffer, by which King meant no resort to exclusion. "There is nothing to fear from Japanese immigration," he recorded later, "so long as wise councils of conciliation and moderation are brought to bear and the arts of diplomacy substituted for obnoxious measures that would prove more ineffective."

In a message clearly designed for the ears of Roosevelt, Komura also labelled as curious an apparent US assumption that Japan's investment in its navy was directed against the United States. On this point, King was not so sure. He sensed Japan must be preparing for conflict not only with Russia and China but also, if necessary, with the US.

> It is perfectly clear that the Japanese must have some area for expansion. If they do not find it in Asia they will find it in America, and it is better for Canadian interests that the struggle should be centred in the east than directed toward Canadian shores . . . At the moment I am inclined to believe that within another 10 years Manchuria will be the occasion of one of the world's greatest wars.

King's musings were off, but only by a couple of decades.

All in all, King came away feeling rather conflicted. He enjoyed his time in China; there was something about the Chinese character that appealed to him. But he found conditions there deplorable, in contrast with orderly, progressive life in Japan. He also liked Japanese better than expected. On moral grounds he could not condone Japan's control over Korea nor its intended seizure of Manchuria, but on practical grounds he could not bring himself to condemn these aggressions. When he asked himself what he would do if similarly placed, he hesitated to pass judgment.

What seems to have made the biggest impression on King was Japan's rising economic power. He was amazed by the extent of Japan's industrialization, as evidenced by huge numbers of factories and ships. "One is right in assuming," he noted in another prescient observation, "that the centre of industrial greatness is going to shift gradually from Europe to Asia, once there is political security in Asia."

He was especially struck by a visit to a cotton mill that employed some 3,000 workers, over two-thirds of them female. Indentured for three years they worked 12-hour days, while little girls sat on the floor cleaning cotton from boiled cocoons for a pittance. He was also told of a creek at the base of Mount Fuji where the bodies of some who ran away could be found.

This was the less attractive underbelly of Japan's remarkable transformation: the exploitation of millions of textile workers, mostly women, who bore the brunt of the massive drive to industrialization. But where some rushed to judgment, King was more inclined to draw parallels. He saw nothing peculiarly Japanese about the textile workers' plight; it was a phenomenon that had its counterpart everywhere in the industrialized world, including Canada.

LEFT Count Komura Jutarō represented Japan in the negotiated settlement of the Russo–Japanese War presided over by US president Roosevelt. *Diplomatic Archives of the Ministry of Foreign Affairs, Japan*

RIGHT William Lyon Mackenzie King in 1910, the year after he visited India, China and Japan. *Library and Archives Canada, William James Topley, PA-25970*

> I could not help thinking that except for the wages, the conditions of the girls in the cotton mills of Japan were very similar to what they are in the cotton mills of the Province of Quebec. At best it is industrial slavery . . . It is difficult to know what force will be strong enough to bring home to the conscience of men their responsibilities through gaining wealth in this way.

Learning that the Japanese mill had attracted British investment, he drew practical implications.

> The real peril so far as the Orient was concerned, lies, to my mind, not in the possible movement of labour from Asia to America . . . but in the almost certain movement of capital, not only from America but Europe also, to Asia, once the industrial possibilities of these continents become better known and a greater degree of stability

and security of investment is afforded. This is a phase of the problem which Canadians interested in the future industrial greatness of our Dominion will do well to consider.

Here was King the industry and labour theorist, the future author of *Industry and Humanity* (1918), his personal manifesto for social and economic change. To his mind everything—the recent trouble in Vancouver, Japan's expanding economy, the evolving strategic equation in the Pacific—was intertwined and explainable by universal economic and social conditions. Restricting immigration, he rationalized, was a given and a necessity, but this should be recognized for what it was: an economic matter rather than one of race or colour or creed.

In the end sentiment won out. King thought he would never forget his last glimpse of Japan. "A mist had gathered over the shore as the sun was setting, and one could see through it and the haze created by the sunlight as the great ball of fire sank below the horizon, the outline of Fujiyama, just such a scene as one sees depicted on a Japanese screen."

• • •

There was one more King who travelled to Asia in the spring of 1909, and that was King the nascent nationalist. While Canada at the time controlled its domestic affairs, in international matters it was still under London's thumb—a situation that grew increasingly untenable as it became evident that Britain could not always be counted on to serve Canadian interests.

Laurier was a staunch supporter of the British Empire, but even he resented the way London expected Canada to fall into lockstep with imperial priorities. He also chafed under the British proclivity for enhancing power and prestige by centralizing control, while marvelling at their capacity to turn on the charm. "It is hard," Laurier once remarked after returning from a visit to London, "to stand up against the flattery of a gracious duchess. Weak men's heads are turned in an evening, and there are few that can resist long. We were dined and wined by royalty and aristocracy and plutocracy and always the talk was of Empire, Empire, Empire."

King, in contrast, was attracted to just this kind of high society. An admirer of the British upper classes, he liked nothing better than elegant London life and weekends in fine country houses. At the same time he loathed being treated as a colonial by condescending British bureaucrats, which nettled his own considerable vanity. Before leaving for the Far East he decided to use his

RIGHT During his 1909 visit, William Lyon Mackenzie King attended a celebration of the wedding of Nose Kama, daughter of the recently returned Japanese consul general in Canada, and the son of Baron Iwasaki, head of the Mitsubishi Company. *United Church of Canada Archives, 1999.054P/47*

BELOW King saw parallels between conditions in Japanese textile mills, like the one shown here, and those in Quebec. *United Church of Canada Archives, 1999.054P/44N*

trip to float the possibility of Canada taking more direct responsibility for its own interests abroad, including but not confined to immigration.

To what extent this idea, which amounted to placing Canadians in British diplomatic missions, was his own or Laurier's is unclear, but it was well received when King raised it with the British foreign secretary in London. The response in Delhi and Peking was also positive. In Tokyo, however, the British ambassador was so patronizing that King was put off, grumbling that it was the sort of thing that made Canadians feel they should rid themselves of colonial status and become partners rather than daughters in the imperial scheme.

Nor was King reassured by what he heard and saw. Everywhere he went he was told about US inroads in trade while Canada, which produced many of the same goods, lagged behind. He also arrived in Tokyo on the heels of the "Preston affair," the foofaraw that ensued when Canada's special trade representative insisted on the right to export directly to Japan without going through foreign agents. King received an earful from local ambassadors who made clear they regarded Preston as a troublemaker and, in the words of the British ambassador, "a damned nuisance." Komura told King that he thought Preston had gone too far. On the other hand, Tamura Shinkichi, the largest exporter of Canadian goods to Japan, defended Preston strongly, noting that he had not made any enemies among Japanese.

King felt Preston's ideas were on the right track, though he had doubts about his methods. And whatever Preston's shortcomings were, they paled in comparison with what King discovered in China, where he was told of a Mr. Craig, who had allegedly made a good deal of money reselling loot during the Boxer Rebellion and running the blockade during the Russo–Japanese War and gone off to St. Petersburg to collect. He also heard that the Canadian government trade commissioner in Shanghai rarely set foot in the office. When King arrived there he was dismayed to find shabby premises fronted by a rough wooden sign, staffed by the man's daughter and an 18-year-old Japanese Eurasian.

King returned from his trip to Asia with his instincts reinforced: Canada needed to take more direct responsibility for its own international interests—seeds of an idea that would resurface after he came to power as prime minister in 1921. By then, however, international dynamics had shifted profoundly.

• • •

The world before the First World War was a colonial one that accepted, even welcomed, Japan's special interests on the Asian mainland. Japanese suzerainty over Korea and part of Manchuria was a check on the Russians as well as a means of bringing much-needed order to confusion and chaos. Japan, however, had the misfortune of entering the colonial game at a time when the ground was already largely occupied. The post-war world still took colonies and spheres of influence for granted, but it was caught short by Japan's assumption of control over former German possessions in the region as well as its issuance of the famous "Twenty-One Demands" to China. On a collision course with European and US interests, Japan was increasingly viewed as an aggressor nation, not fully trusted.

At the same time, the refusal of the 1919 Paris Peace Conference to recognize the principle of racial equality was a blow to Japan's hard-won international prestige that hardened attitudes at home. And while the international community partially accepted Japan's territorial demands against the vociferous objections of a rapidly crumbling China, it did so reluctantly to secure Japanese support for Woodrow Wilson's showpiece, the newly minted League of Nations—which in the end the United States did not join. With the optimistic new world of the League, the language of international relations itself also changed as the talk became less and less about territorial possessions and more and more about territorial integrity and collective security.

The old Anglo–Japanese Alliance, the longstanding lynchpin in Japan's international relations, also ran its course. During the First World War nervous BC residents had reason to be grateful for the *Izumo* and the *Aso*, Japanese cruisers that patrolled the Strait of Juan de Fuca. And in what surely ranks as one of the more bizarre episodes in Canadian military history, a hastily assembled collection of Canadian military and RCMP went to Siberia after the Russian Revolution as part of an Allied force formally under the command of a Japanese general, Otani Kikuzo, aimed at protecting the Trans-Siberian Railway. In the early 1920s the Alliance was allowed to lapse in favour of the shiny new promise of the League and the new collective security treaties emerging from the 1922 Washington Naval Conference.

The new global mix—an ambitious and frustrated Japan, a wary United States, a watchful Britain and an untried multilateralism—was full of uncertainty, as realization sunk in that future issues of war and

Looking east, south and west in 1936: Prime Minister William Lyon Mackenzie King (seated) with the ministers of France, the United States and Japan, and O.D. Skelton, undersecretary of state for external affairs. *Library and Archives Canada, C-098305*

peace were as likely to revolve around Tokyo as Washington, London or other world capitals.

• • •

We are as intimately associated as possible with Great Britain. In regard to France we are in the exceptional position of being related by kinship, by past tradition, by sentiment and by language in large part . . . In regard to the United States we are so situated geographically that between us we occupy practically the whole of this continent . . . Now it so happens that Japan is our nearest neighbour across the Pacific. Thus as a country we are situated, so to speak, in the centre of the four great powers . . . that are instrumental in controlling world affairs as far as they relate to peace and war.

With these words Prime Minister William Lyon Mackenzie King rose in the House of Commons in January 1928 and announced his government's decision to establish Canadian diplomatic legations in Washington, Paris and Tokyo.

Like some kind of portly latter-day archangel, hovering with wings extended somewhere over Hudson Bay, he conjured a vision of Canada at the centre of a kind of world amphitheatre, surrounded on three sides by great powers; its frontiers, of necessity, completely exposed. In friendship and nothing else lay its security. It is a Canadian foreign-policy self-image that has endured ever since, distinguished by the extent to which subsequent archangels have been inclined to shift their gazes more south, east, west or north at various points in time.

The decision, however, was not as obvious at the time as it may seem in hindsight. Canada had long been represented in London, and since 1924 in Geneva. The establishment of a legation in Washington, where Canada had much ongoing business, was natural and uncontroversial, as was upgrading the status of Canada's longstanding commissioner-general in Paris. But Japan, a country with which Canada's connections were still, by comparison, slight? To opposition leader R.B. Bennett it looked suspiciously like the thin edge of the wedge, a wily move by King destined to lead to nothing short of dissolution of Canada's historic ties to Britain and the Empire, if not the Empire itself.

As Bennett railed on, King, in the convoluted verbiage he employed on such occasions, split hairs over theories of empire while waxing eloquent about the importance of immigration and trade. It would not be surprising if on these points he also had some sense of déjà vu. As Canadian exports took off in the 1920s, Laurier's prediction of booming trade across the Pacific was finally coming true. Immigration pressures also resurfaced after the US decision to ban all Asian immigration in 1924—a road King's government went down with respect to China but resisted in the case of Japan, preferring instead to tighten the more diplomatically palatable Gentlemen's Agreement in 1928.

As a rationale for establishing formal diplomatic relations, however, the demands of trade and immigration alone were rather thin. Nor was Japan top of mind for most Canadians. King's announcement also spoke to a larger

Baron Tomii, Japan's minister to Canada, shown above (left) with Prime Minister William Lyon Mackenzie King admiring the abbey ruins at Kingsmere in 1938.
Library and Archives Canada, Matsunaga photograph, PA-134795

picture: the profound shift taking place in the structure of global power and Canada's future place in it.

By the time King took office in 1921, Canada had already earned a seat at the international table in the First World War, albeit at a cost of thousands killed and wounded on the battlefields of Europe. The days of "ready aye ready" were drawing to a close, but they were not yet gone; Canada was still expected to march to the imperial tune. At the 1923 Imperial Conference in London, King astounded other participants by insisting on Canada's right to equal status with Britain. When the Conference met again in 1926 he effectively won the point, which remained only to be formally codified in the 1931 Statute of Westminster.

Winning the principle, however, amounted to little without action to give it effect. "The solution," King confided to his diary in 1925, "is to gradually expand the Canadian diplomatic corps and establish legations where Canadian interests are most directly affected."

What the 1928 announcement was fundamentally about was Canada's international coming of age, with a Pacific as well as a North American and Atlantic face. It was concrete evidence, a signal no one could miss, that Canada was taking responsibility for its own role in the world within the British Empire.

FLAMING PASSION

By the time Caroline Macdonald died unexpectedly in 1931, she was one of the best-known foreigners in Japan.

News of her death was reported in the *New York Times*, the *Times* of London and the Japanese press. A thousand people turned out for her memorial service, from ordinary workers to the Japanese vice-minister of foreign affairs. She had recently received a high honour from the emperor as well as special recognition from the Japanese Ministry of Justice. She was also the first woman to receive an honorary doctorate of laws from the University of Toronto.

What would have meant most to her, however, were more than 50 letters placed, Japanese fashion, before her photograph—letters from grateful Japanese convicts.

• • •

From the beginning, Caroline Macdonald was unique. In 1901, when few Canadian women went on to higher education, she graduated from the University of Toronto with an honours degree in mathematics and physics and a prize for a paper on banking.

Three years later her life took a surprising turn when she went to

Caroline Macdonald, who went to Japan in 1904, become a well-known prison reformer and labour activist. *University of Toronto Archives, A73-0026/259(90)99-40#1*

Tokyo to help establish a branch of the Young Women's Christian Association (YWCA). Just why she did this is unclear; the idea seems to have arisen at a meeting she attended in the Ottawa drawing room of Elizabeth Sifton, the wife of Interior Minister Clifford Sifton, in 1903—the same year Canada participated in the Osaka industrial exhibition and began hatching visions of vast new trade across the Pacific.

Soon after arrival Macdonald fell in with a group of leading Japanese educators and reformers that included Japan's foremost female educator, Bryn Mawr–schooled Tsuda Ume, who in 1900 had recently established Japan's first private women's college, the forerunner of Tsuda University. Accepting an invitation to teach English literature there, she continued to do so on and off for years, exposing successive classes of young Japanese women to the delights of Tennyson and Browning. She was also plugged into the Keio modernizers through Shidachi Taki, a daughter of well-known Meiji reformer Fukuzawa Yukichi, who chaired the YWCA board, and her husband Shidachi Tetsujiro, a prominent socially-minded businessman and financier.

Another friend was Nitobe Inazō, a prominent Japanese educator and the author of the famous *Bushido, the Soul of Japan*. Macdonald was regularly invited to join his international circle at his summer home in Karuizawa. It was also Nitobe who encouraged her to become proficient in Japanese by spending six months in the home of a retired newspaper proprietor and his family in a remote village on the other side of the mountain.

Like others of her time and station, Macdonald was perturbed by the state of Japanese womanhood, lamenting that twice as many girls were working as geisha, licensed prostitutes and bar girls as went to high school. She also had little patience with the prevailing Confucian-based ideal, with its emphasis on obedience, self-effacement and frugality. "Girls," she observed, "are lectured about being good wives and wise mothers until in their desperation they go off on the rebound into the wildest excesses; boys, who might do well to listen to a few lectures on the duty of being good husbands and wise fathers, are taught nothing which even remotely approaches the attitude men ought to take toward women."

This perspective tended to overlook the extent to which the nuclear family was a Western model introduced into a society that had long relied on a broader, more collective view of kinship and familial relations. Western society also tended to assume that sex, social stability, love and companionship could and should be found in one person, the spouse, while looking the other way when reality fell short of the mark. In Japan, family life, love life and sexual life had historically been more differentiated.

The role of Japanese women, however, was changing. The Good Wife and Wise Mother of Martha Cartmell's day had been an upper-class, quasi-Confucian ideal designed to shape Japanese women who would take their place alongside modern Japanese men—a view that always sat a bit incongruously with the way most Japanese women lived their lives, especially those who toiled in the countryside or flocked in growing numbers to urban factories.

By the turn of the century, the ideal Japanese woman was still firmly anchored in home and family, but she was also likely to be a higher school graduate, an effective household financial manager and an investor in the postal savings system, Japan's nationwide household savings institution. She might also be active outside the home, particularly after the 1904–05 Russo–Japanese War, when many women heeded the emperor's call for a nationwide effort by taking up nursing, bandage rolling and similar patriotic activities. As Japan's expanding economy took men into the private sector, small numbers of women graduates began taking on traditionally male functions like teaching and office work.

At the same time, conventions were being challenged by the controversial "New Woman" debate associated with the feminists of the Seito ("bluestocking") movement that emerged during the more liberal Taishō era, which coincided with the reign of the new Emperor Taishō (1912–26) following the death of the Emperor Meiji. More independent-minded and equal to her husband, the New Woman wanted to attend political meetings and vote. She might even show interest in the forbidden subject of birth control.

Macdonald dabbled in the radical end of the New Woman debate, joining Margaret Sanger when she arrived to discuss birth control with its chief Japanese advocate, Baroness Ishimoto. But for the most part she remained at the conservative end of the feminist spectrum, sharing the view of people like Tsuda and Nitobe that a precipitous move to women's suffrage could undermine the fabric of Japanese society.

The Tokyo YWCA made its formal debut in the autumn of 1905 at a "chrysanthemum garden party" given by Count Ōkuma Shigenobu, a former prime minister and founder of Waseda University. Designed to provide a safe and wholesome environment for young women arriving in Tokyo to work or study, the initiative had great appeal to foreigners and socially conscious Japanese alike.

Among the institution's key benefactors was Hirooka Asako, a daughter of the Mitsui family. Separated from her husband, Hirooka was something of an advertisement for the New Woman herself. One of Japan's few female entrepreneurs, she managed coal mines, a bank, an insurance company and an agricultural enterprise in Korea. She also lived in a lavish Western-style house with a staff of 24.

• • •

While Macdonald came from the same Protestant, middle-class Ontario background as the female missionary teachers who flocked to Japan from the 1880s onward, what she was really about was universal social reform. "One soul," as she once put it, "is a step toward saving the whole world."

Exchanging costumes: Hirooka Asako of the Mitsui family and Caroline Macdonald at a YWCA Conference in 1912. *United Church of Canada Archives, 76.001P/4149N*

In 1917 her life took another astonishing turn when her focus shifted from middle- and upper-class Japanese women to Japanese men, specifically those at the bottom of the social ladder: the inmates of Japanese prisons. It began when she started visiting a young man of her acquaintance who was in Kosuge Prison for the murder of his wife. Each morning at five o'clock the prison guards watched as a tiny, bespectacled foreign woman lined up at the gate. Finding she had a beneficial effect on prisoners, they invited her to visit regularly. Day after day she sat in a small cubicle separated by wire mesh from some of the most hardened criminals in Japan, giving encouragement to those awaiting release and helping those facing death come to terms with their fate.

Her celebrity arose from a relationship with one particular prisoner, Ishii Tokichi, a habitual offender who was in jail on a relatively minor charge of theft. Overhearing one day that a man had been jailed for the murder of a geisha, an act that Ishii himself had committed, he was stricken with

Macdonald worked with Arima Shirosuke, the governor of Kosuge Prison, ca. 1915. *United Church of Canada Archives, 86.298P/1*

conscience and confessed. Duly sentenced to death, he was befriended by Macdonald, and under her influence he is said to have undergone a kind of catharsis during which he became a Christian and found inner peace. When his final moment came he bequeathed to her all his earthly possessions: a one-*sen* coin that she wore thereafter on a chain around her neck.

While awaiting execution, Ishii wrote his story, *A Rascal Becomes a Saint*. A touching tale that captured the public imagination, it was translated into English by Macdonald and published in New York by Canadian George Doran as *A Gentleman in Prison*. The book gave her tremendous notoriety; anyone who was anyone in Tokyo in 1917 had heard of Caroline Macdonald—or, as some began calling her, the White Angel of Tokyo.

She personally was not very keen on this label, nor were conversions her principal preoccupation. The prisoners and prison officials who converted to Christianity on her watch never amounted to more than a handful, and those who did may well have been equally influenced, if not more so, by a Japanese propensity for adopting the beliefs of a superior.

Arima Shirosuke, the prison governor, was both a Christian and a man with a reputation for humane treatment of prisoners. He was also a friend who visited Macdonald's home regularly for English lessons, dinner and what she called their "discussions of the cosmos." Working with him she became Japan's international eyes, ears and sometimes voice on prison reform. No longer the brutal, feudal places of popular imagination, Japanese prisons by that time, though dismal and depressing, were arguably no worse than their counterparts in Europe and America. Travelling, making connections and translating documents, Macdonald kept Japanese prison and judicial officials abreast of developments in other countries while ensuring that Japanese advances were recognized abroad.

Arima's methods received widespread attention around the world in the upheaval that followed the Great Earthquake of 1923, when 1,300 inmates of Kosuge Prison remained in the open yard for three days and three nights without guards or restraints of any kind. They did not even try to escape.

• • •

When Macdonald shifted into prison work, her YWCA role was assumed by Emma Kaufman, a home economics graduate from Kitchener, Ontario, who fell in love with Japan during a visit and stayed to teach at Tsuda in 1909.

As much of a powerhouse in her own way as Macdonald, Kaufman was also her polar opposite. While Macdonald lived in a couple of rooms in a Japanese-style house that she happily shared with a steady stream of visitors in need of bed and board, Kaufman built a well-appointed Western-style house complete with North American furniture, a cook and a chauffeur. She also owned "the Ark," a cottage in Karuizawa where she entertained her friends, including the Nitobes. Where Macdonald was frugal to a fault, Kaufman gave lavish dinner parties with fine china and silver in her large dining room. And when Macdonald got tired of walking, Kaufman magically produced an automobile.

Indeed, as time went on, Macdonald came to appreciate that she owed much to the Kaufman family, who had made a fortune in rubber, a growing Canadian export to Japan. They supported a number of philanthropic causes in addition to the YWCA, including Tsuda and Women's Christian universities. Emma Kaufman spent much of her own considerable inheritance on a new YWCA headquarters, as well as a rest house, an apartment house and hostels near the Yoshiwara, Tokyo's licensed pleasure quarter. She and her family also sent Japanese women abroad to study and brought Canadian and American women to work in Japan.

More than a dormitory, the YWCA was an exercise in leadership-building among middle-class women, which the institution's backers hoped would eventually spread to their sisters in factories, commercial enterprises and hospitals. Its new headquarters in Tokyo's Kanda district was a large,

Emma Kaufman (above left) with her visiting sister, shown in a *jinricksha* in 1917, became a driving force in the Tokyo YWCA and other social causes. *University of Waterloo Library, Special Collections, Augustine Ham Kaufman family fonds, GA138 2004*

modern facility designed to Kaufman's specifications with Western and Japanese-style rooms, a night school and home economics, English and business departments, as well as something new: a swimming pool.

She also introduced young YWCA women to the joys of camping, once outfitting an entire peninsula on Lake Nojiri with tents and canoes. "It was an exciting and new experiment," she noted. "Some campers wore kimono while the foreign leaders dressed in shirts and knickerbockers."

• • •

When Macdonald's house was destroyed in the 1923 earthquake she decided to realize a long-held dream of establishing a settlement house. Capitalizing on concern over the thousands left homeless and destitute, she tapped her contacts in Mitsui, the judiciary, the Tokyo government and the Imperial Household, as well as her Canadian supporters.

Modelled along the lines of similar institutions sprouting up in Chicago and other North American cities at the time, the Shinrinkan was part dormitory, part school and part refuge, a place where the poor and out of luck could find a bed, a meal, an English class and, with luck, help in finding a job. It also responded to the exploding number of factory workers in Tokyo,

The Shinrinkan (Home of the Friendless Stranger) was located in Tokyo's Shiba district behind Alexander Shaw's St. Andrew's Church. *United Church of Canada Archives, 86.298.1*

which by then had reached about 1 million, fed by growing unrest in the countryside. While the 1920s spelled prosperity in most industrialized countries, Japan's first real spurt of economic growth was running its course by that time. Instead of enjoying the benefits of economic and social transformation, farmers and factory workers found themselves poorly paid, with miserable housing and working conditions, in an era when social support was still largely the responsibility of the family, not the state.

From social work it was a short skip and jump into the world of Japan's incipient labour movement. Soon the Shinrinkan was being used as a meeting place for one of the more moderate labour unions, Sodomei, as well as a school for workers. While Macdonald was necessarily more of a labour sympathizer than an active organizer, she involved herself in labour protests, usually to urge non-violence. On one memorable occasion she addressed several hundred strike-weary, red-headbanded strikers of the brewer's union during their dispute with the soy sauce–producing Kikkoman Company, one of Japan's longest and most memorable strikes.

As incongruous as the sight of a foreign woman addressing striking Japanese workers, however, was the sight of one accompanying the leader of Sodomei to a meeting of the International Labour Organization (ILO) in Geneva in the late 1920s.

Following Caroline Macdonald's death in 1931, her friend Arima Shirosuke, the governor of Kosuge Prison, found himself asking questions. How was it that a woman had come to Japan and devoted herself to prisoners, people on whom Japanese society was inclined to turn its back? "Her conduct appeared at first sight to be that of an insane person," he reflected. "But she had a plan which she executed resolutely and bravely, with flaming passion."

Passion alone, however, did not explain how a foreigner, especially a foreign woman, was able to gain such a level of acceptance or such a wide range of personal and professional connections. Fluency in Japanese was undoubtedly a factor, as was her manner. But there had to be more to it than that.

Macdonald was driven. Macdonald was formidable. Macdonald was fearless. In a society where imprisonment was traditionally associated with an intense sense of shame, her house became a refuge for recently released convicts and their families. A foreign visitor who stayed overnight reminded her to lock the door. "Why bother?" she replied. "The criminals are all inside."

She knew everybody. People approached her in the streets to ask for help. Businessmen gave her donations. Government officials showed up on her doorstep for English lessons, advice and a chat. The Mitsukoshi Department Store band occasionally dropped by to play for her. She described the endless series of visitors who showed up during a typical day at the Shinrinkan in one of her letters home.

> Before . . . breakfast . . . an official from the Prefectural office called to get information about the settlement. While he was here the first installment of detectives arrived. The women strikers themselves were arriving all the time . . . About eleven a graduate of Tsuda College turned up and asked me to read *Rabbi Ben Ezra* with her, which I did. Rabbi's "turning earth's smoothness round" is very apropos of our present circumstances. One of the strike leaders dropped in to report progress (or rather lack of progress) . . .
>
> Mr. Shidachi, a well known economist and financier and member of the settlement committee, dropped in to see how the strike was progressing and also to talk over with me the educational work for the autumn. Before he had gone an official from the Dept. of Justice arrived . . . to ask me to help him with a translation of American

prison pamphlets . . . Mr. Uchida, a former employee of the Japan Electric Co. . . . dropped in to commiserate with me on the length of time the strike is lasting . . . and to beg my continued kind offices for the women . . .

Hard on his heels came Ikematsu-san, a young scamp who got out of prison five months ago and . . . has not mended his ways. Came to say that he has sold his sister into some disreputable place in Shimonoseki and wished me to get her out! I suggested he telegraph his father from whom the girl had presumably run away and that if he didn't have money to send him the telegram I'd do it for him. He didn't take my offer . . .

While he was still here Dr. Hora of Nagasaki Medical College came in . . . He has made post mortem examinations of men who have undergone capital punishment. He is . . . visiting reformatories and juvenile prisons and testing the mentality of these young offenders. We have much in common as we are both keen on crime!

Macdonald, it seemed, was everywhere. When not managing the Shinrinkan, visiting prisons or working with labour activists, she was busy canvassing her wealthy friends for jobs for wives of convicts, addressing students at Keio University, counselling young offenders or promoting a proposal for a juvenile court. She travelled back and forth to Canada, the United States and England to raise funds. She even found time for a sabbatical at Aberdeen University in Scotland, where she earned a doctorate in divinity.

In a society where hierarchy mattered, she paid remarkably little heed to social or class distinctions. A Christmas at the Shinrinkan was a motley mix of several hundred people, including students from the labour school, members of the knitting class, ex-prisoners and prison officials, students, businessmen, bureaucrats, the vice-mayor of Tokyo and an Anglican bishop. Macdonald herself admitted to being struck sometimes by the anomalies.

Once the governor of the prison, my beloved Mr. Arima, Yamada San and I had lunch together. Yamada San [the murderer responsible for her original involvement in prison work, subsequently released on good behaviour] was still in his prison clothes as his ordinary ones hadn't arrived. As this is a very great public holiday in Japan the governor was in his very grand regimentals, with his Imperial

Decorations around his neck . . . I don't think the combination could have happened anywhere else on earth.

One of the most striking things about Macdonald was her ease with Japanese men. While she had many female friends, some of her most enduring connections were with men, who seem to have treated her not so much as a woman or even a foreigner but as a respected professional, a helpful colleague. Indeed, if anyone belied the conventional wisdom that foreign women cannot thrive in Japan's male-oriented society, it was Caroline Macdonald. In addition to Nitobe, Arima and others, she was close to Uemura Masahisa, one of Japan's leading Christians and her spiritual confidante. The only foreign member of his independent Presbyterian church, she even became a church elder, something that would have been impossible in a Canadian church at the time.

It is also tempting to wonder whether somewhere along the way at least one of these friendships might have developed into something beyond the professional and platonic. A relationship between a foreign woman and a Japanese man, while far from common, was not unheard of. Nitobe, for example, was married to an American. There is no indication, however, that Macdonald's inclinations ever veered in that direction. Her heart, she once confided, firmly belonged to a Scottish widower and professor of theology at the University of Aberdeen, for whom she maintained a lifelong and apparently unrecognized and unrequited ardour.

• • •

Before she died Macdonald herself speculated about the reason for her success. She thought it lay in her refusal to admit any differences between foreigners and Japanese. In a world ridden with views of racial and cultural superiority and inferiority, she saw only similarities and possibilities. "Any fool can see the differences," she once wrote. "It takes a loving heart and a well balanced head to see that we are all one."

Arima Shirosuke, who puzzled so much about Macdonald following her death, had a further thought. Japanese were impressed by this woman because there was no contradiction between her words and her actions. She simply lived what she believed.

THE GREAT QUAKE AND COMMERCE

According to myth, the Japanese archipelago is inhabited by a giant catfish pinned down under a powerful rock by the Kashima god. Whenever the god lets down his guard, the catfish thrashes about and causes earthquakes.

At two minutes before noon on September 1, 1923, the catfish must have done a back flip. The massive earthquake that struck the Kantō plain left an estimated 143,000 dead, another 100,000 injured and a further 2 million homeless. Much of the damage came from the fires that ravaged vast sections of Yokohama and Tokyo, as the earthquake struck just when hibachis were being lit to cook the mid-day meal.

Samuel Robinson, captain of the Canadian Pacific *Empress of Australia*, was loading passengers in Yokohama at the precise moment the earthquake struck. He and his crew watched the impact unfold minute by ghastly minute, recording their observations in the ship's log: "The vessel shook all over in a most terrifying fashion, and also rocked very quickly and violently until it seemed as though the masts and funnels must carry away." The long wharf beside the ship simply vanished.

> Three or four hundred people were on the wharf . . . saying good-bye to their friends, with paper streamers in their hands, when the earth-quake happened. A number fell, or were thrown by the motion, down the fissures as they opened and closed as the land waves passed—some of the openings being three or four feet wide—either disappearing into the water below or being crushed to death. In one case a motor car and its occupants, ready to drive off the wharf, disappeared entirely.

He also watched the impact unfold on Yokohama itself. "A dense pall of dust rose up hundreds of feet above the town and a terrible roar came from it,

Samuel Robinson, captain of the Canadian Pacific *Empress of Australia*, received great acclaim for his actions following the Great Earthquake of 1923 and was recognized by the emperor for his services. *Vancouver Maritime Museum*

which was probably caused by the simultaneous falling of hundreds of brick and stone buildings in the Settlement, also possibly by the earthquake itself."

Only after the wind dropped in mid-afternoon, however, did the full magnitude of the disaster become apparent. The entire town was destroyed, including the residential district on the Bluff. Fires burned fiercely along the foreshore and in all directions for miles around. A northward glare in the sky in the direction of Tokyo and Yokosuka indicated they, too, were burning.

He and the crew also soon realized their own danger, as gusts of intensely hot air and burning matter threatened to set fire to a nearby freight shed. The *Empress* itself was then struck heavily by a large Japanese steamer, the *Lyons Maru*, which had lost its moorings. Securing themselves as best they could, they turned to the task of rescue, launching lifeboats through the night to bring survivors back to the ship and ferrying fresh water to those huddling in Yokohama Park.

The danger, however, was far from over. Toward morning a huge, furiously burning mass was spotted near the foreshore about half a mile away. Initially thought to be drums of stored paint, it turned out to be fuel oil from burst storage tanks floating in the harbour. Thick, greasy, rolling flames shot up in a whirling column of fire a hundred feet wide and several hundred feet high. As the fiery masses roared toward them, Robinson realized they had to get away as fast as possible. "We had then over 2,000 people on board and I was very anxious."

Eventually the ship was manoeuvred to safety beyond the breakwater, where it became the headquarters for rescue work until the immediate crisis

The devastated port of Yokohama in the aftermath of the 1923 earthquake, seen from the Canadian Pacific *Empress of Australia*. *Vancouver Maritime Museum, 5861*

passed. The first merchant vessel to arrive after the earthquake was another Canadian Pacific *Empress* bringing a Canadian gift of condensed milk, canned fish, flour and relief supplies from the Canadian Red Cross and the Japanese Canadian community, along with two Vancouver nurses.

• • •

The Great Earthquake of 1923 was the end of old Yokohama. Visiting what remained of the city in the days that followed, Robinson and his party found the devastation absolute. It was a tumbled mass of debris, and only someone with a thorough knowledge of the streets and buildings could distinguish where the foreign settlement had even been. Picking their way through the tangle of fallen wires and piles of brick and stone, they located #14 on the Bund, the site of the Canadian Pacific office, which had been there since the 1890s and also housed the Canadian government trade office. The building had simply disappeared. Looking about, they came upon the charred remains of two staff members; they covered them up and located a burial party.

Elmer MacDowell, the resident Alcan (Aluminum Company of Canada) representative, was far luckier. On a visit to Tokyo the day the earthquake struck, he watched in horror from a seven-storey building as an adjacent one disintegrated before his eyes. After spending the night with thousands of others in a park, he walked the 25 miles back to Yokohama, where he could find no trace of his office, of the club where he lived or of any of the 12 men with whom he had breakfasted the previous morning. Locating a rowboat, he made his way out to Robinson's ship in the harbour.

W.D. Cameron, the Sun Life Assurance representative, was walking home after a swim at Hakone, the mountain resort south of Yokohama, when he felt the earth suddenly move beneath his feet, he recounted in the eyewitness account he prepared for his company.

> Crouching, I watched as the house wrenched about, swinging and jumping much like a rat shaking in the grip of a relentless terrier's mouth. To stand or walk was a physical impossibility. Those who did not crouch in terror the instant the shock began were thrown violently to the ground. The earth split and cracked in all directions, oozing water from some of the deeper fissures . . . Living as we have so long in this country, it might be supposed that we have long since become accustomed to earthquakes, but this awful shake was so infinitely worse than anything before experienced or imagined by any of us that it bore about the same relation to an ordinary quake as a terrible shipwreck to a stormy but safe sea voyage.

More than two-thirds of the village, including the newly built three-storey Hakone Hotel, crashed to earth with a thunderous roar. Huge landslides in the surrounding mountains suggested the awful possibility that the entire district might be swallowed by the lake, itself of volcanic origin, mysterious and seemingly bottomless in parts.

> Immediately the shock subsided we rushed out and lay flat in the middle of the village street, and what a sight met us there! Houses sprawled in fantastic shapes testifying to the violent manner in which they were hurled to destruction; terror-stricken inhabitants and visitors huddled together, many praying to God and Buddha—a scene hardly to be equalled by the ravages of modern warfare.

Mounted Samurai Watching Geese, a hanging scroll by Yorada Keishu, was painted around 1900—the same time that Nitobe Inazō wrote his famous *Bushido* in an effort to explain Japanese values in terms of the code of the cultured samurai warrior.

Art Gallery of Greater Victoria, Robert Miller collection, gift of Paul Watson, AGGV 2005.047.006

ABOVE "If sincere, you never fail" is the inscription on a scroll that hung in a martial arts hall in Kamakura in the 1920s. It depicts the figure of Daruma, considered to be the founder of Zen Buddhism, which strongly influenced the development of bushido.
Art Gallery of Greater Victoria, gift of Judith Pratt, AGGV 2000.001.002

RIGHT This samurai suit of armour, like many, was assembled over time as pieces wore out and were replaced. The helmet and face mask are the oldest parts of the suit, dating from the 16th or 17th century. The armour with lacquered iron and silk braid is from the 18th or 19th century. *Art Gallery of Greater Victoria, gift of Professor Peter Moogk, AGGV 2008.026.001.11*

"NO LIMIT: JAPAN—I see your cruisers and raise you a dreadnought!" was the caption on a cover of *Puck* magazine in 1909, by which time Japan had risen to the rank of major power following its victory in the 1904–05 Russo–Japanese war. Emperor Meiji (centre) is shown raising his bid in a high-stakes poker game with Uncle Sam, German Emperor William II, King Edward VII of Britain and Émile Loubet, president of France.

Library of Congress, AP101.P7 1909 (case X) [P&P]

A Japanese mother and son are the subject of *Courtesan Dandling a Child*, a woodblock print by Kitagawa Utamaro II (Koikawa Shuncho), ca. 1806–20. *Royal Ontario Museum, Sir Edmund Walker collection, 926.18.439*

Preparing to take a stroll, a married woman in the Meiji Period, a woodblock print by Yoshitoshi Tsukioka (Taiso), 1888, captures the spirit of the modern Japanese woman.
Art Gallery of Greater Victoria, gift of Elizabeth Marsters and Senora Ryan, AGGV 1995.033.001

TOP Images of a woman, Mount Fuji and a *torii* gate are powerful lures in this 1920s-era travel poster. *UBC Library, Rare Books and Special Collections, Chung collection, CC-OS-00239*

ABOVE This art-deco-style Canadian Pacific brochure from 1929 celebrates the impressive new second *Empress of Japan*, launched after the original was scrapped in 1922. *Canadian Pacific Archives, BR62*

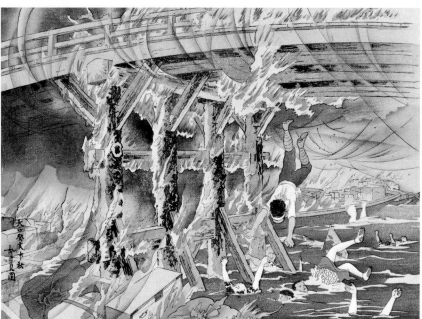

LEFT Namazu is the giant catfish who, according to Japanese mythology, lives in the mud under the islands of Japan and causes earthquakes. This print belongs to a popular genre of woodblock prints that are often unsigned.
UBC Library, Rare Books and Special Collections, George Beans, Disaster Prints, 3 DRUM 9

BELOW *Fire on the Bridge— Great Kanto Earthquake*, a woodblock print by Josen Hamada in1926, illustrates the great earthquake of 1923 and accompanying fires that devastated Yokohama, Tokyo and surrounding areas.
Art Gallery of Greater Victoria, gift of Barry Till, AGGV 2008.030.006

A Canadian Pacific brochure from 1936 draws travellers across the Pacific, even as conditions deteriorated during the 1930s. *Canadian Pacific Archives, Maurice Logan, White Empress Route, A-15381*

Suspecting the event was probably a local occurrence, Cameron headed south on foot with his wife, Alice, and their four young children. Struggling over landslides and fallen trees, the earth shaking beneath them from the aftershocks, they eventually reached Shizuoka where they learned for the first time of the extent of the catastrophe. This aroused new anxieties, as they had family living in Yokohama.

After dispatching Alice and the children by train to safety farther south in Kobe, Cameron joined forces with Arthur Bryan, the Canadian trade commissioner in Yokohama. Stuck in a car in a garage that miraculously did not collapse, Bryan had also survived and made his way along the coast. Together they begged and battled their way onto a crowded Japanese steamer bound north for Tokyo.

Three days had elapsed and still the fires burned, a shocked Cameron observed.

> Capital of a mighty empire, combination of ancient and modern—Yedo, relic of the Shogun's power and Tokyo—comparable with London or New York—in the grip of relentless fire. "Flowers of Yedo" is the fanciful name given by the citizens to fire from which the city has suffered heavily from time immemorial. Flowers! That imagination could possibly compare such tokens of innocence with the devouring, never satisfied monster roaring and licking up the city before our eyes!

Unable to land, they jostled their way onto a vessel bound back to Yokohama, where an even worse sight awaited: a heap of smoking debris was all that remained of the great port city.

> We saw at once that the destruction was complete—a work which it is doubtful if an army, equipped with all modern engines of destruction, could have performed in months. It was a blazing day and with heavy hearts we landed. We were promptly surrounded by Japanese refugees begging for food, drink and smokes. Money for the time being had lost its value and nothing was to be bought. Corpses of men, women, and children were lying everywhere in attitudes grimly suggestive of the terrible way in which death was met. Owing to the great heat decomposition had set in and the odour was frightful.

Remarkably, Cameron's entire extended family survived, including some who were waving goodbye to the Canadian Pacific *Empress* on the wharf that sank beneath their feet. The single sad note was the death of a devoted household *amah*, who had perished while re-entering a house to rescue a child. "On hearing of the family's safety the awful strain under which I had been suffering for four days was relieved and perhaps it is hardly necessary to say I completely broke down," Cameron confessed. "Physically, too, I was a wreck and was glad to be taken off to the *Empress of Australia*." But it was still not over. The British consul, who had set up shop on the ship, begged Cameron and Bryan, both fluent Japanese speakers, to return to Tokyo with messages for the British Embassy.

This time they managed to land, and the British produced a car to convey them through the smoking ruins. Locating his house, Cameron found it still standing. But the Sun Life office was completely demolished, as were surrounding buildings in what was left of the Nihombashi district, including the huge Mitsukoshi Department Store, the Mitsui Bank and part of the Bank of Japan.

Arthur Bryan, meanwhile, was at the British Embassy sending a message to Canada, where it was assumed he had perished. "Bryan given up for dead," ran a headline in the *Ottawa Journal*. "I am safe but lost absolutely everything send immediately funds," he cabled. By "everything" he meant his office, the office records and his own cottage by the sea. Following the quake, the Canadian trade office, like much of the Yokohama foreign business community, shifted to Kobe.

• • •

Earthquakes in Japan are a given, an unfortunate feature of life along with typhoons, tidal waves, volcanic eruptions and other calamities on a sometimes staggering scale. The impact of the 1923 earthquake was so devastating, however, that it became a defining moment in Japanese history. While the immediate challenge was recovery, the tragedy presented an opportunity for reconstruction along new lines, with modern networks of roads, trains, parks and public services. In the process, so much of the old was swept away, and so different did things look afterward, that it became commonplace for decades to refer to places and events as being "before" or "after" the Great Earthquake.

At the same time, the earthquake also served as a watershed in Canada's trade relationship with Japan. Canada's role as an importer of tea, silk and other luxuries, a transportation corridor through which consumer goods passed on their way to the United States and Europe, was a largely pre-earthquake conception that was already turning around in response to export opportunities associated with Japan's growing economy. In 1922 Canadian exports to Japan surpassed imports for the first time, led by rising shipments of wheat.

The huge demands associated with post-earthquake reconstruction accelerated the trend. Eight million dollars in 1920, Canadian exports to Japan galloped to a record $42 million in 1929. In the larger scheme of things this was still modest, just 3 percent of total Canadian exports, which remained oriented to Britain and the United States. The breakthrough, however, was significant; only one-thirtieth of US volumes in 1914, Canada's exports to Japan rose to one-tenth by 1929, roughly in line with the relative size of the two economies (although such figures did not factor in additional trade that passed through US ports).

In particular, post-earthquake demand was instrumental in the making of budding lumber magnate Harvey Reginald (H.R.) MacMillan, one of Canada's most successful businessmen. While Canadian lumber first reached Japan in the 1880s, when the tall trees of the Pacific coast were exported for use as ships' masts, the early lumber trade languished; British Columbia's milling capacity was still small and Japan was initially able to meet most of its needs from its own forests. As the Japanese economy expanded, however, it turned increasingly to imports, particularly the abundant and relatively cheap lumber coming out of the new mills of the Pacific Northwest—though as MacMillan, then BC's young chief forester, pointed out, "British Columbia only got the orders the United States didn't want and none of the cream."

Engaged by the Canadian government to travel the world in search of markets for Canadian lumber, he quickly came to a conclusion: Canada had the product; what was missing was the capacity to sell.

> I must confess that it made me almost indignant when I saw, practically everywhere I went, that the lumber, including British Columbia's product, is sold through United States firms. The importers . . . did not know that any of it came from this Province. We have the raw materials, but sadly lack organization to sell it to the world.

Disappointed when his recommendations elicited little immediate action, MacMillan decided to go it alone. In 1919 he and a partner established the MacMillan Export Company. A small lumber brokerage firm that arranged contracts, shipping and financing for lumber exported from BC mills, it was the first of its kind in the province and a forerunner of industrial giant MacMillan Bloedel.

On learning of the earthquake, the company immediately redirected two ships already on the Pacific loaded with lumber to Yokohama. Large orders mushroomed from there. So did the confusion, as an initial hysteria of purchasing gave way to a realization that lumber had been vastly overbought. The market was glutted, orders were cancelled and prices plummeted.

Worried about the huge contracts he had just entered into with Canadian mills, MacMillan set out for Yokohama the following April. "Obliteration complete," he cabled his partner. "Cleaning up still proceeding—found bodies in ruins of Grand Hotel today." He also discovered stacks of lumber stretching a mile beyond the docks. Canadian lumber evidently would not sell itself.

US lumber interests, who blitzed Japan after the earthquake, also gained a leg up when a New York adviser was engaged to assist with rebuilding Yokohama and Tokyo along more modern lines. US mills, however, were not geared to produce the special cuts required by the Japanese building trade. Recognizing an opportunity, MacMillan insisted on exporting lumber specifically tailored to the Japanese market. "I want it cut *exact*," he ordered the BC mills. Soon his company was exporting "Japanese squares," beams precisely 2 feet square and 40 feet long that buyers could trim on arrival to their own requirements.

From 1924 to 1926, Japan purchased a billion board feet of lumber from Canada and MacMillan opened offices in Tokyo, Yokohama and Kobe. Two lumber cargoes a week left Vancouver's Japan Wharf for Yokohama, where regular customers included Mitsui and Mitsubishi. By the end of the decade Japan was Canada's second largest lumber market, setting the stage for further expansion after the Pacific War when Canada's lumber exports to Japan surpassed those of the United States.

To meet competition in Japan and other markets, MacMillan also established his own shipping line. By 1927 the Canadian Transport Company with its company flag, a green fir on white ground, was one of the biggest charter shipping companies in the world, with services through the Panama Canal to the West Indies, Britain, Europe and South Africa as well as US and

JAPAN BOUGHT FROM CANADA DURING 1925 AGGREGATED SUM OF $ 30,000,000.00 = LUMBER, PLUP, WHEAT, FLOUR, MARINE PRODUCT, BUTTER, CHEESE & ETC.

Canadian east coast ports, and across the Pacific to Australia, Japan, China and India. As the *Canadian Lumberman* noted in 1929, "MacMillan would be selling to the moon if he could get delivery."

In the process the six-foot-four-inch, bushy-browed MacMillan learned something about what it meant to do business in Japan in the rough-and-tumble 1920s. As MacMillan told the story, during one visit he was set upon by ruffians hired by a disgruntled European agent to whom he had refused to pay a commission when the agent failed to produce results.

When I returned to Japan in 1927 he was on the warpath. He had a hired ruffian—a known type, something sounds like Feroski—German helmet, glazed jackboots, carried a club. He threatened my safety, tried to take me out of my hotel room, also attacked me in public hall at entrance dining saloon on *Empress*. Also tried to pull me out of my room onto the gangway from ship to wharfside, but was each time ejected by a Japanese "gens d'armes" who while a foreign ship is in port maintains law and order.

As the years passed, the story acquired even more drama. In one account MacMillan discovered someone trying to climb into his hotel room window and unceremoniously dumped him into the flower bed below. The next morning he was alarmed to see the same gang flying down the wharf in *jinricksha*, two of whom seized him by the legs while he held on to the ship's railing for dear life until the police arrived. Another version had a gang of up to 50 thugs chasing MacMillan around the ship, nearly succeeding in dragging him back to shore, while Bryan went for help. Whatever the details, the episode was, MacMillan confessed, one of the most frightening of his life.

What stands out about MacMillan, apart from the scale of his operations, is the way he aggressively sought out global buyers—in contrast to much of the Canadian business community, which was more comfortable sticking to US and other markets closer to home.

Another company that actively worked the Japanese market was Alcan, which began exporting there in 1901 when its new smelter at Shawinigan shipped 67,000 pounds of ingot to Yokohama. As the pace of Japanese industrialization picked up, growing Japanese imports were sourced from Canada, mostly through New York export houses. In 1917 a prominent Japanese scientist interested Alcan's parent at the time, US-based Alcoa, in exploring prospects for establishing an aluminum smelter in Japan; a team spent two months traversing the country by train, car, *jinricksha* and canoe in what turned out to be a futile search for a suitable source of hydro power.

Elmer MacDowell, the man who miraculously escaped a Tokyo office building during the earthquake, was the recently arrived representative of Alcan's own distributing agent, the Asia Aluminum Company, established in 1921 in response to the growing demand for aluminum ingot. Under his watch Alcan developed a close relationship with the powerful Sumitomo group; Sumitomo was big in copper and Alcan was able to offer aluminum

Visiting the General Motors plant in Osaka: Hugh Keenleyside (left) and James Langley (right) of the Canadian Legation in Tokyo which opened in 1929. *Library and Archives Canada, e002712820*

at competitive prices. In 1927 an agreement was successfully concluded with Sumitomo Electric Wire and Cable for the manufacture of electrical conductors. At the same time, rapid electrification of Japan, combined with growing demands in Korea and Manchuria, enhanced demand for aluminum wire.

Alcan and Sumitomo took the partnership further in the early 1930s when they embarked on a fabricating joint venture involving the forerunner of what became Tōyō Aluminium K.K. Substantial differences in Canadian and Japanese business philosophy and corporate structure required large doses of mutual trust and creativity in structuring the partnership. Formally, Alcan owned 50 percent of the company and Sumitomo owned the other 50 percent; in practice, management was largely in Sumitomo hands. Alcan had a majority of members on the board, but one of the Alcan directors had to be Japanese. The company also went by different names: in Japanese it was Sumitomo Aluminium; in English, Aluminium Sumitomo Limited.

● ● ●

The 1920s established Canada as a key supplier of agricultural and resource products to the Japanese market. Commercial interests in Japan, however, extended beyond the resource boom. Indeed, the Canadian display said to have attracted most attention at a 1925 trade exhibition was not grains or lumber or metals and minerals; it was automobiles.

Winners of the monthly flag, Manufacturers Life Insurance Agency staff in Yamagata in 1918. Note the maple leaf and snowdrift. *Manulife Financial Corporate Archives*

In addition to autos and parts, Canada exported substantial quantities of other manufactured goods: rubber tires and shoes, electrical equipment, chemicals and photographic film. Some resource-based exports also contained a substantial value-added component; by the 1930s, for example, Canada supplied over 80 percent of Japan's newsprint.

Another dimension of Canada's commercial presence in Japan was life insurance, whose introduction into Japan coincided with the rise of the Canadian life insurance industry. Conducted largely by local agents visiting Japanese homes, it proved highly profitable.

W.D. Cameron, the Sun Life (now Sun Life Financial) representative who provided the riveting account of the earthquake, worked for a company that began doing business in Japan in 1893 and established its own office in Yokohama 10 years later. Manufacturers Life (now Manulife Financial) appointed its first agent in Japan in 1898 and opened an office in 1901. Soon Canadian life insurance representatives were scattered from Fukuoka in the south to Sendai in the north as part of a global expansion of the Canadian insurance industry that extended to China, Hong Kong and the Philippines, as well as other regions.

While the impact of the great earthquake was understandably huge, the payout fell more heavily on the non-life side, especially fire.

● ● ●

The 1929 trade high did not last. The impact of the major stock market crash in October that year sent Canadian trade with Japan reeling. Exports plunged from $42 million in 1929 to $10 million in 1930. Japan fared even worse as Canadian markets dried up, particularly for silk.

What rose instead was protectionism, as the two countries fell into a protracted and nasty trade war sparked by devaluation of the Japanese yen, followed by Canadian tariff hikes on Japanese imported goods, which triggered taxes on Canadian resource products. The dispute was resolved only after William Lyon Mackenzie King returned to power as prime minister in late 1935.

The spat revealed a deepening regional cleavage between the interests of Western resource producers, who depended on the Japanese market, and central Canadian manufacturers, who viewed it as a growing source of competition. Canada was less affected than the United States when the foreign automobile industry was driven out of Japan in the 1930s, but the textile industry in Quebec and Ontario felt the pinch of lower-cost Japanese imports. And while roughly half of the record $42 million that Canada sold to Japan in 1929 was wheat, much of it was milled in Japan's new flour mills and re-exported to China and elsewhere. The only Canadian exports that took off in the 1930s were metals, until these were finally shut off on the eve of the Pacific War.

Pre-war trade dynamics also contained the seeds of a trade pattern that emerged afterwards, when Canada resumed the role of resource supplier for Japan's massive post-war reconstruction, and the tea, silk and oranges of the early import trade gave way to their post-war equivalents: the cheap toys of the 1950s, cameras of the 1960s, automobiles of the 1970s and consumer electronics and high technology goods of the 1980s and '90s. For Canada, there would also remain aspirations that went back to Laurier's time, visions of trans-Pacific trade yet to be fully realized.

SIR HERBERT AND THE LEGATION

As the Canadian Pacific *Empress* neared Yokohama, Hugh Keenleyside could barely contain his anticipation. From the prow he watched the rising sun dissolve the morning mist over Mount Fuji—a sure sign of welcome. A small cloud, however, had already crossed the young diplomat's horizon in the form of a telegram inviting him to stay with the British ambassador.

The advance man for the opening of Canada's new legation in Japan, Keenleyside was not entirely sure what he was supposed to do after he arrived; "use your head and send a cable if you run into difficulties," had been Ottawa's best advice. But he was acutely aware that the British were not keen on Canada's new diplomatic presence in Japan. Indeed, over a year had passed since Prime Minister King's announcement as London had niggled over the details. And he was quite certain that taking up residence with the British was not what King had in mind. He insisted instead on being taken to the Frank Lloyd Wright–designed Imperial Hotel, which had survived the 1923 earthquake and was now the unofficial centre of Tokyo international life.

British reservations resurfaced a few days later, when Keenleyside was invited to luncheon at the ambassador's residence following an introductory call on Japan's foreign minister. "Quite unnecessary, you know," the ambassador's wife sniffed. "So silly of you." Another embassy wife took up the chorus.

> You know we don't mind looking after things for you, and, of course, we have had long experience . . . When we heard that a Canadian diplomat was coming to Japan, we just didn't know what to expect. When I came here to lunch today, I was wondering if you would be wearing spurs and a cowboy hat and—what do you call them—chaps? And here I find that you have written a book! And you're fun, in spite of those awful clothes.

July 1, 1929: Hugh Keenleyside raised Canada's flag in Japan in the company of assembled Canadians, including Mrs. Richard Hubert and C. Julian. *Library and Archives Canada, PA-202773*

Keenleyside already had reason to regret his formal attire on a hot, sticky Tokyo summer day, an experience he likened to wearing an Arctic parka in a sauna. More to his taste was his first semi-official function a few days later, umpiring a softball game between the US Embassy and the Japanese Foreign Ministry on the grounds of the Meiji Shrine. The record does not indicate who won, although abuse is said to have been hurled at Keenleyside with equal vigour by both sides.

He soon found living quarters in the Nagai compound, a housing enclave up the road from Shibuya Station. There, on July 1, 1929, he officially raised Canada's flag for the first time in Japan, as "O Canada" and "God Save the King" rose from over 60 assembled Canadians.

● ● ●

While Keenleyside did the groundwork, Herbert Meredith Marler was in London purchasing a diplomatic uniform with 20 pounds of gold braid, white silk breeches and stockings, and a hat topped with a plume of white ostrich feathers. On September 16, 1929, the Imperial Hotel was bedecked in Japanese and Canadian flags as Marler set off to present his credentials to the young Showa emperor as Canada's new minister plenipotentiary to the Empire of Japan.

Marler was not, perhaps, the most obvious choice for his role. A notary from Montreal who had served briefly in King's cabinet, he was a staunch anglophile who initially opposed establishment of the legation. He was, however, an ideal candidate in one important respect. From a prominent Quebec family, he was a person of considerable social standing, as was his wife, Beatrice Isabel of the Allan shipping family. More remarkable was Japan's choice of its first minister to Canada, Prince Tokugawa Iyemasa, the grandson of the last shogun.

History has not been kind to Marler. "Tall, handsomely tailored and shod, rather stiff in figure and face," was Keenleyside's summation. "In a somewhat wooden way he looked like the conventional idea of an ambassador, although his lack of facial mobility and sparkle gave the impression that he might not be much concerned with either people or ideas."

Keenleyside may have been merciless, but he was not alone. James Manion, a young trade officer who joined the legation in the early 1930s, described Marler as "amusingly pompous, a case of someone born with a legalistic mind further enhanced by incipient megalomania . . . Any time I or anyone is alone with him he talks as though we were an audience of two hundred people." A secretary once remarked that Marler read the Sunday lesson at church as though he were God and had written the Bible himself. Not that Keenleyside was beyond reproach; one wit dubbed him "Canada Dry" for his teetotaller habit of serving ginger ale in the champagne glasses.

Obsessed with status and precedence, the Marlers brought much of this kind of criticism on themselves. They had barely set sail for Japan when Beatrice Marler decreed they should be addressed at all times as "His and Her Excellency." Bells were installed in their bedrooms labelled "His Excellency's Room," "Her Excellency's Room" and, in the case of a visiting son, "His Young Excellency's Room." Soon after arrival Marler mounted a campaign for a British knighthood, which he duly received, becoming "Sir Herbert." When the British ambassador died, Marler also preposterously suggested he might replace him.

The matter, however, went beyond personal idiosyncrasy. Marler had an old-school view of diplomacy as an arena for gentlemen, a vocation properly limited to those of wealth, manners and social breeding—in other words, to people like himself. This did not sit well with the young men being drawn into the fledgling Canadian Foreign Service, whose backgrounds were by and large more modest and whose instincts more egalitarian.

LEFT Beatrice Marler in the garden. *Library and Archives Canada, William Lyon Mackenzie King collection, PA-120417*

RIGHT Herbert Meredith Marler, Canada's first minister to Japan, arrived in September 1929. *Canadian Embassy, Tokyo*

Symbolic of the chasm was a debate over whether Canadian diplomats should adopt diplomatic uniforms. While soon to drop out of fashion, the extravagant outfit Marler sported was still *de rigueur*. Senior representatives of leading countries, with the exception of the United States, wore them on ceremonial occasions, as did senior Japanese and, for that matter, members of the Canadian cabinet. When it came to style and comportment, Marler was literally cut from the same cloth as the patricians who represented Canada in London, Paris and Washington, who all dressed in a similar way.

Oscar "O.D." Skelton, the Queen's University professor, enticed by King to head up the new Department of External Affairs, personally had little patience for such sartorial folderol. A man whose own favourite headgear was an old peaked cap pulled down over his eyes, he was known to muse whether

TOP The Marlers were welcomed with a banquet at the Imperial Hotel. *Library and Archives Canada, Hugh L. Keenleyside collection, C-00283101*

ABOVE Wearing uniforms: Herbert Marler greeting Prince Fushimi, with the British ambassador (behind) and the rector of St. Andrew's Church. *Canadian Embassy, Tokyo*

"it might be better for Canada to adopt the frock coat of the Americans or even the overalls of modern democracy."

To be fair, however, Marler had a tough row to hoe. Dropped into a world in which he was expected to be the instant embodiment of Canada's new international persona, his recourse was to be as British as the Brits. And perversely, it was only by taking on British trappings that he could hope to be treated as an equal rather than as some jumped-up quasi-colonial. That, at least, was how Marler played it. His five and a half years in Tokyo were a saga of relentless determination to ensure he was never, ever perceived as inferior to the British ambassador.

It largely worked—though it needled the British endlessly. As the British ambassador of the day, Sir John Tilley, once remarked ruefully, "Herbert Marler makes me feel like a man who late in life finds that he is a twin."

● ● ●

Herbert Marler departed from the British mould in one vital respect. Senior British diplomats were typically men of letters who immersed themselves in history and culture and the great issues of the day. Even commercial officers were sometimes of this bent; the senior British commercial representative in Tokyo in the early 1930s was the well-known Japan historian George Sansom.

Marler, in contrast, was very much the model of a modern trade ambassador. En route to Japan he chivvied Canadian business into looking beyond traditional British Empire and US markets to Asia. Immediately after arrival he embarked on a vigorous program to assess commercial prospects from Hokkaido in the north to Nagasaki in the south.

His ambitions went well beyond the staples of the resource trade. Manion, the junior trade officer, found himself promoting an astonishing array of products: bond paper, carbon paper, hectographic paper, toilet paper and lithographic pictures for Christmas cards and papermakers' felts; surgeons' gloves and rubber gloves; frozen beef, tallow, whisky, barley, tobacco, butter, cheese, macaroni, oatmeal and catsup; linoleum, wallpaper and gas and coal stoves; hairpins, razor blades, ice skates, boots, hockey sticks and an ice planer for a hockey rink; and four silver foxes and five mink imported for breeding purposes. He was also amazed to discover in the Japanese market 132 copies of the Canadian Club whisky label on recycled bottles.

Marler viewed himself not simply as Canada's minister to Japan, but also as a kind of super–trade emissary to Asia as a whole. He was especially keen on China, though he soon came to realize it was too internally chaotic at the time for anything approaching orderly trade relations.

Ultimately, however, destiny dealt Marler a bad hand, for he arrived in Japan a mere month before the stock market crash sent the world's economic and financial system into a tailspin, precipitating the Great Depression. Dismayed, he watched Canada's ballooning trade with Japan tumble, while similarly embattled American, Australian and other competitors worked to scoop hard-won Canadian markets.

● ● ●

As the Depression cooled one dream, Marler turned to another. A man with a personal predilection for grand houses, he was convinced that nothing would convey Canada's presence in Japan better than an imposing building. Before departing Canada he had presented King with a large leather-bound volume lettered in gold, in which he had meticulously set out his requirements, including drawings by a Montreal architect.

The notoriously penny-pinching King went along with most of it. But he drew the line at expensive real estate and Marler had to content himself with a European-style house in Nishi-machi (Azabu) formerly occupied by the Romanians and an office in the Imperial Life Insurance building in the Marunouchi business district. He continued to sniff around, however, and eventually found a magnificent property in one of the city's most prestigious areas on Aoyama Dori in the Akasaka district, across from the home of Prince Chichibu, the emperor's brother. When the government, by then headed by R.B. Bennett's Conservatives, balked again, Marler came up with an irresistible proposition. He threw in $25,000 of his own money and undertook to raise up to $200,000 on his personal credit, to be repaid to him by the government over 10 years.

The project, consisting of a large residence and a smaller chancery or office, was put in the most prestigious hands Marler could find. Antonin Raymond, a student of Frank Lloyd Wright, drew up plans from drawings by a Montreal architect, while a professor at Waseda University advised on making the buildings fire and earthquake-resistant. Marler personally oversaw every aspect of construction, poring over each drawing and sample. What could not be located in massive shopping expeditions to China for furniture and carpets was sourced through purchasing agents in London.

The Canadian residence in Tokyo, now called Marler House. In 1989 the adjacent chancery building, which had become too small to house Canada's growing interests in Japan, was replaced by a new building designed by architect Raymond Moriyama of Toronto. *Canadian Embassy, Tokyo*

Most remarkable, in retrospect, is that the project was undertaken at all. Even if the government was spared direct financial outlay, the political optics of erecting grand buildings halfway around the world during the Depression, when many Canadians were jobless, homeless and driving "Bennett buggies" (cars hitched to horses), were, at best, challenging. Marler's moment of triumph was dampened when his description of the final product came under the astute eye of Skelton in 1933.

"Prune off some of the verbal foliage," Skelton directed; "make His Majesty less Britannic and more Canadian, and make clear that the move was justified for business reasons not to provide Marler with more comfortable quarters." Marler: "The Canadian Minister's residence stands with majestic dignity further down the tree lined driveway." Skelton: "Omit majestic dignity." Marler: "A long corridor, illuminated in the evening glow of concealed lights, and carpeted with a heavy Chinese rug of a rich deep red and furnishings in soft tints, leads to the three main rooms on the main floor." Skelton: "A long corridor leads to three main rooms on the main floor. Omit heavy."

The original members of the Canadian Legation in Tokyo: (from left) Kenneth Kirkwood, Hugh Keenleyside, Herbert Marler and James Langley. *Library and Archives Canada, PA-120407*

It went on. Marler: "The second floor is devoted to the private quarters and guest rooms. In one wing is the Minister's suite, including bedrooms, bathroom and library. In another wing are a number of private guestrooms or guest suites, each with separate attached bathroom, and spacious cedar-lined closets. From one end of the upper floor, the Sacred Mountain Fuji-yama can be distinctly seen." Skelton: "Omit including bedrooms, bathrooms and library and guest suites through to storage closets and stick to the Sacred Mountain of Fuji-yama which cannot cause any qualms in the mind of the Canadian taxpayer."

It was as well Marler left out any reference to the ballroom, which, when not used for dancing, was where he and Beatrice liked to entertain guests at cards.

• • •

Part of the former estate of Viscount Aoyama Tadayoshi, the last feudal lord and 13th daimyo (land-owning noble) of the Sasayama clan in Kyushū, the legation property came with an impressive lineage. According to legend,

Tokugawa Ieyasu, the first shogun, was out hawking one day in the early 1600s with two generals. Near the top of Akasaka Hill, he challenged them to demonstrate how far each could ride in a day. Aoyama Tadanari rode west while his companion rode east. The following day Ieyasu granted each the respective lands they had covered.

While Beatrice Marler maintained that Canada came by the prestigious site as a result of a providential golf game between her husband and the then current Count Aoyama, there was a back story. Prime Minister Yoshida Shigeru related to Canadian diplomat Arthur Menzies in the early 1950s that, as the vice minister of foreign affairs at the time, he was acquainted with a family that was experiencing difficulty selling a well-situated property because it was haunted by the ghost of two people who had comitted suicide.

"Then it came to me in a flash that the property could be sold to the Canadians, since Westerners apprehended the presence of ghosts only when they heard the thud of heavy feet. Japanese ghosts however, make no heavy footfalls but move silently on a wisp of smoke. I arranged to sell the property to Marler."

Ghost stories are a common theme in Japanese folklore, and one of the most famous is indeed associated with the Aoyama family. Immortalized in the kabuki play *Bancho Sarayashiki*, it is the story of Okiko and the Nine Plates. One popular version, though situated in Himeji Castle near Osaka rather than Tokyo, has Okiko as a servant of a daimyo named Aoyama Shuzen. On learning she has overheard his intentions to kill his master and reported it to her lover, a loyal warrior, he takes revenge by accusing her of stealing 1 of 10 valuable Dutch plates. In desperation Okiko throws herself into a well and drowns. Her ghost returns every night to count the plates, howling and sobbing, while Aoyama goes insane from the nightly apparitions. Another version has a happier ending: an Aoyama family friend stands beside the well and when the plate count reaches 9, shouts, "10!"—and the ghost is seen no more.

Ghost or not, construction was barely completed when the Marlers were struck by a series of illnesses. Keenleyside then stumbled across an unexplained item in the legation accounts and discovered that Marler had quietly arranged for the buildings to be cleansed and blessed by Shinto priests, a common custom.

Marler also turned out to be right. The Canadian residence in Tokyo proved a highly effective setting for pursuing Canadian interests in Japan.

•••

The original members of the Canadian Legation were a remarkable mix of talents. Dr. Hugh Keenleyside was from British Columbia and had taught at eastern American universities. James Langley, who previously headed the Canadian trade office in Kobe, was a fluent Japanese speaker and the legation's Japan hand; he received the rare honour of an audience with the emperor and empress when he left Japan in 1937. Kenneth Kirkwood, a more eclectic personality, possessed degrees from the London School of Economics and Columbia, and had previously worked as a journalist in Turkey as well as in the Canadian Legation in Washington.

Unfortunately their talents were never fully utilized. In the beginning King commented personally on their reports. But Depression-era Ottawa was detached from the intricacies of the Far East, and they soon wondered if anything they wrote was read at all. Increasingly, they turned to sidelines. Keenleyside wrote a book on the Japanese education system. Langley devoted his energies to the legation building project. Kirkwood produced a great array of writings, some published, some not, while teaching English literature at a girls' college.

Avid travellers all, they covered the length and breadth of Japan, as well as China, Korea and Manchuria, for both business and pleasure. The old capital of Kamakura and the nearby seaside resort of Hayama were favourite destinations, as was the new foreign enclave at Lake Chuzenji above Nikkō, which some considered preferable to the increasingly "socialite" atmosphere of Karuizawa.

It was not simply travel, but also the travel experience that appealed, observed Kirkwood, who visited everyone from the Ainu in Hokkaido, to the poverty-stricken miners of northern Japan, to the mountain people of the Japan Alps.

> No sooner does the Japanese traveller embark than he proceeds to change from the street or office clothes into his home clothes. He disrobes in embarrassed but surprising insouciance; he doffs his shoes for slippers, obligingly provided for every passenger by the car conductor; he dons a light kimono, as though he were settled in his own home; he spreads comfortably over the seat, the heels tucked under him, with his papers or his fan in his hand; and thus he is prepared for a day and a night (in Japan journeys do not last longer) in easy comfort.

A massive metropolis of over 5.5 million, Tokyo itself was awash in entertainments. The summer of 1929 witnessed not only the opening of the legation but also an opening of a quite different kind. The new Casino Follies was part of a huge complex of music halls, theatres and movie houses that drew thousands to the district of Asakusa, the heart of what used to be old Edo. In a back street on the second floor of an aquarium, the casino was next door to an entomology museum known as the Bug House. "It came to be," wrote the novelist Kawabata Yasunari, "that the girls of the Casino Follies passed the fishes in their tanks and turned in by a model of the sea king's palace on the way to their dressing rooms." They also had to pass dusty cases of flies, beetles, butterflies and bees.

It was the era of *ero-guru*, the acronym for the erotic and the grotesque, a kind of Japanese version of the flapper age when people drowned their sorrows in pleasures and distractions. The eroticism was modest by today's standards, mostly legs and a lot of promise; even kisses were not shown in Japanese movies until after the Pacific War. For anyone interested in real eroticism there was plenty to be had in back-alley sideshows, bars where girls sat barelegged on tables, and the archery tents around the Kannon Temple in Asakusa, which served as fronts for prostitution.

The city centre was also shifting as the remains of old Edo, which had largely disappeared with the 1923 earthquake, were overtaken by a reconstructed Tokyo of paved streets and European-style buildings. Increasingly, the place to go was Ginza, home to Hibiya Hall, the Kabuki-za and other theatres, movie houses and huge department stores. Its denizens were the freewheeling *moga* (modern girls) and *mobo* (modern boys) who came to shop, amuse themselves, be seen and have their pictures taken. Farther out on the periphery, Shinjuku and Shibuya gave Ginza a run for its money, but nothing could compete with *gimbura*, or "cruising around Ginza."

Not only the young flocked there. Tiny intimate doorways, many with exotic-sounding French names, drew businessmen into Ginza's narrow alleyways. Cafés that had catered to intellectual discussion and debate in the Meiji era were now bars or cabarets. For those with less money and simpler tastes, there were the *kissaten*, or tea shops.

By the early 1930s Ginza was also a major stop on the international celebrity trail, playing host to a non-stop flow of everyone from Charlie Chaplin and Noël Coward to Babe Ruth, the Lindberghs and George Bernard

Shaw. Kabuki was giving way to the movies; hostesses and mama-sans were replacing geisha; and baseball began drawing bigger crowds than sumo.

After 1935 the dynamic shifted again as a new mood of reaction set in. But in the late 1920s and early '30s it was all there: the old and the new, the East and the West, the sublime and the profane. And while elements resurfaced after the Pacific War, things were never quite the same.

• • •

The legation members had their own place in this multi-ringed circus. Diplomatic life at the time was still glamorous, a vestige of the striped-pants era that would soon largely die away. Business and pleasure intertwined in endless rounds of luncheons, dinners, dances and soirees, punctuated by intriguing characters and witty conversation. It was an intimate world where everyone knew everyone else and constantly ran into each other at dinners, hotels and resorts. It was also part of the tight little sphere of the Tokyo elite of foreigners and Japanese who shared values and interests.

The Foreign Ministry and the Imperial Household did their part to keep the diplomatic community entertained. The most unusual event was a duck -netting party, a throwback to the feudal era. It began with the arrival of some diplomats in official morning dress at the Hama Detached Palace, the emperor's waterside retreat that dated to the days of the shoguns. Armed with nets and poles the party made their way toward parallel dikes half-filled with water, into which ducks, mostly mallards, had previously been lured. When a loud clatter sounded, the frightened birds took to the air and the hunters swung their poles, Keenleyside explained.

> After the sport was over each member of the diplomatic corps was given, not the birds he or she had snared but the number of ducks to which his rank entitled him. Skill was not rewarded, failure was not penalized. Ambassadors were presented, via their chauffeurs, with eight, ministers with six, and charges d'affaires with four birds.

The imperial function itself was an object of fascination. The emperor sometimes passed below the legation's first office quarters located in the old Imperial Life Insurance building on his way to Tokyo railway station. Finding that the Japanese staff sometimes peeked as the procession passed, Canadians did the same. From his rented summer villa in Hayama near Kamakura, Keenleyside

The Canadian hockey team in Tokyo in 1937. *Canadian Embassy, Tokyo*

also observed the emperor wading in the water in the distance, engaged in his hobby of marine biology. An invitation to an imperial garden party provided a view at closer range; Kirkwood recalled watching him walk down a grassy lane, Japanese bowing low in respect on one side, while he shook hands and conversed with foreigners on the other in a most democratic way.

When the whirl of Tokyo life became too much, there was the option of retreating into the cultural security of a hockey game. In a letter home, Manion wrote,

> You will be surprised to learn that we are playing ice hockey in Tokyo. There are two excellent indoor artificial ice rinks, and we've organized a pick up Canadian team, mostly Legation people bolstered by CP and CN representatives. We have been challenged twice by Japanese university teams, and the first time we won handily enough. The second time, however, the Japanese had learned their lesson about the Canadian style of play, and just about massacred us . . . Persistence is the key word. Every evening hundreds turn out for skating, most of whom have never done it before and can barely keep afloat. But having done it, it becomes a challenge, and they're going to keep at it until they learn, by gum, even if it takes until doomsday.

As Kirkwood observed after returning from a vacation in 1937, life in Tokyo was, all in all, a congenial existence.

> I was so disillusioned about London, Paris and Ottawa, that I find myself only too glad to be able to return to my Tokyo post for another year or so. It has more exotic oriental appeal; is sufficiently remote from local Ottawa politics and uncertainties and dullness; and it has a life of its own into which I have settled.

• • •

Beneath the surface ran the increasingly harsh realities of the 1930s. As US and European markets fell, thousands of Japanese factory workers found themselves out of work, while declining rice prices led to serious deprivation in the countryside. And while North America reacted to the Depression by turning inward toward Franklin Roosevelt's New Deal and Canada's social democratic movement. Japan, in contrast, turned outward in the direction of long-held territorial ambitions on the Asian mainland, as well as backward into the militarism of its feudal past.

A series of political assassinations in the early 1930s, including of two prime ministers, challenged domestic stability under civilian government. Meanwhile, the infamous "Mukden Incident" in 1931, sparked by an explosion along the South Manchurian Railway, signalled Japan's expanding reach into the Asian mainland. Marler and Keenleyside debated endlessly every Chinese complaint and Japanese justification, every twist and turn of who had done what to whom, every nuance of how the British and the Americans were responding and what the rest of the world in the form of the League of Nations could or should do about it—which in the end was to chastise Japan, precipitating its withdrawal from the League in 1933.

Nonetheless, the early 1930s remained a time of optimism, and the international community naturally gravitated to those who put their faith in international cooperation. Keenleyside was a strong admirer of Baron Shidehara Kijurō, Japan's foreign minister and a former ambassador to Washington, who sought to restrain military power.

> Of all the Japanese statesmen of his era, Shidehara was, in Western terms, probably the most enlightened and certainly among the most courageous . . . He was deeply concerned in 1931 when he began to

hear rumours of impending direct action by the Japanese Army in Manchuria, and after the Mukden Incident in the fall of that year he made strong efforts to find a peaceful solution to the new problems that it had created.

The Foreign Ministry, however, was a divided house. In Hayama, Keenleyside found himself sharing his evening walks along the rocky beach with Shiratori Toshio, a member of the Foreign Ministry sympathetic to extreme elements in the army. An advocate of military expansionism, Shiratori actively counselled an alliance with Nazi Germany and Italy and was sentenced after the war to life imprisonment as a war criminal.

> Of all the Japanese I knew, Shiratori was the least inhibited in his statement of the extreme Japanese case against both China and the West, and was the toughest, though not most sophisticated, defender of Japan's expansionist policy. This officially correct though bitter and angry man could easily be imagined as an intelligent but badly warped terrorist from the Black Dragon Society. Yet we never parted in anger, and on several occasions in subsequent years he greeted me with an apparent friendliness that was only slightly touched with irony.

The early strains of mounting militant nationalism do not seem to have had much impact on daily life. "Despite all this ferment," Manion wrote of the 1931 assassinations, "there is no evidence of any kind of ill feeling toward individual foreigners. I've been in all parts of the town, from the poorest to the best, and I have never seen one of those hostile looks which we might expect." Langley, who lived in a Japanese-style house in a Japanese neighbourhood, left his car beside a local park; it was never bothered.

All the same, there was a palpable sense of growing disenchantment. As Kirkwood observed in 1935: "Patriotism in Japan is no respecter of honour, law or rights . . . It assassinates its Premiers, its Ministers; it mobs government offices; it violates diplomatic immunities; it assaults businesses, individuals— either Japanese or foreign; and invades diplomats' houses."

● ● ●

Elizabeth "Topsy" MacDougall, Herbert and Beatrice Marler's 22-year-old niece who arrived from Montreal in 1935, found herself in a ringside seat as the tenuous mid-1930s reached a turning point.

For Topsy, Japan was one exciting, exotic social whirl in which she had the greatest of fortune to participate. Her arrival was heralded in the newspapers and kicked off by a dinner for 38 in the residence, followed by a seemingly endless round of lunches, teas, cocktails, dinners, concerts, musicales, tennis matches and long card games after dinner that, when she was lucky, helped finance the next day's activities.

In her eyes, Herbert Marler was not a stiff patrician but a benevolent uncle who found time to take her golfing and show her the Meiji Shrine. Beatrice Marler was "dear, warm, understanding Aunt Bea," who kept her social calendar full and packed her and her friends off on excursions with well-stuffed picnic hampers.

Topsy went shopping. She shopped with Aunt Bea. She shopped with her new American friend Mildred. She shopped for prints, for a kimono, for presents to send home. She visited the restaurant at the top of the Mitsukoshi Department Store for ice cream sodas, strawberries and French fruit pie. She recoiled at the taste of Japanese tea, finding it even more diabolical than its jade-green colour. She visited the shrine of the Forty-Seven Ronin and the Tokugawa tombs. She attended celebrations for the wedding of Tokugawa Toyo with her new friend Sunoko. She went to lectures on Japanese printmaking and had long conversations with Aunt Bea's friend Mrs. Sugimoto, a Japanese author who talked of old Japan and showed her a poetry card game.

She went to the Kabuki-za, where the male actors fascinated her, as did the jazz and tap dancing of the all-female Takarazuka Revue. She dined *à la Japonaise* in local restaurants. She visited dim hostess bars and crossed the forbidden portals of the Florida, Tokyo's taxi-dance hall. When she got homesick she ducked out to catch the latest Fred Astaire or Carole Lombard movie.

She travelled with her new friends, delighting in Japanese inns and sleeping on futons. She shed her inhibitions and slipped naked into steamy Japanese baths. She visited the Tokugawa Shrines at Nikkō and played on the beaches at Kamakura and Enoshima. She went by train to the Japan Alps to ski, in an open roadster to Hakone and Mount Fuji and by horseback up the volcano at Mihara. She even capped off her Japan adventure with an exciting side trip to China with Mildred.

Through it all floated young men—lots and lots of young men. There was Ken of the frustrated passions, James the wicked baron of the diplomatic set,

Jerry the schnapps-and-vodka-drinking art collector who led her out under the stars and told her Japanese fairy tales—as well as Keith the deadly attractive, Jeff the impossible, Cecil the intriguing and Gil the attentive (albeit with "a way of avoiding entanglements"). There was also the New Zealand rugby team. The conventional wisdom that single foreign women in Japan are destined to lead lonely lives had apparently not yet been invented.

It was all lighthearted and terribly good fun until Topsy awoke one morning in February 1936 to learn that a group of junior army officers had set out to assassinate senior members of the government and the Imperial Household before being crushed by Imperial Guards. Among the victims was Finance Minister Takahashi Korekiyo, an advocate of reducing military expenditures, who lived next door. The city ground to a halt. Telephones no longer worked, trains stopped running, schools closed. Streets, barricaded with barbed wire and sandbags, were lined with soldiers and tanks. Guards were posted at the legation gates, its residents advised not to leave the compound. Inside, Sir Herbert continued his poker game.

The emperor, furious at the loss of trusted advisers, denied the rebels the honour that came with ritual suicide. Instead, the ringleaders were executed following secret courts-martial, their bodies cremated and their ashes disposed of without being returned to their families.

Even the perceptive Keenleyside, however, admitted he could not have predicted what was coming when he left Japan later that year.

> I feared but did not really believe that war in all its dimensions of horror was about to descend upon us. I knew that over the last few years conditions in Japan and on the mainland so close across the narrow waters were worsening with every passing month. But that this sad trend would continue and spread until the whole world was engulfed I could not accept. Surely some solution short of this final insanity would be found. And yet . . .

• • •

The events of February 1936 marked the beginning of the end. A year later the military gained the upper hand. All-party participation in cabinet was eliminated and the government was brought firmly under the control of an army general. By July 1937 Japan was engaged in full-scale war with China.

By then Herbert Marler had left Japan to take up a long-coveted appointment as Canada's ambassador in Washington. His replacement was Randolph Bruce, a former lieutenant governor of British Columbia. A fine and popular man, Bruce was 73 years old and almost completely blind when he was appointed. He was also a novice in the pitfall-laden world of pre-war diplomacy, and it was only a matter of time before the trap door opened.

When the *Toronto Star* reported in 1937 that Bruce held opinions favourable to Japan's invasion of China, he was widely criticized. The decade drew to a close with the sad image of Bruce sitting alone in his study, patiently waiting for someone to read him papers, taking his cues from the British Embassy and hoping he would be allowed to return home, which he finally did in 1938.

He was not replaced. As the situation deteriorated, the legation carried on under a *chargé d'affaires*, D'Arcy McGreer, the great promise of 1929 put on hold.

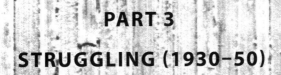

PART 3
STRUGGLING (1930–50)

THE DARK VALLEY

In 1898 a young man passed by train through the Canadian Rockies on his way home. He was Nitobe Inazō and he was about to write *Bushido: The Soul of Japan*, possibly the most famous book ever written about what it means to be Japanese.

Originally published in English in 1900, *Bushido* ("the way of the samurai") dazzled. Here, in a short 127 pages, was an explanation of Japanese values in terms that foreigners could understand. Nitobe's samurai was schooled in the virtues of courage, loyalty and self-control; a man of honour and benevolence; someone who carried a sword but also wrote poetry— rather like a Japanese version of the ideal medieval knight.'

The right book at the right time, *Bushido* also helped the world understand Japan's stunning victory in the Russo–Japanese War of 1904–05. US President Theodore Roosevelt is said to have been thunderstruck by the similarities between Nitobe's samurai and his own Rough Riders.

Decades later the cult of the samurai remained alive and well in Kurosawa Akira's *Seven Samurai*, which inspired *The Magnificent Seven* and other westerns in a similar genre. Like the geisha, the samurai stereotype took on a life of its own.

Born into a samurai clan in Morioka, north of Tokyo, Nitobe came to embody the disparate and increasingly contradictory streams that coursed through pre-war Japan. One of the Meiji-era young men who received a Western education, he studied in Tokyo and at Sapporo Agricultural College in Hokkaido before going on to Johns Hopkins University in Baltimore and to Germany. In America he also joined the Quakers, whose simplicity he admired, and married the daughter of a prominent Quaker leader.

On return to Japan he was appointed principal of Ichiko (First Higher

Nitobe Inazō, the future author of *Bushido: The Soul of Japan*, with his adopted son, Yosho, on a trail near Glacier House in the Selkirk Mountains in 1898. *Whyte Museum of the Canadian Rockies, Vaux family fonds, V653/NG-511*

School), the preparatory ground for entrance to prestigious Tokyo Imperial University, where he quickly rose to prominence as a leading educator and shaper of the modern Japanese man. As a professor at Tsuda University and the first president of newly established Tokyo Joshi Dai (Women's Christian College), he also became a leading proponent of education for women. Housewives wrote to the good doctor by the thousands and lined up to discuss their problems with him in the Nitobe living room.

His professional forte, however, was agriculture, which led to an appointment as head of colonial studies at Tokyo Imperial University. From his perspective there was no inconsistency between his progressive views and Japan's growing control over Taiwan, Korea and Manchuria. Agriculture, in particular, had the happy faculty of improving the lot of the colonized while meeting Japan's chronic preoccupation with food security.

In the 1920s Nitobe was transformed again, this time into Japan's leading internationalist. Named one of five undersecretaries of the new League of Nations in Geneva, he quickly emerged as a much-admired exponent of the gospel of international peace and the necessity of collective security.

By 1926, however, Nitobe had had enough. Discouraged by what he perceived as condescending attitudes toward Japan, and outraged by the US action in 1924 to ban Asian immigration, he quit the League in disgust. He returned to Japan, where he was appointed a peer and began writing a column for a leading newspaper, *Osaka Mainichi.*

By then, however, the tension inherent in Nitobe's persona caught up with him. For all his internationalization, he remained an intensely Japanese Japanese. He was accepting, for example, when General Nogi Maresuke shocked the nation by committing ritual suicide with his wife on the death of the Emperor Meiji in 1912 as a supreme act of loyalty, as well as in atonement for perceived mistakes he had made in the course of his military career. "Looking back at General Nogi's last act," Nitobe noted afterward, "we can say that it represents the model of the old *bushi* and that Nogi may have been the last *bushi.*"

At the same time, *Bushido* came back to haunt him. Originally written to explain that Western concepts like justice and compassion were not alien to Japanese, the samurai code in Nitobe's mind was less about using the sword than the moral fibre that controlled it. Instead, the relatively pacifist book was hijacked by militant nationalists who drew on it to justify the doctrine of intense loyalty to the emperor.

To his supporters, both Japanese and foreign, Nitobe was an advocate of reason and peace in a world that would soon lose its grip on both. At the same time, skeptics questioned the sincerity of his views. Hugh Keenleyside of the Canadian Legation, for one, in 1931 dismissed Nitobe's writing as proving "what I have long contended, that he is a good example of the 'fake liberal.' It is an apologia in the same spirit as his earlier *Bushido.*" His colleague Kenneth Kirkwood, on the other hand, saw Nitobe as an outstanding liberal statesman and scholar, one of the few left to lift his voice against the dangerous course Japan was on. Nitobe, it seems, could not please everyone. Early in life he had consciously set out to make himself "a bridge across the Pacific." Now he was more like the frustrated engineer, desperately trying to straddle a wobbly structure whose ends were pulling inexorably apart.

After voicing criticism of the actions of the Japanese military in Shanghai in 1929 and Manchuria in 1931, he was forced to give in to pressure and apologize. Fearing for his safety, in an era fraught with political assassinations, friends arranged for him to leave in 1932 on a speaking tour of North America that included visits to Ottawa and Vancouver, where he lectured at the University of British Columbia.

The line between explaining and defending Japan's historical rights and its actions in China and Manchuria, however, proved a fine one. What Nitobe intended by way of clarification came out sounding to some more like rationalization of military aggression and a threat to the interests of the other major powers. He was also preaching to an audience that had largely already made up its mind. Influenced by China's version of events, North American sentiment was increasingly with the underdog.

For his part, Nitobe despaired over what he perceived as self-justification and blinkered double standards.

> Many honest Americans thought it terrible and inhumane for Britain to insist on ruling India, yet believed it to be the duty of their country to interfere in Cuba. Similarly, some regarded Japanese treatment of China as cruel and unreasonable, yet justified the US Monroe Doctrine on the ground that a "civilized" power has a moral responsibility toward nations that cannot put their own houses in order . . . There is no feeling as comfortable as that of self righteousness. When this is combined with a sense of superiority, we reach a height from which it is easy to fall.

Returning to Japan, he found the situation changed for the worse. Party politics had ended and Japan had formally withdrawn from the League of Nations over Manchuria. Distraught, he laid blame equally on the League for steering the matter badly and on Japanese diplomacy for failing to explain adequately the complexities of the issue to the international community.

In late 1933 Nitobe crossed the Pacific again, this time to Banff for a meeting of the Institute of Pacific Relations (IPR), the private association of influential public figures, businessmen, academics and journalists from

LEFT Nitobe Inazō, Japan's eminent and controversial pre-war educator and internationalist. *US Library of Congress, LC-B2-1227-6 P&P*

RIGHT University of British Columbia president Norman MacKenzie (right) with Prime Minister Yoshida Shigeru and UBC chancellor Sherwood Lett in front of the Nitobe lantern in the university's Nitobe Memorial Garden in1954. There is another monument and garden dedicated to Nitobe in Victoria, which is twinned with Morioka, Nitobe's birthplace. *UBC Library, Rare Books and Special Collections, Japanese Canadian photograph collection, JCPC 41.005*

both sides of the Pacific who strove to promote mutual understanding from the mid-1920s onward. Canadian IPR participants were a virtual pre-war who's who: former Conservative prime minister Robert Borden, prominent Toronto lawyer Newton Rowell, *Manitoba* (later *Winnipeg) Free Press* editor John W. Dafoe, future University of British Columbia president Norman MacKenzie—as well as the prime Canadian organizer, former Vancouver journalist turned Sun Life publicist John Nelson.

Following the meeting Nitobe took another trip through the Rockies on his way back to Japan. By then in his 70s and in failing health, he was visiting Victoria when he suddenly died. And with his death Japan took a further slide into the *kurai tanima*, the dark valley of the 1930s that preceded the Pacific War.

• • •

The 1930s was a decade of changing perceptions. At the outset, many foreigners still subscribed to the longstanding perception of Japan as a civilizing force in Asia, a "Britain of the East" destined to bring order to warlord-plagued Manchuria as it had already done in Taiwan and Korea, and a contrast to disorderly China. The turning point came in mid-decade after the young officers' abortive coup of 1936, followed by escalation of the Sino–Japanese dispute into a full-scale undeclared war in 1937. Even so, many in the resident Canadian community of roughly 500—mainly missionaries, educators and social workers—hung on, committed to the causes to which they had devoted much of their lives.

How such people dealt with the unravelling decade can be discerned from letters and reports of Canadian faculty at Kwansei Gakuin, the Canadian Methodist–sponsored liberal arts college in Kobe that achieved university status in 1932. A letter Professor Harold Woodsworth wrote home that year reflects the common early-1930s perception.

> It was rather interesting to get into Korea again and hear more of Manchuria. I think I came away more sympathetic with Japan than when I left. She has done a splendid piece of work in Korea and undoubtedly would repeat as best she could in Manchuria. Technically she may be wrong but I wonder if she is not right in a practical way . . . There is something to be said for security.

In 1937 Woodsworth reported that the war with China and increasing totalitarianism in Japan had affected the university "hardly at all . . . Several years ago we realized that an extreme nationalism would place its hand most heavily on our institutions. Fortunately as yet the paternalism is kind. We have found our position tenable if somewhat uncomfortable."

Escalating demands from Japanese authorities were handled pragmatically. A requirement that students participate in military drill was rationalized as being not materially different from similar exercises in some Canadian private schools. The regular Wednesday morning prayer meeting was moved up a half hour to provide time for an expanded ritual: first everyone turned and bowed in the direction of the Imperial Palace, then sang the national anthem; a Christian hymn and a scripture reading followed.

Kwansei Gakuin University students on an outing to a shrine with Professor Harold Woodsworth (far right) during the 1930s. *Courtesy of Sylvia Bews Wright and the Woodsworth family*

A government directive requiring students to visit Shinto shrines did not pose an insurmountable obstacle. "From time to time," Woodsworth explained, "our students have been called to [Shinto] shrines to offer prayers. This was not a problem which troubled most Japanese Christians because they accept the theory of the non-religious character of the shrines . . . Whether we like it or not we must suffer with this country."

Indeed, mental cartwheels were turned to empathize with the situation in which the students found themselves, as reflected in a 1938 report from Howard Outerbridge, the university's second-in-command.

> The voice of authority in Japan is the Emperor, just as the Bible, conscience or the Pope is to us. No texts had been preached more often in recent years than those which claim that we must "fear God and honor the king, render unto Caesar," etc. I believe it is just as hard for a Japanese to reconcile himself to what he believes to be the crime of disloyalty as it would be for me to commit murder.

Even as militant nationalism gained the upper hand, the university's president, Cornelius John Lighthall Bates, remained upbeat. "We have had a very good year in the school," he reported as late as the spring of 1939. "The loyalty, fidelity and kindness of our friends are very wonderful. It is a good fellowship. We have been singularly free from internal troubles at Kwansei Gakuin."

Far from insensitive to the storm gathering around them, Woodsworth, Outerbridge and Bates were acutely aware of it, especially as reports of the Japanese military's actions in China filtered back to Japan. Their alternatives, however, were limited. They could speak out, which risked endangering their Japanese associates and students, as well as themselves. Or they could leave, which most eventually did when it became clear their continued presence risked doing their friends, as well as themselves and their families, more harm than good.

Daily life, for the most part, also remained reassuringly normal. Like foreigners generally, the Kwansei Gakuin faculty were routinely watched and questioned, but ordinary Japanese remained polite and friendly and incidents were few. The position of foreigners in Japan did not become seriously strained until 1940, after 30 British businessmen were arrested in Kobe on suspicion of espionage.

When the few foreigners still remaining in administrative roles in Japan were required to surrender their positions in 1939, Bates finally resigned. He remained until the end of the year, departing on the last Canadian Pacific *Empress* liner to leave Japan, along with other participants in the quietly mounting pre-war exodus. A talk he gave on CBC Radio in 1942 summed up what many returnees probably felt about the war. "The tragic and pathetic fact is that Japan made the wrong choice and threw in her lot with the nations that she judged would be victorious, but that are surely doomed to defeat. Many Japanese saw the mistake but they were powerless to prevent it."

● ● ●

Bates, who had the unusual distinction of serving as a Canadian president of a Japanese post-secondary education institution from 1920 until the eve of the Pacific War, was one of the missionary educators who had been part of the Canadian community in Japan since Meiji times. A graduate of Queen's University in Kingston, Ontario, who arrived in 1902, he was a big man with an even bigger personality. He was also a talented college administrator, who developed a relationship with a generous supporter who was also one of Japan's keenest businessmen, Kobayashi Ichizo.

A graduate of Fukuzawa's Keio Gijuku, Kobayashi absorbed the lessons of material progress well, parlaying a regional electric railway into the enormous Hankyū empire. In 1929, when Kwansei Gakuin's original 23-acre premises in central Kobe became too cramped, he purchased the property for an amount considerably greater than the cost of a magnificent new 70-acre site near Nishinomiya, midway between Kobe and Osaka in the lee of the Rokkō Mountains.

This loaves-and-fishes miracle owed more to the entrepreneurial than the philanthropic spirit. Of the "build it and they will come" school of economic prosperity, Kobayashi pioneered the strategy of locating department stores, amusement parks, zoos, hotels and other attractions along its railway lines.

Located along Hankyū's latest branch line, the new Kwansei Gakuin campus guaranteed steady ridership. The next stop, the hillside village of Takarazuka, was home to another of Kobayashi's ventures, the Takarazuka Revue, the popular musical theatre company he founded in 1913 in which all the roles are played by women—in contrast to kabuki, where they are all played by men—notably the debonair *otokoyaku* (man players), the idealized heroes of Japanese romance novels. The students, the players and the patrons travelled together up and down the line, and Kwansei Gakuin, the Revue and Hankyū all prospered.

Educators like Bates responded to one calling; the growing number of social workers in the 1920s and '30s responded to another. From the same middle-class element that fostered the rise of the social democratic movement in Canada, they transplanted themselves and their values to Japan, working with Japanese colleagues who shared their passion for social welfare and reform.

Their inspiration came from three quarters. One was J.S. Woodsworth, Canada's leading social democrat and founder of the CCF (Co-operative Commonwealth Federation) party, and the brother of Harold Woodworth, the Kwansei Gakuin professor. Another was Kagawa Toyohiko, a charismatic Christian socialist and pacifist who lived "in a box"—a six-foot-square shed in the Kobe slums. Kagawa organized unions, supervised social work and established credit unions, schools, hospitals and churches; he also wrote best-selling books and gave spellbinding speeches during the 1920s and early '30s. A third inspiration was Canada's own social activist prototype in the person of Caroline Macdonald, whose death in 1931 was deeply affecting.

The social fallout from Japan's rapid economic advancement was greatly worsened by the economic hardship associated with the Depression, which hit Japan hard. In Tokyo's poor factory districts and slums, where every second building seemed to be a bar or a brothel, the Canadian Methodists (United Church after 1925) supported a chain of four hostels. One, the Aiseikwan (House of Love and Purity), was a place of refuge operated by Annie Allen. Located along the mud and canals of Kameido, the main factory district at the edge of the city, it was a microcosm of the social ills that beset the poorest districts of Tokyo: mothers in trouble, labourers in need of a meal, street walkers dropped off by the police, young women rescued from prostitution, children in need of birth certificates to register for school.

In the mid-1930s, Kwansei Gakuin University established a similar institution, the Gyomeikan, located on one of the small islands in the old quarter of Osaka that was home to those truly on the bottom of the Japanese social ladder: Liu Chu islanders, Koreans and *burakumin* (the traditional outcaste class).

A response to the growing need for social welfare, a responsibility that traditionally belonged to the family or clan, such institutions were treated as an integral part of Japan's expanding social welfare system. Financial support came from the Home Ministry, the metropolitan government, the Imperial Household and wealthy Japanese benefactors, as well as from abroad.

Tokyo street children were part of a growing problem of widespread poverty and labour unrest during the 1920s and '30s. *United Church of Canada Archives, 1999.054P/46N*

As valuable as these initiatives were, they were a drop in an increasingly leaky social welfare bucket. Some Canadians joined with like-minded Japanese in an effort to plug the larger holes. Ned Hennigar from New Brunswick was

LEFT Children of the Aiseikwan. *United Church of Canada Archives, 2000.017P/3920N*

RIGHT Ken and Mary Woodsworth, children of Kwansei Gakuin professor Harold Woodsworth, dressed for graduation day at the Canadian Academy in Kobe in the 1920s. *Courtesy of Sylvia Bews Wright and the Woodsworth family*

active in campaigns to abolish legal prostitution, which gave brothel owners the right to pursue women who ran away. Historically, Japanese viewed prostitution less as a moral issue than as a social inevitability; far better, the saying went, for a poor girl to spend a few years as a prostitute earning money for her family than try to survive in the rice fields or mines, or worse, starve. This attitude fell away, however, as deteriorating economic conditions in the countryside forced growing numbers of young women into the city.

By the early 1930s, 48,000 girls in Tokyo's licensed quarters were serving some 22 million visitors a year, and thousands more were working in unlicensed premises. The Yoshiwara had also become a much coarser place. Gone was the former park-like setting with its gravelled streets, trees and gardens; in its place was a crasser atmosphere of neon lights and advertising.

Hennigar also took up the temperance banner, travelling from village to village preaching the virtues of the local option of "going dry." The economic motivation for temperance in the thrifty, impoverished countryside was a powerful one. First to heed the call was Kawaidani, a poor village in Toyama Prefecture. Heavily in debt, Kawaidani took the pledge as a means to raise money for a school.

• • •

The most famous Canadian in Japan in the 1930s, though no one could have predicted it at the time, was Paul-Émile Léger. The man who went on to become one of the most famous cardinals ever appointed in the Roman Catholic Church began his career in Japan.

In contrast to Canadian Protestants, who began arriving in Japan in the 1870s, Roman Catholics did not come in significant numbers until the 1920s. The respective contexts were also different: while Protestants were inspired half a century earlier by the vision of a modernizing Japan as a platform for the spread of Christianity throughout Asia, Roman Catholics viewed Japan as a bulwark against the spread of international communism following the 1917 Russian Revolution. The theme, common at the time, also meshed with long-standing Japanese preoccupation about Russian, now Soviet, strategic ambitions vis-à-vis Japan and China.

The first Canadian Roman Catholic in Japan, Hélène Paradis, arrived in Kumamoto in 1898 with a French order. By 1921 Canadian Franciscans had established themselves in Nagasaki and Kagoshima on the southern island of Kyushū, where Catholicism was first introduced in Japan; Dominicans reached Hakodate in the north in 1928. Other orders followed, including large numbers of nuns.

Léger was a student at the huge Sulpician seminary outside Paris when he first learned of a proposal to build a seminary at Fukuoka in Kyushū to train a Japanese ministry. The project, said to have the backing of Rome, was the brainchild of the local bishop, a Frenchman named Breton. The idea caught Léger's imagination, and in September 1933 he and a colleague, Charlie Prévost, boarded a Canadian Pacific *Empress* for Japan.

What they discovered on arrival in Tokyo gave them pause. Watching Japanese bow and clap at shrines, and observing the hustle and bustle of

Cardinal Paul-Émile Léger began his illustrious career as a parish priest in Kyushū in southern Japan. *L'Oeuvre Léger*

the city, Léger confessed privately to some misgivings. The idea that Christianity could make any significant inroads in a society so entrenched in its own traditions and so advanced in material culture seemed little short of folly. "What could a young missionary with no experience do in a country rich in 2,000 years of culture?" he asked himself. In his long priest's robes he felt distinctly out of place. That night he slept on *tatami*.

The venture took another leap backward when Léger arrived in Fukuoka and learned the seminary project had been shelved for lack of funds. Instead of teaching, he found himself working as a parish priest in the local community. Sometimes he travelled about the region visiting temples and getting to know Buddhist priests. Occasionally he went to Tokyo, where Hugh Keenleyside recalled looking forward to visits from an unassuming, intelligent young man who turned up from time to time at the legation, eager for conversation.

In time Léger realized he had come to Japan under false assumptions, when he discovered that Breton expected Léger's order in Montreal to provide the thousands of yen needed to build the seminary. During a visit home in 1935, he then learned the order had lost the bulk of its finances when an investment turned sour during the Depression.

Commandeering the family Oldsmobile, Léger spent the spring touring Quebec giving slide shows and lectures about life in Japan, raising enough money to keep himself and his fellow Canadians, who by then numbered five, in operation in Fukuoka. That still left the seminary, so he went to Paris to find out what could be done. In the end Rome came through, and Léger was able to see it completed in 1938, and to teach there.

Léger came to feel at home in Japan, and even contemplated remaining for the rest of his life. He does not seem to have experienced the kind of heavy police surveillance and occasional harassment that affected other Roman Catholic orders in the vicinity, like the Canadian Franciscans in nearby Kagoshima, who decamped farther north in 1936. Kyushū was a historic gateway for Catholicism, but it was also a strategic shipping base for the war in China. In 1939, however, Léger was asked to return to Canada, something about which he later felt guilty, as Prévost and other colleagues in Fukuoka ended up spending the duration of the Pacific War in prison. It is said he retained a deep nostalgia for Japan, and was even known to occasionally turn up to class in Montreal in the 1940s in Japanese dress and speaking Japanese.

• • •

In two decades Canada and Japan had gone from being allies to enemies. Those returning to Canada on the eve of the war also found themselves in a country that was entering a dark valley of its own. The war in China had spilled over into the domestic arena, hardening public attitudes toward Japan. Public pressure mounted for boycotts of Japanese goods and bans on Canadian exports, particularly metals and minerals.

At the same time, the possibility of war fostered growing insecurity about the vulnerability of Canada's largely undefended Pacific coast. Increasingly, the spectre of fear shifted to the approximately 22,000 people of Japanese origin living mainly in British Columbia whose forcible evacuation from the coast became, for many Canadians, the defining issue of the Pacific War.

Hugh Keenleyside, who returned from the Canadian Legation in 1936, was among the more enlightened members of the Ottawa establishment who fended off pressures to take action against Japanese Canadians, until the bombing of Pearl Harbor let loose a surge of pent-up anti-Japanese feeling. Keenleyside acknowledged there was a rationale for legitimate security precautions, possibly even some deportations; war, after all, was war. But he was against taking measures aimed at people, 75 percent of whom were Canadian citizens, simply to assuage hostile feeling in British Columbia. In his view, King ought to have shown more courage; he also suspected him of racism. Most objectionable was the appalling way in which the relocation was carried out. Even more disturbing, he wrote afterward, investigations into allegations of disloyalty and subversion came to naught.

The Canadian security services had in fact made strong and repeated statements that there was no evidence to justify the belief that such a movement was necessary. Looking back, it is hard to avoid the conclusion that the relocation of the Japanese was both unnecessary and unjust, especially in the case of those who were Canadian citizens. The only possible justification was the depth of the fear and hysteria aroused by the leaders of the long campaign against orientals in British Columbia and the danger of possible civil disturbances.

King, who seemed at times possessed of a remarkably double-jointed mind, apparently saw no inconsistency between his government's treatment of the Japanese Canadians and his own longstanding regard for Japanese people. During the early months of the war he carried on a cordial relationship with the Japanese minister in Ottawa, Yoshizawa Seijiro. When Yoshizawa was repatriated to Japan in 1942, King telephoned him in Montreal to apologize for not saying goodbye in person, assuring him that their relations had always been wholly honourable and pleasant. "When all this war is over," King confided afterward in his diary, "we may wish to bind together the different countries and Yoshizawa might be helpful in that way, if his faith in me were not destroyed . . . Besides, I did not want him and his wife to go away with a pain in their hearts which I could have spared them."

As Keenleyside noted, it would be reassuring to think a similar pain in King's heart extended to the thousands of Japanese Canadians in Vancouver's Hastings Park awaiting transportation to relocation camps away from the coast.

John Fraser, who returned to Vancouver with his family in the mid-1930s, recalls local feelings ran so high before the war that anything or anyone associated with Japan came to be viewed with suspicion, sometimes even the Frasers themselves. The day after Pearl Harbor, he was beaten up several times at school because he was "Japanese."

His father, Clarence Fraser, the well-known representative of the MacMillan Export Company in Tokyo before the war, was realistic about the course Japan's military leadership was on and wrote to King to that effect. At the same time, he was also determined that his son appreciate the home-grown tragedy unfolding around him. In 1943 he took him to Vancouver's Stanley Park and pointed out the monument honouring Japanese Canadians who served in Canadian forces in the First World War, whose light had been turned out in the early days of the war.

A lone Japanese man leaving Hastings Park in 1942. *Vancouver Public Library,* Province *newspaper collection, VPL 1400*

Fraser never forgot his father's condemnation of the internment. He was present as a federal government minister when the light on the monument was turned back on in a ceremony in 1985—which also honoured former Sergeant Mitsui Masumi, who had been so enraged by the expulsion order 40 years before that he had thrown his hard-won medals onto the desk of the administering official. He was also present when the Canadian government announced its formal apology and compensation to Japanese Canadians in 1988.

WAR AND RECONCILIATION

On the morning of August 9, 1945, an air strike formation—two flights of four Corsairs, each carrying two 500-pound bombs—headed toward the northeast coast of Japan. Three days earlier the atomic bomb had been dropped on Hiroshima. The war was almost, but not yet, over. The word was to take no unnecessary risks.

The formation leader, Robert Hampton Gray, had been a medical student at the University of British Columbia before the war. Finding himself "getting a little mad at Mr. Hitler," he had joined the Royal Canadian Naval Volunteer Reserve, which lent him to the British Royal Navy. By 1945 he was serving as a senior pilot with the British Pacific Fleet aboard the aircraft carrier HMS *Formidable*.

Beneath his affable exterior lay the cool, deadly aim of a bomber pilot; "Hammy" Gray was one of the best. By day he led strikes pounding airstrips on the islands between Taiwan and Okinawa. By night the airstrips were rebuilt and the process began all over again. The greatest danger came from determined young kamikaze pilots who relentlessly attacked *Formidable* and other ships, in their words, falling like cherry blossoms in suicide missions.

As the final Allied assault on Japan mounted in the summer of 1945, the British fleet moved north, running bombing raids against airfields and coastal shipping facilities on the Japanese mainland. In July Gray wrote to his family that he sensed the war was coming to an end; he was looking forward to coming home.

As the formation made its way up the coast, it came across Onagawa Bay, a small relay point on one of the last Japanese shipping lanes still in operation, which contained a heavily armed destroyer, *Amakusa*, and smaller ships. Skirting the steep hills and ravines, Gray came in low, as he had so many times before. By then, however, he had been spotted.

Streaking down, he struck anti-aircraft fire but continued straight for *Amakusa*. One bomb was shot off; the second was a direct hit. As the ship sank he pulled up and headed out to sea. It was too late; his plane burst into flames and plunged into the water. He was gone. A Japanese gunner who was close enough to see Gray's face as he went down later marvelled at the pilot's audacity.

Meanwhile, his fellow airmen could hardly believe their eyes. Turning around, they bombed the bay repeatedly before heading back to *Formidable*, where they learned a second atomic bomb had just been dropped on Nagasaki. Forty US planes completed the Onagawa bombing later that day; one Japanese submarine chaser survived. The following evening, August 10, Japan signalled its acceptance of the terms of surrender; the war was over, although the official surrender ceremony would not take place for three more weeks, on September 2.

In recognition of Gray's brilliant fighting spirit and leadership in action, he was posthumously awarded the Victoria Cross. He also received the Distinguished Service Cross for his earlier role in the bombing of the German battleship *Tirpitz* in a Norwegian fjord. A mountain in the Kokanee Glacier region near Nelson, British Columbia, his hometown, was named for him and a brother who died fighting in Europe. His sunny face now stands out among the Canadian war heroes near the national cenotaph in Ottawa and in a photograph in the BC Legislature.

It is one thing, however, for a country to honour its own war dead. It is virtually unprecedented to honour those of the enemy. A more remarkable monument to Gray is one erected in 1989 that overlooks Onagawa Bay near another honouring the 157 members of the Onagawa Defence Squadron who died that day in battle. The monument is made of granite donated by the BC government and supported by contributions from Canadian businesses and individuals.

How the people of Onagawa decided to accept a monument to the enemy pilot who attacked them is an extraordinary story of post-war reconciliation. It began when the Canadian War Museum decided to investigate the possibility of recovering the wreckage of Gray's aircraft, which proved infeasible after unexploded bombs were discovered in the bay. In the process, however, a cordial relationship developed between Canadians and residents of Onagawa, including Japanese veterans of the battle.

Lieutenant Robert Hampton Gray died in an attack on Onagawa Bay in August 1945 as the Pacific War was ending. The remarkable monument erected to Gray in 1989 was toppled but not destroyed by the March 2011 tsunami, which devastated the town of Onagawa. *Library and Archives Canada, Department of National Defence collection, PA-133296*

When retired Canadian navy pilot Stuart Soward floated the idea of erecting a monument to Gray instead, local reaction was understandably less than enthusiastic. Opposition gradually melted away, however, under the leadership of former Japanese army warrant officer Kanda Yoshio, who had manned one of the anti-aircraft guns during the battle. Broader public consultations undertaken by the mayor of Onagawa, Suda Zenjiro, yielded a favourable consensus: "Paying respects to the great Canadian naval hero through erection of a monument," Suda announced, ". . . is a most relevant and really excellent thing to do." Haruna Kazuo, chairman of giant trading corporation Marubeni, himself a former sub-lieutenant in charge of one of the anti-aircraft batteries, lent influential support.

To Canadians involved, the process seemed to help the Onagawa veterans close old wounds by providing an opportunity to talk about the battle after a silence of more than 40 years. Following the dedication ceremony, Captain T.C. (Terry) Milne, military attaché at the Canadian Embassy in Tokyo at the time, watched in wonderment as Japanese veterans and surviving Canadian pilots celebrated together at Kanda's house—old men sharing experiences through an interpreter, re-enacting gunfire through hand gestures and mime over glasses of sake and Canadian whisky.

To some, there was also something about it all that seemed to imply an almost samurai-like Japanese respect for Gray. After the ceremony, Shinto priests invited members of his family to join in launching candlelit paper boats bearing messages to the troubled and angry spirit of the bold warrior who remained unburied in the bottom of the bay. It was as if to say everything was all right; former enemies had become friends.

• • •

For Canada, the Pacific War was mainly a defensive one, driven by concern about the vulnerable Pacific coast. As Hong Kong, Malaya, Singapore and the Philippines fell to Japan one by one after Pearl Harbor, nervous British Columbians came to believe it was only a matter of time before they, too, were invaded. Air-raid sirens were installed, blackout curtains covered windows and wardens patrolled the streets. A militia of fishermen, farmers and trappers looked out for subversive activity, while Prince Rupert gained new life as an air defence staging point. Over 30,000 Canadian troops, 14 air force squadrons and 20 warships reinforced Pacific coastal defences.

In the end, the much-feared attack never came. The closest call was in June 1942 when a Japanese submarine lobbed a few shells at the isolated Estevan Point lighthouse on Vancouver Island, which heightened concern but caused no damage or casualties. What did materialize was an invasion of an unexpected kind. During the last months of the war, thousands of *fugo*, unmanned balloons carrying small bombs, were released in Japan and carried on the prevailing winds over the Pacific Northwest. Apparently intended to set fire to the landscape, they had little impact. Small demolition teams scoured the landscape on snowshoe and dogsled with the help of Aboriginal guides, while their existence was kept secret from the public—though information leaked out when one bomb was accidentally exploded by picnickers in Oregon.

An unmanned Japanese balloon (*fugo*) recovered at Hay River, Northwest Territories. Of 9,300 launched, some 300 are known to have landed, many in British Columbia and some as far away as Manitoba, Michigan and Mexico. *Library and Archives Canada, Department of National Defence collection, PA-203245*

Canadians certainly identified with Allied fighting in the Pacific, and some like Hammy Gray served with Allied forces. Royal Canadian Air Force transport squadrons flew supplies in India and Burma and communications specialists assisted the Australians. In 1943 Canadian and US forces joined to attack a Japanese garrison on Kiska in the Aleutians, although by the time they arrived the island was deserted. Toward the end of the war, a lone cruiser, the HMCS *Uganda*, was dispatched to reinforce the British Pacific Fleet.

For most Canadians, however, the 1930–45 period began and remained largely about a European conflict. Already heavily committed with troops there when war with Japan broke out, Canada had no fighting force of its own in the Pacific War. This was set to change in the spring of 1945 as hostilities in Europe wound down and the Canadian government made plans for massive redeployment of some 80,000 battle-weary troops from Europe to the Pacific.

Colonel Richard Malone was dispatched to the Philippines to pave the way with US General Douglas MacArthur for the arrival of Canadian forces. Malone knew generals; in Italy he had served on the staff of Field Marshal Montgomery. But he got nowhere with MacArthur, who, while hospitable, was never keen on sharing the Pacific theatre with anyone. As it turned out, the plan was overtaken when the war ended.

A journalist before the war, Malone managed to finagle his way onto an accompanying press plane on the first US landing, doing double duty for Canadian Press. There were, he reported, no last-ditch stands.

> As our plane swung in from the ocean, and the Japanese shore and outline of Mt. Fujiyama loomed out of the dawn there was a little concern over the threatened action by the Japanese Kamikaze pilots. One anti-aircraft gun on the coast loosed off a few rounds at a plane flying on our left. The transport planes being completely unarmed, our pilot swung wide of this position and a few minutes later landed us perfectly on the Japanese airfield.

Billed by MacArthur as a stupendous undertaking, the landing itself seemed to Malone more chaotic than impressive; enterprising GIs took joy rides in jeeps, while the Japanese in a friendly gesture sent in several hundred prostitutes, who were turned away.

It was impossible, however, not to be moved by the drama of the surrender ceremonies on the USS *Missouri* a few days later, set against the backdrop of the weather-beaten American flag flown by Commodore Perry when he sailed into Tokyo Bay almost a century before. As the grim-faced participants completed the formalities, all eyes were sharply drawn upward as 1,500 planes flew over in tight formations, Malone recalled. "I had witnessed the great German air raids on London, the thousand Allied bomber attacks on German cities, and the great air armadas that launched the attack at Arnhem but never had I witnessed such an awesome display of air power, staged in a matter of minutes."

Colonels Richard Malone and Moore Cosgrave raising Canada's flag over the Canadian Legation in 1945. A journalist by profession, Malone became publisher of the *Winnipeg Free Press* and publisher and editor-in-chief of the *Globe and Mail*. *Library and Archives Canada, Department of External Affairs collection, e008444150*

• • •

Shortly afterward, Malone and a colleague circumvented a ban on leaving the US base by orchestrating an invitation from Prince Tokugawa, the former Japanese minister in Ottawa, to go to Tokyo.

Among the first Allied troops to enter the city following the intense US firebombing in the final months of the war, they found a scene of devastation far greater than anything witnessed in Europe. The city was a wasteland, a junk heap of corrugated iron and cardboard shacks. Some 2 million homes had been destroyed and 200,000 people had died—twice as many as died in the atomic bombing. Hundreds of Japanese soldiers roaming the streets greeted them with curious and hostile stares.

As they approached Tokugawa's office in the Japanese Diet building, an armed Japanese sentry put up a show of resistance. Doing some quick thinking, they removed their belts and pistols, and the much-relieved guard let them pass. Tokugawa himself they found stiff and expressionless, though honour-bound to receive his Canadian visitors with courtesy.

Next on their list was the Canadian Legation, among the few buildings still standing in that part of Tokyo. In the hallway lying on a silver tray was the calling card of Japan's minister of foreign affairs, Shigemitsu Mamoru, apparently one of the last visitors. Malone's companion, Moore Cosgrave, a trade commissioner in Shanghai before the war, had crossed paths with Shigemitsu before. Indeed, a few days earlier their eyes had met briefly on the *Missouri* in startled mutual recognition—which may explain why Cosgrave signed the surrender document on Canada's behalf on the wrong line, causing a chain reaction of misplaced signatures on the Japanese copy, an inadvertent historical curiosity.

The legation's elderly Japanese caretaker, who had faithfully looked after the property and put out fires during the war, burrowed deep into the bowels of the residence and brought out a bottle of Suntory Whisky. He also came up with a Canadian flag, which Malone and Cosgrave raised over the legation buildings once again.

The legation members themselves had, of course, long since departed. Trapped behind enemy lines when war broke out, their main challenge had been boredom. Work was impossible and excursions beyond the gates were limited to visits to doctors and dentists. Once there was a game of golf, and on four occasions, movies.

Conditions, however, were tolerable in the circumstances. Supplies of food and fuel oil arrived regularly, though the latter was in such limited supply that it was used mainly to heat water for bathing. The buildings remained unheated throughout the winter except on Christmas—which also saw the arrival of a large turkey, an unexpected gift from the wife of the vice-minister of foreign affairs.

Most other Canadians still in Japan when war broke out were placed under house arrest and interned. Sybil Courtice, the long-time principal of the Shizuoka Eiwa Girls' School, joined fellow teachers and other female internees, including 20 Quebec nuns, in Sumire Camp on the outskirts of Tokyo. There she shared a Western-style room heated with a small hibachi and received Western-style food, though she would have preferred Japanese. A local dairy sent daily bottles of milk, while the neutral Swiss, who assumed formal responsibility for Canadian interests in Japan during the war, supplied occasional jars of marmalade and cans of oatmeal. Courtice was also appointed camp interpreter, largely, she suspected, because the commandant's wife and daughter had been pupils at the Shizuoka and Tōyō Eiwas.

In one surreal moment, Courtice found herself conspiring with a guard who invited her on a cabbage-picking expedition at a nearby farm. "We ate those cabbages a leaf at a time," she recalled afterward. "I still hate to cut a cabbage."

ABOVE "Welcome Mr. Bott": A popular social worker in Tokyo before the war, George Bott was one of the first to return afterward, as a senior administrator of civilian relief through LARA (Licensed Agencies for Relief in Asia). *United Church of Canada Archives, 2000.01P/3428*

RIGHT A woman and child searching for food in Tokyo after the war. *Library and Archives Canada, Department of National Defence collection, PA-206847*

Unusually, two Canadian United Church teachers and social workers, George and Edith Bott, were not interned, although they had to give up their work—his with Japanese social agencies and a teaching post at Waseda University, and hers at the Women's Higher Normal School. They were repatriated in June 1942 on one of the Japanese ships bound for Lourenço Marques in Mozambique that rendezvoused with the *Gripsholm*, a Swedish ship carrying returning Japanese.

Among the few who remained behind was Agnes Wintemute Coates, the Methodist wife-cum-nutritionist, who resisted entreaties by her family to return and who died in Tokyo toward the end of the war. Another was Margaret Elizabeth Armstrong, the operator of a popular kindergarten in Toyama on the Japan Sea coast, who opted to stay after she retired in 1940. Unusually, she was also permitted to take out Japanese citizenship. On August 1, 1945, it was Toyama's turn for the terrifying US firebombing. Running from place to place, dropping flat in the dust, creeping and crawling, and dipping an old quilt into vats of water placed along the streets, Armstrong and a fellow teacher managed to survive. The Occupation forces later appointed her official interpreter for Toyama Prefecture, and in 1953 she was honoured by the emperor.

Some 60 Roman Catholic priests and nuns, who declined repatriation on the ground that their primary allegiance was to Rome, spent the duration of the war in prison.

• • •

Malone's purpose in searching out Prince Tokugawa was to obtain his help in locating the near-forgotten Canadian prisoners of war (POWs), survivors of the ill-fated defence of Hong Kong in late 1941. Members of the Winnipeg Grenadiers and Royal Rifles of Canada, they had been transported to Japan in 1943 to help meet its growing shortage of labour.

The first Malone found were 20 or so pathetic men stretched out on small bunks, dressed in rags, their bodies emaciated and discoloured with sores. A few got unsteadily to their feet in an effort to stand to attention. "When I tried to talk to them," Malone recorded afterward, "there was no response; their faces remained vacant, zombie-like. They couldn't tell me their names, their regimental numbers or even the names of their units. They were mental cases and also suffering from such things as beriberi. The smell in that hut was indescribable."

The horrific conditions the POWs endured are well documented. What also stands out in their later recollections, however, are the remarkable shafts of human light that occasionally shone through the darkness.

Captain John Reid, a medical officer who led incoming POWs through Osaka, was astounded when a member of the elite Japanese Imperial Guard identified himself as an acquaintance from university days in Canada: "What an odd place to meet!" the man exclaimed. In Hong Kong the POWs had suffered the brutalities of an infamous guard known as the Kamloops Kid, who had grown up in British Columbia. This guard, in contrast, was anxious to help, and supplied the prisoners with thick army greatcoats and a bonanza of fluffy sweet buns.

As their train whizzed through a panorama of peasants in cloaks and broad straw hats, the guards chatted and offered cigarettes while warning that the POWs would soon be meeting "some very bad men in the regular army." In Yokohama railway station they marvelled at the bustling crowd—a group of bedraggled, freakish, sickly giants among pretty, kimonoed women.

Finally the POWs reached their destination: Camp 3D in an industrial area in Kawasaki, a dismal compound with two long, unheated huts and cinders underfoot, without a blade of grass or tree in sight. Signalman William Allister soon found himself suspended on a wobbly plank high above the ocean painting a ship in the Nippon Kokan Shipyards, the unanticipated outcome of having entered "painter" in a space for "occupation" on a form. Before the war he had been an artist.

The "paint master" in charge was an older civilian in a black jacket, khaki army pants, frayed white socks in shiny shoes, a polka-dot bow tie and a straw boater; to Allister he seemed straight out of a Renoir. Allister also soon discovered a shared interest in literature with Kondo, the *hancho* or foreman, the only person he met since joining the army, aside from some Russian POWs in Hong Kong, who had read Maxim Gorky. During the daily 15-minute rest, Kondo shared the latest news. He also delighted in Allister's Harpo Marx imitation, joining in the daily routine. "Arisuta Hawpo-ka?" Kondo would ask, and the two would shuffle forward, imaginary pistols drawn, followed by peals of laughter—two strangers driven toward each other by a mutual symbol of zany playfulness that was the antithesis of the circumstances in which they found themselves.

The general manager was part of an older, polite and formal generation, with an inner dignity and sense of fairness despite a gruff facade, and the POWs liked and respected him. At the same time, Allister found the man troubling: "Where did he come from? This country, this alien, hostile, menacing land had made him. He upset me, induced an unpleasant softening, a dissolving, an urge to weep. I could hug this man. And I could kill those soldiers. Was my view darkened and twisted? Which was the true Japan?"

On the other hand, a camp corporal once beat Allister severely for no apparent reason other than disapproval of his new Red Cross–supplied hat.

While treatment of POWs varied from guard to guard, it also varied from camp to camp. The commandant of Camp 3D allowed Reid to leave the camp to purchase medicines and ordered guards to apologize for some of the worst treatment; Reid later intervened on his behalf during the Tokyo war crime trials, observing that in comparison with others he had been "fair and considerate." By general consensus the worst was Camp 5B on the outskirts of Niigata, where one commandant was later convicted of war crimes.

Even dreaded Niigata, however, was inconsistent. Rifleman Kenneth Cambon recalled a commandant who allowed POW officers to purchase musical instruments and organize

ID photo of POW Kenneth Cambon in Camp 5D near Niigata where his weight fell to 68 pounds. Only 17 when he went to Hong Kong, he became a medical doctor in Vancouver. *Courtesy of Austen Cambon and the Cambon family*

a small combo—an enormous boost to camp morale. One guard was "an evil looking, paranoid schizophrenic," while another was "a good egg," a much-decorated, twice-wounded veteran who allowed the POWs to rest and shared an occasional cigarette. Another guard, a young socialist, confided his opposition to the war and his disgust with the way POWs were treated; at great personal risk he brought medicine purchased on the black market, as well as news of the war.

The POWs found their own small revenges in the form of quiet acts of sabotage, like overloading electrical circuits and causing coal cars to jump the track. Cambon helped steal a commandant's prize chicken and have it blamed on the guards. Allister and friends took to pissing into a particularly nasty guard's tea.

Liberated Canadian prisoners of war receiving new clothing in Yokohama in 1945.
Library and Archives Canada, PA-114876

● ● ●

A multinational hodgepodge of Allied prisoners taken throughout the Far East, the camp inmates organized themselves as if in response to some innate tribal instinct of their own. Americans were the entrepreneurs and individualists who worked the system. The British maintained their hierarchy. The Dutch got some of the best jobs, while Canadians, Australians, Poles and others buddied up in twos and threes to survive.

Some Canadians sensed they were not viewed quite the same as others. Inasmuch as there was a Japanese hate list, Americans were at the top at 10 points, the British next at 8 and Canadians merely at 1. Mostly there was confusion about why Canadians were there at all. "This is something the Japanese couldn't understand," recalled Company Sergeant-Major Cecil

"Red" Windsor. "It was explained to them to the best of our ability that Hong Kong was an English colony, and we were a member of the Commonwealth of Nations, and we felt it as our duty to help England out. The Japanese couldn't understand that."

The Japanese question, however, was reasonable. Before the war, Hong Kong's tactical position had been acknowledged as hopeless; it was Singapore, not Hong Kong, that was supposed to be impregnable, although that, too, proved an illusion. The decision to go to Hong Kong was also out of character for Prime Minister King, who customarily tippy-toed around anything to do with the Far East. He was especially leery of British intentions and what he called "the China trap," confiding to his diary in 1937 that "British interests in China will not be sufficient ground for our participation in a war in the Orient."

What seems reckless in hindsight, however, presumably made more sense in the precarious context of the time, when any prospect of deterring war must have seemed like a straw worth grasping. The plan—sending a group of Canadian, Scottish and Indian troops to defend a British colony—proved disastrous, a situation some likened to the Charge of the Light Brigade.

Less than eight hours after Pearl Harbor, a Japanese force swept south to Hong Kong. The Canadians held out for an astonishing 17 days in what turned out to be some of the fiercest hand-to-hand combat of the war. A Japanese commander, Colonel Shoji, was so impressed with their courage that he ordered the Canadian commander, Brigadier J.K. Lawson, buried with full military honours.

The Japanese ethic that honoured those who died in battle did not, however, extend to the defeated. Enemy soldiers who chose the ultimate shame of surrender over death with honour were viewed as being without dignity. Many of the Hong Kong wounded were bayoneted, the rest rounded up into miserable makeshift prison camps, where still more died.

• • •

Already severely weakened by years of imprisonment in Hong Kong, the POWs worked long, punishing days shovelling coal, pushing cars along trestles and riveting ships as unpaid labour. The chronic problem was malnutrition, which worsened dramatically as food dried up in Japan in the latter part of the war. Private Don Wilson believed he was starving to death; 183 pounds when he went to Hong Kong, he was only 90 when he came home.

"But in one sense they weren't doing much better themselves," he allowed of his Japanese guards, "because they didn't have much to eat either." Survival became a matter of food tactics.

> One day they brought us in some fish heads and guts. And they put that in the soup. There were maggots floating on top. It was the thickest soup I'd had so far . . . (Corporal Jack Willis) . . . You do all kinds of darned things when you're hungry. Like on the way to work there was a sort of swamp near the camp. Whenever you got a chance you'd stuff your pockets with frogs . . . (Private Bill Savage). One of my boys caught a rat and cooked it, and he saved me a small portion. I sat it on top of my rice while it was still hot, so I could taste that flavour through the rice . . . (CSM Red Windsor). In season they'd give us the Japanese orange, say, one orange a month. Now a Japanese orange would last the average prisoner of war two weeks . . . (Bandsman Art Young). Sex! God, a dirty old crust of bread, or the most glamourous star in Hollywood, there'd be no choice! You'd go for the bread . . . (Private Fred Reich).

Left briefly unsupervised one day, Allister hit the jackpot: steaming lumps of coagulated noodles in the camp garbage cans.

> I wanted to whoop—this was my day! I threw a quick glance over my shoulder toward the kitchen doors, then dove in, scooping up huge gooey globs of hot noodles, cramming them feverishly under my shirt, wet and sloppy against my chest . . . Then I dashed away, hugging my precious cargo under my jacket, making for the *benjo* [toilet] to hide . . . I darted into the first narrow cubicle and locked the door. The stench was thick enough to drive nails into. I kept a lookout for the guards through a tiny shoulder-high window as I straddled the magic mountain and leaned against the moving wall of worms, squishing them underfoot. Then out came the lumps of half-raw noodles. I joyfully gobbled and gurgled my ravenous way toward the ultimate, the prisoner's Nirvana . . .

Jack Willis was no stranger to worms. " . . . apparently these worms get into you through your pores. The poor old worms were starving to death too, you know. You'd go to sleep at night, and you'd get a worm . . . up your esophagus.

Once I scratched my nose and pulled a two-inch worm out of my nose. He was hungry, because he had nothing in me to eat."

As the months wore on, their lives became a medical textbook of diseases: tropical ailments like chronic dysentery, malaria and beriberi; symptoms of vitamin deficiency and malnutrition like swelling, blindness, "hot feet" and "strawberry balls"; and diphtheria and tuberculosis. The deterioration was not only physical; it also attacked the mind and spirit. Some POWs became so depressed that they lost the will to live. One by one they died, one young man after another, lost in drawn-out, horrible deaths while their friends watched, wondering who would be next. "After you were in there for a while you got the idea that Canada never existed," recalled Private Gordon Durant. "After the years went on, you thought it was a dream, Canada was just a dream. It didn't exist."

What is surprising is not that so many died but that so many mustered the inner strength to survive.

As hostilities hurtled to their finale in the summer of 1945, Sergeant Major George MacDonell found himself in a kind of triple jeopardy. The senior Canadian among 68 POWs at a remote underground iron ore mine at Ohasi in northern Japan, he realized he was unlikely to survive if the war lasted much longer. He also shared the general suspicion that POWs were likely to be killed in the event of an Allied invasion. Perversely, he found himself constantly diving for cover from machine gun fire and bombs launched by low-flying US fighters. "It seemed to me ironic," he wrote afterward, "that as the Allied Forces grew stronger and stronger and the possibilities of rescue increased, our chances of survival were diminishing." Nonetheless, he believed there was still a chance of rescue.

The basis of this strand of optimism was a clandestine naval radio receiver set, whose components had been smuggled into the camp by American prisoners and hidden high in the rafters, allowing a handful of POWs to track the war's progression. In early August MacDonell heard of the atomic bombs and that negotiations for Japan's surrender were underway. On August 15, he and his men were assembled in an isolated section of the mine—to what end they did not know. When they were released, the Japanese foreman of the machine shop informed him of the emperor's famous broadcast to his people, and quietly whispered with a wink: "*Hancho*, you go Canada now."

For a week the camp remained guarded, and eerily quiet. Then the radio told them a massive American grid search for Allied POWs was underway.

Bedsheets were quickly placed on rooftops with huge letters directing passing US planes to their location. Before long, the sky rumbled as bombers began parachuting in supplies to theirs and other camps. Huge drums bounced off pavements and occasionally crashed through roofs in a great shower of boots, clothing, magazines, cigarettes, cheese, milk, cookies and drums of fruit salad, as well as two items not seen before: penicillin and Spam. In the days that followed, the well-meaning generosity became overwhelming, as well as dangerous. ". . . the camp had begun to look like it had been shelled by artillery," MacDonell recalled. "So we painted two words on the roof: NO MORE!"

Following evacuation to hospital ships and brief recuperation in the Philippines and Hawaii, the surviving veterans of Hong Kong finally went home. Before departing, MacDonell went back to say goodbye to the foreman of the machine shop and promised to take his advice and return to school when he got home. "I developed no hatred for the people of Japan," he reflected afterwards. "Most of them were as kind to us as they could be under the harsh rules of their military dictatorship . . . it was the common people of Japan who paid the terrible price for the military imperialism of their ruling elite."

He also visited the camp cemetery. Of the approximately 1,975 Canadians who sailed to Hong Kong, a quarter never returned home; of these, 137 POWS died in Japan. Many of the survivors would suffer the after-effects of imprisonment for decades.

● ● ●

Most former POWs, understandably, never went back to Japan. For a few, however, the path to reconciliation with the past lay in confronting it directly.

William Allister, the Kawasaki "painter," returned to the Nippon Kokan Shipyards in 1973. Instantly he felt himself transformed into someone with a Japanese number on the back of his shirt, trudging along in baggy pants, gut-hungry, surreptitiously diving in the street for cigarette butts and orange peels. He also found himself confused by his Nippon Kokan hosts, who sent a representative to assist him and showered him with kindness and hospitality. Some Japanese also expressed shame about how he had been treated.

Mentally clapping his hands in a Kyoto shrine to summon the Shinto gods, it finally came to him. "Harmony is all," their voices murmured. "Anger, bitterness, hatred have no place in the smooth running universe."

And they drove away the mists, revealing the outlines of a grand design . . . As an artist I would paint a path toward peace, paint as I'd never painted before, stretching to the limits, soaring, exploring new forms, new harmonies. Visions of giant canvases marrying East and West unfolded before me . . . Who knows? These tiny flute notes of reconciliation might stir a calming breeze somewhere along the discordant winds of the planet. It was worth a try.

Allister produced 20 huge canvases in all, four feet by six feet, framed by his experience.

Kenneth Cambon, who survived Niigata, also vowed not to return to Japan. But in 1980 he, too, went back. Met by a limousine and presented with keys to the city, he found nothing familiar. The town of narrow streets and thatched roofs had given way to a city of steel and glass and pulsating traffic. "How silly of me to expect to find oxcarts, women in long bloomers, men in army style dress with the inevitable military cap. I wonder what happened to all those caps. Not one was to be seen."

The yards where he had shoved coal cars around a track had been transformed into a modern port facility. No trace could be found of the three camps he had been in, nor could any of the older Japanese with whom he spoke remember a prison ever having been in the area. That night he scarcely slept, and it was not the hard Japanese pillow that kept him awake.

The next evening he found himself dining with a Japanese family. After a wonderful feast of seafood and sake, his host pulled out a bottle of Courvoisier and proposed a toast to two prisoners of war—revealing that he himself had been a Russian POW for four years. The experience triggered the closure Cambon needed.

After a few more brandies my Japanese of forty years ago returned— or, perhaps, it just seemed so. We shared experiences, capping each story with another brandy. The evening ended with an empty bottle, with Mr. Suda singing a Russian song and me singing one of the Japanese Army's marching songs . . . I slept well and miraculously awoke in the morning with a clear head.

More formal steps toward reconciliation have taken longer. In 1998 the Canadian government provided compensation to the surviving Hong Kong POW veterans. The Japanese government offered an apology in December 2011.

NORMAN *SENSEI*

When Herbert Norman plunged to his death from a Cairo rooftop in 1957, reactions around the world differed widely.

In the United States, where he was being pursued by Senator McCarthy's communist witch hunt, the news of his death was quickly leaped upon as proof of his guilt as a communist spy. In Canada, he was seen as the victim of a crazed American right wing.

In Japan, saddened friends floated small bamboo boats among the rice fields in his memory. Which raises a question: just how Japanese was Herbert Norman—and what bearing did this have on his life and its tragic and controversial end?

• • •

There is, of course, no real way in which a foreigner can "be Japanese." Herbert Norman, however, was not a typical foreigner.

In the early days of the Pacific War he was one of the diplomats trapped in the Canadian Legation in Tokyo, awaiting the repatriation ships that would take him home. As he whiled away the days, entertaining his fellow inmates with repartee and conserving food and bathwater, he had no way of knowing he was about to burst onto the international stage as the pre-eminent Western authority on modern Japan. A recent graduate from Harvard, his doctoral dissertation had just been published as *Japan's Emergence as a Modern State*—and unlike most doctoral theses it turned out to be a blockbuster.

Norman came by his topic naturally. He was "BIJ," shorthand for foreigners born in Japan, in his case in Karuizawa, the resort village in the Japan Alps near Nagano where his father, Daniel, was a Methodist missionary. There the Norman family carried on a kind of hybrid life typical of expatriates. Their

E. Herbert Norman, before he burst onto the international stage as a leading expert on modern Japan. *UBC Library, Rare Books and Special Collections*

house was a large wooden structure that resembled an Ontario farmhouse of its day. Herbert was educated at home using an Ontario school curriculum until he was old enough to go to the Canadian Academy in Kobe. The family ordered its clothes from the Eaton's catalogue and Kate, Herbert's mother, imported baking powder from Canada for her biscuits.

Like many of his contemporaries, Daniel Norman lived in the straitjacket of his religious convictions. He evinced little interest in Japanese religious beliefs and spoke almost no Japanese. Nor was he a particularly successful missionary as measured by conversions. He was, however, a man of deep social conscience with a natural empathy for people, who spent much of his life among the poor farmers of the district.

More isolated than their contemporaries in the cities, the Normans were also more integrated into the local community. Daniel Norman was saluted

The Normans of Nagano, with friends and household members: Herbert (with dog), father Daniel, mother Kate, brother Howard and sister Grace. *United Church of Canada Archives, 2000.017P3158N*

as he got on and off the local railway, which issued him a lifetime pass. A story is also told of a boy who spotted him in the street and cried out, "There's a foreigner!" to which the response is said to have been, "That's no foreigner, that's Mr. Norman."

This was Herbert Norman's world, one of people not much different in essentials from himself. Like all foreigners, he was an outsider. But he was an outsider who instinctively viewed Japan from the inside out, rather than the outside in. And this, at the end of the Pacific War, made him a hot commodity.

• • •

Japan's Emergence, as Norman's book came to be called, was a godsend for the US-led Occupation (August 1945–April 1952), looking for insights on how to deal with the shambles that was post-war Japan.

Its central theme—that an enlightened but essentially autocratic Meiji government had set the stage for Japan's spectacular economic transformation, but also for future repression—did much to answer the nagging question of "what went wrong" during the 1930s. At the same time, his characterization of the Meiji Restoration as "an incomplete revolution" provided the intellectual bedrock for the Occupation's determination to ensure that post-war Japan would not simply revert to pre-war Japan.

Issued in a shorter version in 1945, *Japan's Emergence* became the de facto textbook of US Occupation forces, recalls John Howes, a former GI who went on to teach at the University of British Columbia. "The many others who earlier pored over the copy I read had caused the binding to disintegrate." The Americans, however, were not only interested in Norman's book. They wanted the author himself. In September 1945 he was back in Japan, seconded to the Occupation authority headed by US General Douglas MacArthur.

On the face of it, Norman the scholar diplomat and MacArthur the imperious Supreme Commander were an odd match. But they had something in common. They were both committed to the early Occupation's twin program of demilitarization and democratization, albeit from different perspectives—MacArthur because his military judgment told him this was the only way to preclude the possibility of another war, and Norman because of what the lessons of history taught. They also shared an understanding that the forces that came to dominate pre-war Japan would inevitably seek to reassert themselves, and that the answer was to encourage pre-war voices of democracy that had been quashed during the 1930s as a counterweight.

As the civilian head of a US army intelligence unit, Norman was entrusted with the sensitive task of preparing dossiers on suspected war criminals. His influence, however, was wider. The autocratic MacArthur did not listen to many people, but he was known to respect and listen to Norman. The Canadian was also the first person to whom MacArthur spoke following the memorable call on him by Emperor Hirohito.

Where Norman and MacArthur parted intellectual company was over a key issue of the Occupation, the instrument for effecting change: the proposed new Japanese constitution. In MacArthur's mind democracy was in the nature of a gift bestowed from above. Norman believed democracy could succeed only to the extent that it carried the support of the Japanese people expressed through a constitutional assembly or referendum that would take more time.

When MacArthur presented his draft constitution to the Japanese Diet in February 1946, Norman was in Washington representing Canada at the Far Eastern Commission, the group of Allied powers under the assumption that it was responsible for Occupation policy. Indeed, Norman happened to be chairing the commission at the precise moment its astounded members learned of MacArthur's *fait accompli.*

ABOVE Herbert Norman with US
General Douglas MacArthur at the
Canadian Legation in Tokyo, July 1,
1947. *US Army photo, Library and Archives
Canada, Department of National Defence
collection, PA-187690*

RIGHT Herbert Norman greeting
Minister of External Affairs Lester
Pearson as he arrived in Tokyo to
confer with General MacArthur in
1950. *Canadian Embassy, Tokyo*

Six months later Norman was back in Tokyo with his wife, Irene, this time representing the Canadian government's interests in Occupied Japan. His personal relationship with MacArthur resumed. By then, however, US policy was already beginning its dramatic "reverse course" in response to the emerging Cold War. Increasingly, the early Occupation's ambitious democratization agenda took a back seat to Japan's strategic importance as a Pacific bastion against Soviet aspirations in Asia, an alternative to revolutionary China in the Far East and an ally in the Korean War. War criminals were rehabilitated and the huge Japanese business conglomerates, or *zaibatsus*, re-energized as Japan turned to the massive task of post-war reconstruction under successive governments of conservative Prime Minister Yoshida Shigeru.

When MacArthur was famously fired by President Harry Truman in 1951, Norman wrote a scathing critique for the Canadian government of the departing general's swan song to Congress.

● ● ●

When Norman's diplomatic posting in Japan ended in 1950, some 200 Japanese professors turned out to bid him farewell. To them he was *Habaato Noman Sensei*, the honorific reserved for gifted scholars and teachers.

In their eyes he was also a scholar of a different kind. Before Norman, students of Japan tended to be Tokyo-centric, concerned principally with the great men and events that shaped the course of Japanese history from the capital. With his roots firmly entrenched in rural Japan, Norman naturally looked beyond this central march of Japanese history to its impact on the rest of the country—on farmers, townspeople and workers who found their lives changed but not necessarily much improved by Japan's transition to modernity.

He admired the great Meiji reformers who wrested Japan from the rigidities of Tokugawa feudalism. But he instinctively sensed that the rapid pace of change, combined with external pressures, had forced the country to revert to an authoritarian style of government at the expense of democracy. He felt that Japanese history could best be understood as a dynamic interaction between the strains of Tokugawa feudalism and the forces of liberalism on the part of those outside the governing elite.

Prior to Norman, foreign study of Japan had also largely been the purview of Japan specialists who focused on the country's uniqueness, complexity and particularities. Norman took a broader view. "I do feel," he once remarked, "that foreign observers should guard against viewing the Japanese as a mysterious and inscrutable people whose behaviour and institutions are immune to rational analysis and understanding."

Instead he placed Japan in the broad stream of human history. His writings are full of references to European history and philosophy. *Japan's Emergence discusses the Meiji Restoration in the context of the French Revolution and* the growth of British liberalism. A speech he gave to the students at Keio University on the death of Fukuzawa Yukichi in 1948 compared Fukuzawa with Thomas Jefferson. It also extolled the virtues of free speech.

> I urge you to be brisk and diligent in defence of liberty; by making Japan a citadel of freedom and free culture you can prove yourself to be the finest patriot . . . The world is tired of war and force . . . Persuasion is not only the only way of reason and humanity, it is now the sole path of self preservation. Thus we are, all of us, whatever our nation or status, faced with the same alternative: PERSUADE OR PERISH.

Unlike most of the Occupation force, Norman could talk with Japanese about the war on their own terms in their own language. During a 1947 visit back to Nagano he spoke frankly about the tendency of any repressed people to vent their spleen on someone beneath them, as disenchanted former samurai did in the Meiji era when Japan undertook campaigns against Korea and Formosa (Taiwan). He also encouraged with talk of homegrown democratic heroes like Nakamura Takachiro, who campaigned for general suffrage, and the journalist Kinoshita Naoe, who chose Nagano as a base.

At a time when the psychological distance between Japan and the rest of the world could not have been greater, Norman had little patience for the tendency to generalize about the Japanese character.

> A commentator could prove that almost any set of qualities is inherent in the Japanese. For instance one can draw up a list of complete contrasts . . . that Japanese are rigid and highly conventional in their behaviour and, on the other hand, that they are adaptable and quick to change their views; that they are docile and submissive, and again that they are turbulent and easily excitable; that they are painstakingly polite and, on the other hand, insensitive and thoughtless; that they are frugal and thrifty on the one hand and pleasure-loving and lavish on the other; that they are brave and fearless of death, yet are timid, especially

in matters of civic life; that they are highly disciplined, and yet their army has revealed many instances of insubordinate behaviour. This sort of contrast could be extended, and no one would be the wiser for it.

He found his democratic hero in Ando Shoeki, a little-known 18th-century Japanese country doctor who dared to speak out in favour of social justice. Written by Norman in the Canadian Legation and published in 1949, *Ando Shoeki and the Anatomy of Japanese Feudalism* drew attention to a small but significant Japanese tradition of liberal populism and was greeted with interest by the post-war Japanese intelligentsia.

As a democratic hero in the modern sense, Ando may be a bit of a stretch. But the book helped Japanese to think about democracy in their own terms rather than as something gifted by the Occupation.

• • •

Was Herbert Norman guilty? And if so, of what was he guilty? The questions dogged Norman's name for decades after his death.

There is little doubt that he became a communist while studying at Cambridge, but this in itself is not remarkable. Many students turned left during the 1930s in the troubled context of the Depression and the Spanish Civil War. It was the intellectual flavour of the times, a counterweight to rising militarism and fascism.

That Norman may have been an active communist agent after joining the Canadian government in 1940, a mole in the manner of other Cambridge alumnae like Kim Philby and Donald Maclean, is an intriguing Cold War conspiracy notion. But if he was, nothing approaching evidence ever surfaced—not from McCarthy, not in the official Canadian inquiries that exonerated Norman and not in the trail of suspicion and innuendo that dogged his memory for years. The charges brought by Senator McCarthy's committee in 1952 seem to have been little more than a dubious mishmash of circumstantial incrimination: testimony from individuals pressured to name names, confused identities and not a little FBI and CIA mischief. As one CIA agent reportedly admitted off the record years later, the case against Norman was one with neither a head nor a tail.

His Japan connection, which had been his making, also proved part of his undoing. Norman's first brush with the US security establishment was in 1942 when he arrived at the Boston apartment of Tsuru Shigeto, a left-leaning economist he had known at Harvard, and made the fateful mistake of trying to pass his presence off as official Canadian government business. His name would already have been in their files; before joining External Affairs in 1940, he had been courted by the head of the United States Office of War Information, Owen Lattimore, whom McCarthy also later accused.

General Charles A. Willoughby, MacArthur's chief of intelligence, was also a factor. A man of profoundly right-wing persuasion who did not hide his admiration of Spanish dictator General Franco, Willoughby distrusted Norman's democratic sympathies as well as some of the Japanese company he kept. He kept the dossier on Norman that fed the McCarthy investigation, an account that suggested, for example, that Norman had acted personally when he released prominent liberal intellectuals, socialists and communists from prison in the early days of the Occupation rather than on orders from MacArthur. Those around MacArthur also never forgave Norman for warning the general that crossing the 38th parallel would inevitably bring China into the Korean War—especially after it did. There were allegations Norman had passed information to the communists.

McCarthy's case was also partly one of guilt by association; suspicion fell on Norman by virtue of the circles in which he travelled. Specifically, he had the misfortune to be an Asia scholar at a time when Asia scholars generally were distrusted, especially the "China hands" in the State Department who were blamed for the loss of China to the communists.

Japan scholars were not tarred with the same brush, but the Institute of Pacific Relations (IPR) was. And Norman was closely identified with the IPR, which had first published Japan's Emergence, the book that so entranced early Occupation authorities. A regular contributor to IPR conferences and journals, Norman was also instrumental in reviving its Japanese branch at the end of the war, just before it became the target of a virulent assault by McCarthy. Forty-six people associated with the IPR were declared by McCarthy to have been members of the Communist Party.

Even so, Norman might have shaken the charges off—others did. Robert Bryce, a Canadian student at Harvard who introduced Norman to Tsuru, was also named by McCarthy but survived to become one of Canada's most illustrious public servants. Bryce, however, was associated with lower-profile Canadian domestic and economic policy making. Norman, had he accepted the offer of a teaching position at the University of British Columbia, might similarly have slid beneath the radar screen. Instead he was

Egyptian president Gamal Abdel Nasser (second on left) looks intently at Ambassador
Herbert Norman as he greets another Egyptian dignitary in Cairo in 1956.
Canadian Embassy, Tokyo

put in charge of the American and Far Eastern branch of the Department of
External Affairs, a position that carried access to American intelligence and
infuriated the McCarthyites.

In 1957 the McCarthy bag of snakes reopened after Tsuru ultimately
capitulated and admitted to having been a communist, though he, too, sur-
vived the ordeal, later becoming a university president. By that time Norman
was in Cairo as Canada's ambassador to Egypt, busily convincing President
Nasser to accept the first UN peacekeeping force designed to defuse the Suez
Crisis, the initiative that later won Canada's then foreign minister, Lester
Pearson, the Nobel Peace Prize. Cairo was a hotbed of international intrigue.
And Herbert Norman was in the international spotlight again.

• • •

Time and record will show to any impartial observer that I am
innocent on the central issue—i.e. I have never conspired or committed an act against the security of our state or of another state—
Never have I violated my oath of secrecy. But how the issues will be
obscured and twisted! But I am too tired of it all. The forces against

me are too formidable, even for an innocent man, and it is better to go now than to live indefinitely pelted with mud—although so much of it will be incorrect and false . . .

This excerpt from a suicide note left behind by Norman speaks to the desperation and inner torment that preceded his climb to the roof in Cairo that morning. But neither these words nor others he left behind seem to shed much real light on why he acted as he did.

If he was not guilty of anything improper why would he choose to take his own life? The answer is a function of different perceptions of what it means to commit suicide.

In the Christian tradition in which Norman grew up, suicide has historically been regarded as a sin. An innocent man, by implication, would have been able to live with himself. This is what the forces arrayed against Norman implied when they leaped on his action as proof of guilt.

In the tenets of modern psychology, suicide tends to be viewed essentially as an irrational act, something that a well-adjusted individual would not do. This is what his supporters in the Canadian government and elsewhere implied when they characterized his death as the result of stress from overwork exacerbated by the revival of the McCarthy hounding. In other words, he was a victim of a nervous breakdown, a man not entirely in his right mind.

The problem with such explanations is that they do not stack up well against the kind of life-embracing man Norman is known to have been. He was understandably under some stress in Cairo, and the McCarthy hounding had certainly taken its toll. But he was at the top of his game. He also had the backing of Pearson—though by then he, too, had attracted McCarthy's interest.

In the absence of obvious "reasons why," the possibility has even been floated that Norman's suicide might actually have been the result of some drug-induced conspiracy on the part of the CIA, already suspicious of Norman and nervous about what he might be up to in Cairo—but this is merely conjecture.

It may simply be that Norman had a more accepting view of suicide; one born, perhaps, of his formative years in Japan, where suicide has traditionally been viewed as a rational act, a means of preserving honour, an acceptable way out of a hopeless situation. His suicide notes certainly suggest he saw his action as a means of upholding his honour and innocence.

There is no reason to think that Norman had anything like Japanese ritual suicide on his mind when he climbed to the roof that morning. But on the previous evening, he had watched *The Mask of Destiny*, a Japanese film involving suicide, from which he is said to have came away heartened. There was also something about the way he neatly folded and arranged his clothing that suggested to some a possible Japanese ritual aspect. But why Herbert Norman acted as he did, no one really knows.

• • •

The more accepting Japanese view of suicide does not make the act, when it occurs, less regrettable. Maruyama Masao, one of Japan's most influential post-war intellectual historians, provided insight into why Japanese felt so deeply saddened by Norman's death.

Maruyama's sensitive tribute to him, *An Affection for the Lesser Names*, compares his relationship with Norman to the usual one-sided acquaintance-ships with foreign Japan specialists in which he typically got less than he gave. What struck him most was Norman's grasp of history, particularly his never-failing interest in its crooked byways, his affection for history's wing players and "lesser names"—Epicurus and Lucretius rather than Plato or Aristotle, Mo-tzu and Chuang-tzu rather than Confucius or Mencius.

He also admired Norman the man: courteous, with a gentle straightforward-ness and lack of hypocrisy; his store of risqué stories; his taste for life. Had Norman been a solitary melancholic or had a more doctrinaire side to his character, Maruyama suggested, his suicide would not have been such an unbearable shock.

> It is because we knew him as a "quiet optimist," as someone determ-ined never to overlook the brighter sides of human life or the forward-looking movements of history, that the thought of that thing which tortured his mind as he hovered on the cliff-edge of death makes one hide one's head in horror . . . if Herbert Norman, who so loved the good in men, and who had such faith in the power of reason to persuade men, has ended his short life in the midst of fanaticism and prejudices and intolerance, what should we do—we who are left behind?

As Maruyama's portrait suggests, something about Norman seems to have spoken to Japanese concepts of the ideal man: one dedicated to his profession who also indulges in life's pleasures. An honourable man, quick to act but sensitive to his obligations to those around him.

A gathering at Maruyama Masao's house: (from left) Herbert Norman, Nakano Yoshio, Maruyama Masao and Okubo Genji. *Canadian Embassy, Tokyo*

Another professor, Watanabe Kazuo, recalled drinking too much and falling asleep during Norman's birthday party at the legation. When he awakened several hours later feeling distressed and ashamed, Norman simply asked if he had slept well and offered him another drink. The following midnight Watanabe's phone rang; it was Norman asking if he could come by for a moment. Shortly after, Norman arrived at the door with a bottle of whisky. After talking a while, he said he was tired and, at Watanabe's invitation, took a nap. "I couldn't forget this incident," Watanabe said later. "To save my face Dr. Norman tried to lose his."

Recollections of Norman among his legation colleagues are similarly disarming. Like his favourite Greek philosopher, Epicurus, he was a lover of the good life, an enthusiastic party-goer who spent many evenings in bars and geisha houses in the company of friends. His interests were varied: he was a passionate tennis player who had courts installed on the legation grounds, regularly attended kabuki theatre, and spent hours running with Brandy, his Alsatian, in Meiji Park.

Norman's intellectual brilliance seemed limitless. D'Arcy McGreer, who was in charge of the legation during the early months of the war, found him an ideal person with whom to be imprisoned, someone who in a single evening could amuse with talk of Persian poetry, early Italian wines, little-known 17th-century British literary figures and sidelights on Cervantes and Voltaire. Others recall explorations of how the unicorn got its horn, the mating habits of African tribes and the sewage system of ancient Rome. These were not the late-night ramblings of a detained and bored diplomat, but flashes of a sparkling intellect, one that delighted in the ebb and flow of humanity in all its manifestations.

There may even be something in Norman's description of the country doctor Ando Shoeki that verged subconsciously on self-portrayal.

> Reserved but yet not cold, neither haughty nor fawning, humane but not condescending, valuing friends but not ambitious; stoical in manner but sanguine in outlook; studious of books but more of the living world around him; a man who could look with keen but friendly eyes on Nature and his fellow men, learning from them and so able to teach them . . . Above all he was a lover of peace and the pursuits of peace, hence, in the proper sense, a civilized man.

• • •

When Herbert Norman died, more was lost than the man himself. What is remarkable is that his scholarly legacy virtually disappeared, erased by new interpretations of Japanese history that could compete with Marxism and break the influence of leftist thought in an era defined by China's revolution and the Korean War.

In this new climate, Norman's perception of Japanese history as a struggle between the forces of reaction and liberalism gave way to the politically less challenging tenets of "modernization theory" and the jargon-ridden empiricism of the social scientist. His integrative approach to East and West waned in favour of a resurgence of specialization and the time-honoured propensity to explain what was difficult about Japan in terms of cultural difference and uniqueness.

For the new generation of American academics who flocked to Japan in the 1950s and '60s, probing analysis of the broad sweep of Japanese history was less important than exploring the secrets of Japan's rising economic miracle, held up as a model for the Third World and an alternative to revolutionary China. Tainted by the McCarthy charges, Norman's writings were deemed old hat, straw men against which to tout the new orthodoxy. *Japan's Emergence* was dubbed a Marxist interpretation, and *Ando Shoeki* and other works dismissed as inconsequential.

Herbert Norman in discussion with Okubo Genji, who worked with him in the Canadian Legation and preserved his scholarly legacy. *UBC Library, Rare Books and Special Collections*

The issue in retrospect is not whether Norman was right or wrong. It is that he virtually dropped from sight. American historian Edwin Reischauer, another missionary son and a contemporary of Norman's—the two faced each other as teenagers on the tennis court in Karuizawa—dismissed *Japan's Emergence* as an outstanding work of great historical significance that had seen its day. A Reischauer history published in the early 1960s, while he was US ambassador to Japan, did not even refer to Norman in the bibliography.

That Norman's scholarly flame survived at all owes much to his friend and collaborator, Okubo Genji. A young Japanese historian who had worked with the IPR, Okubo was brought into the Canadian Legation by Norman after the war. It was Okubo who eased Norman's entrée to the world of progressive Japanese intellectuals and journalists, and Okubo who did much of the research that underlay Norman's penetrating reporting on the Occupation. He also translated the Japanese edition of *Japan's Emergence,* which appeared in 1947, and supplied much of the original research for *Ando Shoeki*, working with Norman at the legation late into the night.

Determined to preserve Norman's scholarly legacy after his death, Okubo quietly began translating the rest of Norman's work into Japanese.

● ● ●

Herbert Norman is buried in Rome's foreign cemetery, not far from Shelley, one of his favourite poets. His heart, however, seems to belong nearer to Japan, the place that shaped much of his life and conceivably also his death, the place that may have understood him best.

In 1956, the year before Norman's death, a dedication he wrote for a collection of essays was published in Japanese. Translated as *The Face of Clio*, it reads almost like a love letter to Japan or perhaps simply to history, both Western and Eastern.

> In preparing these essays and in my efforts to continue some unfinished work in Japanese history, I seek for inspiration not so much from Clio as from an Oriental goddess of similar spirit. I know this is a new or perhaps strange idea, since the Muses were a Greek conception and described by their ancient poets. But for my purpose I shall look to an Oriental Clio, a Clio of partly Buddhist inspiration but whose features are surely Japanese.
>
> I recall her in the form of that miracle of grace carved in wood—the figure of Kwannon (Miroku) in the Chuguji Nunnery at Nara. Her right hand is raised lightly against her cheek; her lips are half parted in the merest suspicion of a smile; her expression is serene rather than melancholy. She looks out upon human striving, both its follies and its greatness, on the passions and ambitions of this world, with an expression neither indifferent nor disdainful, but rather infinitely patient and compassionate. I can imagine the face lighting up with humour untinged with mockery. Unlike many conventional representations, there is nothing chilly or forbidding in this figure; rather does it radiate warmth and sympathy, more so, it strikes me, than her Greek counterpart.
>
> For me she represents Clio in her Eastern incarnation, as it were, and from her shrine I seek encouragement and understanding. Whatever of historical imagination or significant awareness, particularly of Japanese history, may appear in my work I owe to that Clio of Japan, to the memory of her smiling lips and pensive face.

General Source Materials

Fry, Michael. "Development of Canada's Relations with Japan 1919–1947." In *Canadian Perspectives on Economic Relations with Japan,* edited by Keith J. Hay, 7–67. Montreal: Montreal Institute for Research on Public Policy, 1980.

Ion, A. Hamish. *The Cross and the Rising Sun: The Canadian Protestant Missionary Movement in the Japanese Empire, 1872–1931.* Waterloo, ON: Wilfred Laurier University Press, 1990.

Langdon, Frank. *The Politics of Canadian-Japanese Economic Relations, 1952–1983.* Vancouver: UBC Press, 1983.

Lower, J. Arthur. *Canada on the Pacific Rim.* Toronto: McGraw-Hill Ryerson, 1975.

———. *Ocean of Destiny: A Concise History of the North Pacific 1500–1978.* Vancouver: UBC Press, 1978.

Meehan, John D. *The Dominion and the Rising Sun: Canada Encounters Japan.* Vancouver: UBC Press, 2004.

Neumann, William L. *America Encounters Japan: From Perry to MacArthur.* New York: Harper and Row, 1963.

Norman, Gwen R.P., and Howard Norman. *One Hundred Years in Japan: 1873–1973. Gwen R.P. Norman: 1873–1923: Howard Norman: 1923–1973.* Toronto: Division of World Outreach, United Church of Canada, 1981.

Sansom, G.B. *The Western World and Japan: A Study in the Interaction of European and Asiatic Cultures.* New York: Alfred A. Knopf, 1950.

Seidensticker, Edward. *Low City, High City: Tokyo from Edo to the Earthquake: How the Shogun's Ancient Capital Became a Great Modern City (1867–1923).* New York: Alfred A. Knopf, 1983.

———. *Tokyo Rising: The City since the Great Earthquake.* Cambridge: Harvard University Press, 1991.

Strange, William. *Canada and the Pacific War.* Toronto: Thomas Nelson and Sons, 1937.

Woodsworth, Charles J. *Canada and the Orient: A Study in International Relations.* Toronto: Macmillan Company of Canada, 1941.

Inspired Madness

Cole, Jean Murray. *Exile in the Wilderness: The Biography of Chief Factor Archibald McDonald 1790–1853.* Don Mills, ON: Burns and MacEachern Ltd., 1979.

Lewis, William S., and Naojiro Murakami, eds. *Ranald MacDonald: The Narrative of His Early Life on the Columbia Under the Hudson Bay Company's Regime; of His Experiences in the Pacific Whale Fishery; and of His Great Adventure to Japan; with a Sketch of His Later Life on the Western Frontier, 1824–1894.* Spokane, WA: Eastern Washington State Historical Society, 1923. Reprinted with new foreword and afterword. Portland, OR: Oregon Historical Society Press, 1990.

MacDonald, Ranald. Papers. British Columbia Archives, Victoria, BC.

McLeod, Malcolm. Papers. Library and Archives Canada, Ottawa.

Oliva, Peter. *The City of Yes.* Toronto: McClelland and Stewart, 1999.

Roe, Jo Ann. *Ranald MacDonald: Pacific Rim Adventurer.* Pullman, WA: Washington State University Press, 1997.

Stoldt, Frederik L. *Native American in the Land of the Shogun: Ranald MacDonald and the Opening of Japan.* Berkeley: Stone Bridge Press, 2003.

Van Kirk, Sylvia. *Many Tender Ties: Women in Fur-Trade Society, 1670–1870.* Winnipeg: Watson and Dwyer Publishing Limited, 1980.

Wildes, Harry Emerson. *Aliens in the East, A New History of Japan's Foreign Intercourse.* Philadelphia: University of Pennsylvania Press, 1937. Reprint, Wilmington, PA: Scholarly Resources Inc., 1973.

Wiley, Peter Booth. *Yankees in the Lands of the Gods: Commodore Perry and the Opening of Japan.* New York, London and Toronto: Penguin, 1990.

Those Seductive Treaty Ports

Douglas, Archibald C. *Life of Admiral Sir Archibald Lucius Douglas.* Totnes, Devon, UK: Mortimer Bro., 1938.

Earns, Lane R., and Brian Burke-Gaffney. *Across the Gulf of Time: The International Cemeteries of Nagasaki.* Nagasaki: Nagasaki Bukensha, 1991.

Feifer, George. *Breaking Open Japan: Commodore Perry, Lord Abe and American Imperialism in 1853.* New York: Smithsonian Books and HarperCollins, 2006.

Higuchi, Jiro. "Henry Spencer Palmer Museum," last modified February 24, 2004. http://homepage3.nifty.com/yhiguchi.

Jones, Hazel J. *Live Machines: Hired Foreigners and Meiji Japan.* Vancouver: UBC Press, 1980.

Keene, Donald. *Emperor of Japan: Meiji and His World (1852–1912).* New York: Columbia University Press, 2002.

Manthorpe, Victoria, ed. *The Japan Diaries of Richard Gordon Smith.* London: Viking Rainbird, 1986.

Meech-Pekarik, Julia. *The World of the Meiji Print: Impressions of a New Civilization.* New York and Tokyo: Weatherhill, 1986.

Mizuno, Captain Hironori. "The Japanese Navy." In *Western Influences in Modern Japan*, by Nitobe Inazō and Others, 408–46. Chicago: University of Chicago Press, 1931.

Pyle, Kenneth. *The New Generation in Meiji Japan: Problems of Cultural Identity, 1885–1895.* Stanford: Stanford University Press, 1969.

Tames, Richard. *Encounters with Japan.* New York: Alan Sutton, Stroud, St. Martin's Press, 1991.

Till, Barry. *Japan Awakens: Woodblock Prints of the Meiji Period (1863–1912).* San Francisco: Pomegranate Communications Inc., Art Gallery of Greater Victoria, 2008.

Williams, Harold S. *Foreigners in Mikadoland.* Rutland, VT, and Tokyo: Charles E. Tuttle Company, 1963.

Woodward, Frances M. "Henry Spencer Palmer." In *Dictionary of Canadian Biography Online*, vol. XII, 2000. http://www.biographi.ca/009004-119.01-e.php?&id_nbr=6352.

Missions and Mountains

Copithorne, Tamako. *Unknown Foundation of the Canada Japan Relation (translation of Shirarezaru Nikka no Ishizue).* Tokyo: Mita Hyoron, Keio University (March 2006): 52-56; (April 2006): 46-48.

Fukuzawa Yukichi. *The Autobiography of Fukuzawa Yukichi.* Translated by Eiichi Kiyooka, with an introduction by Shinzo Koizumi. Tokyo: Hokuseido Press, 1960.

Kirkwood, Kenneth P. "Sessho Hut." Kenneth Porter Kirkwood Papers. Library and Archives Canada, Ottawa.

Powles, Cyril Hamilton. "The Development of Japanese-Canadian Relations in the Age of Missionary Activity, 1873–1930." *Kanada Kenkyu Nenpo/Annual Review of Canadian Studies* (1980): 146–65.

———. *Victorian Missionaries in Meiji Japan: The Shiba Sect, 1873–1900.* Toronto: University of Toronto/York University Joint Centre on Modern East Asia, 1987.

Sohō, Tokutomi. *The Future Japan.* Translated and edited by Vinh Sinh with co-editors Matsuzawa Hiroaki and Nicholas Wickenden. Edmonton: University of Alberta Press, 1989.

Suzuki Bokushi. *Snow Country Tales; Life in the Other Japan.* Translated by Jeffrey Hunter with Rose Lesser. New York and Tokyo: Weatherhill, 1986.

Weston, Walter. *Mountaineering and Exploration in the Japanese Alps.* London: John Murray, 1896.

No Geisha

Baldwin, Douglas. "Lucy Maud Montgomery's Anne of Green Gables: The Japanese Connection." *Journal of Canadian Studies* 28, no. 3 (Fall 1993): 123–33.

Barr, Pat. *A Curious Life for a Lady: The Story of Isabella Bird, Traveller Extraordinary.* Markham, ON: Penguin Books Canada Limited, 1970.

Bernstein, Gail Lee, ed. *Recreating Japanese Women, 1600–1945.* Berkeley and Los Angeles: University of California Press, 1991.

Bingle, Florence Rothwell. *High Buttoned Shoes and Tabi.* Kingston, ON: Tabi Publishing Co., 1980.

Birchall, Diana. *Onoto Watanna: The Story of Winnifred Eaton.* Chicago: University of Illinois Press, 2001.

Buruma, Ian. *A Japanese Mirror: Heroes and Villains of Japanese Culture.* London: Penguin Books, 1984.

Cartmell, Martha. Papers. United Church of Canada Archives, Toronto.

Coates Family. Papers. United Church of Canada Archives, Toronto.

Finn, Dallas. *Meiji Revisited: The Sites of Victorian Japan.* New York and Tokyo: Weatherhill, 1995.

Gagan, Rosemary. *A Sensitive Independence: Canadian Methodist Women Missionaries in Canada and the Orient.* Montreal: McGill-Queen's University Press, 1992.

Iwao, Sumiko. *The Japanese Woman: Traditional Image and Changing Reality.* Don Mills, ON: Maxwell Macmillan Canada, 1993.

Kajahira, Yuka. "An Influential Anne in Japan." In *Lucy Maud Montgomery Album,* compiled by Kevin McCabe and edited by Alexandra Heilbrun, 443–48. Toronto: Fitzhenry and Whiteside, 1999.

Reischauer, Haru Matsukata. *Samurai and Silk: A Japanese and American Heritage*. Cambridge, MA, and London: Belknap Press of Harvard University, 1986.

Ridout, Katherine. "A Woman of Mission: The Religious and Cultural Odyssey of Agnes Wintemute Coates." *Canadian Historical Review* 7, no. 2 (June 1990): 208–44.

Till, Barry, Michiko Warkentyne, and Judith Pratt. *From Geisha to Diva: The Kimonos of Ichimaru*. Victoria, BC: Art Gallery of Greater Victoria, 2001.

Trillin, Calvin. "Anne of Red Hair: What Do Japanese See in Anne of Green Gables?" In *Lucy Maud Montgomery and Canadian Culture*, edited by Irene Gammel and Elizabeth Epperly, 213–21. Toronto: University of Toronto Press, 1999.

Highway to the East

Allen, Louis, and Jean Wilson, eds. *Lafcadio Hearn: Japan's Great Interpreter, A New Anthology of His Writings, 1894–1904*. Folkestone, UK: The Japan Library Ltd., 1992.

Andrew, Edgar. "Sir William Van Horne and His House." *Montreal Gazette*, April 3, 1971.

Atterbury, Paul, ed. *The History of Porcelain*. London: Orbis Publishing, 1982.

Benfy, Christopher. *The Great Wave: Gilded Age Misfits, Japanese Eccentrics, and the Opening of Old Japan*. Toronto: Random House, 2003.

Chamberlain, Basil Hall. *Things Japanese: Being Notes on Various Subjects Connected with Japan for the Use of Travelers and Others*. London: K. Paul, Trench, Trubel and Co., 1891.

Coleman, D'Alton C. *Lord Mount Stephen (1829–1921) and the Canadian Pacific Railway*. New York: Newcomer Society of England, America Branch, 1945.

Cott, Jonathan. *Wandering Ghost: The Odyssey of Lafcadio Hearn*. New York, London and Tokyo: Kodansha International, 1992.

Gibbon, John Murray. *Steel of Empire: The Romantic History of the Canadian Pacific, the Northwest Passage of Today*. Indianapolis and New York: Bobbs-Merrill Company, 1935.

Glazebrook, G.P. de T. *Sir Edmund Walker 1848–1924*. London: Oxford University Press, 1933.

Hart, E.J. *The Selling of Canada: The CPR and the Beginnings of Canadian Tourism*. Banff, AB: Altitude Publishing Ltd., 1983.

Hosley, William. *The Japan Idea: Art and Life in Victorian America*. Hartford, CT: Wadsworth Atheneum, 1990.

Jenyns, Soame. *Japanese Porcelain*. New York: Frederick A. Praeger, 1965.

Kirkwood, Kenneth P. *Unfamiliar Lafcadio Hearn*. Tokyo: Hokuseido Press, 1936.

Lamb, W. Kaye. *Empress to the Orient*. Vancouver: Vancouver Maritime Museum Society, 1991.

Marty, Sid. *A Grand and Fabulous Notion: The First Century of Canada's Parks*. Toronto: NC Press Limited, 1984.

Meech-Pekarik, Julia. *The World of the Meiji Print: Impressions of a New Civilization*. New York and Tokyo: Weatherhill, 1986.

Rosenstone, Robert A. *Mirror in the Shrine: American Encounters with Meiji Japan*. Cambridge, MA, and London: Harvard University Press, 1988.

Scidmore, Eliza Ruhamah. *Westward to the Far East: A Guide to the Principal Cities of China and Japan.* Montreal: Canadian Pacific Railway Company, 1891.

"Sir Edmund in Japan." In *Current Account* (June 1939), Canadian Imperial Bank of Commerce Archives, Toronto.

Stephen, George. Papers. Library and Archives Canada, Ottawa.

Stevenson, Elizabeth. *Lafcadio Hearn.* New York: Macmillan, 1961.

Till, Barry. *The Land of the Rising Sun, Arts of Japan, Japanese Art in the Collection of the Art Gallery of Greater Victoria.* Victoria, BC: Art Gallery of Greater Victoria, 1998.

Turner, Robert D. *The Pacific Empresses: An Illustrated History of Canadian Pacific Railway's Empress Liners on the Pacific Ocean.* Victoria, BC: Sono Nis Press, 1981.

Van Horne, William Cornelius. Papers. Library and Archives Canada, Ottawa.

Vaughan, Walter. *Life and Work of Sir William Van Horne.* New York: Century, 1920.

Vincent, Mrs. Howard. *Newfoundland to Cochin China by the Golden Wave, New Nippon and the Forbidden City.* London: Sampson, Low, Marston and Company, 1892.

Waterhouse, David. *Images of Eighteenth Century Japan: Ukiyoe Prints from the Sir Edmund Walker Collection.* Toronto: Royal Ontario Museum, 1975.

Wray, William D. *Mitsubishi and the NYK, 1870–1914: Business Strategy in the Japanese Shipping Industry.* Cambridge: Council on East Asia Studies, Harvard University Press, 1984.

Myths and Markets

Collard, Elizabeth. *Nineteenth Century Pottery and Porcelain in Canada.* Kingston and Montreal: McGill-Queen's University Press, 1967.

Dane, Frederick, and R.S. McIndoe. *A Sketch of the Growth and History of Tea and the Science of Blending Particularly Adapted to the Canadian Trade.* Toronto: Department of Agriculture, 1881.

Fisher, Sydney. Papers. Library and Archives Canada, Ottawa.

Gowen, Robert J. "Canada and the Myth of the Japanese Market, 1896–1911." *The Pacific Historical Review* 39, no. 1 (February 1970): 63–83.

Grey, Albert Henry George, 4th Earl. Papers. Library and Archives Canada, Ottawa.

Hill, O. Mary. *Canada's Salesman to the World: The Department of Trade and Commerce, 1892–1939.* Montreal and London: The Institute of Public Administration of Canada, McGill-Queen's University Press, 1977.

Hoffman, Frances. *Steeped in Tradition: A Celebration of Tea.* Toronto: Natural Heritage Inc., 1991.

MacKay, Donald. *The Asian Dream: The Pacific Rim and Canada's National Railway.* Vancouver and Toronto: Douglas & McIntyre, 1986.

Preston, W.T.R. *My Generation of Politics and Politicians.* Toronto: D.A. Rose, 1927.

Reischauer, Haru Matsukata. *Samurai and Silk: A Japanese and American Heritage.* Cambridge, MA, and London: Belknap Press of Harvard University, 1986.

"Report of the Fifth National Industrial Exhibition held at Osaka, Japan, from March 1st to 31st July, 1903." Exhibition Branch, Department of Agriculture Papers. Library and Archives Canada, Ottawa.

Webber, Bernard. *Silk Trains: The Romance of Canadian Silk Trains or "the Silks."* Kelowna, BC: The Word Works Publications, 1992.

King's Japan

Adachi, Ken. *The Enemy That Never Was: A History of the Japanese Canadians.* Toronto: McClelland and Stewart, 1976.

Bailey, Thomas A. *Theodore Roosevelt and the Japanese American Crises: An Account of the International Complications Arising from the Race Problems on the Pacific Coast.* Stanford: Stanford University Press/Oxford University Press, 1934.

Dawson, R. MacGregor. *William Lyon Mackenzie King: A Political Biography 1874–1923.* Toronto: University of Toronto Press, 1958.

Esthus, Raymond A. *Theodore Roosevelt and Japan.* Seattle and London: University of Washington Press, 1967.

Ferns, H.S., and Bernard Ostry. *The Age of Mackenzie King: The Rise of the Leader.* Toronto: Heinemann, 1955.

Granatstein, J.L. *Mackenzie King: His Life and World.* Toronto, Montreal, New York and London: McGraw-Hill Ryerson, 1977.

Hutchison, Bruce. *The Incredible Canadian: A Candid Portrait of Mackenzie King: His Works, His Times and His Nation.* Toronto, New York and London: Longman's, Green and Company, 1952.

Iino, Masako. "Japan's Reaction to the Vancouver Riot of 1907." *B.C. Studies*, no. 60 (Winter 1983–84): 28–47.

King, William Lyon Mackenzie. "Mission to the Orient" (3 vols.). William Lyon Mackenzie King Papers. Library and Archives Canada, Ottawa.

MacMillan, Margaret. *Paris 1919.* New York: Random House, 2003.

McLaren, Roy. *Canadians in Russia, 1918–1919.* Toronto: Macmillan, MacLean-Hunter Press, 1976.

Price, John. "Orienting the Empire: Mackenzie King and the Aftermath of the 1907 Race Riots." *B.C. Studies*, no. 156 (Winter 2007–8): 53–81.

Skelton, Oscar Douglas. *Life and Letters of Sir Wilfrid Laurier, Volume II.* Toronto: Oxford University Press, 1921.

Skilling, H. Gordon. *Canadian Representation Abroad, from Agency to Embassy.* Toronto: Ryerson Press, 1945.

Stacey, C.P. *Canada and the Age of Conflict: A History of Canadian External Policies, Volume 1: 1867–1921.* Toronto: Macmillan, 1977.

———. *Canada and the Age of Conflict: A History of Canadian External Policies, Volume 2: 1921–1948: The Mackenzie King Era.* Toronto: University of Toronto Press, 1981.

———. *A Very Double Life: The Private World of Mackenzie King.* Toronto: Macmillan, 1976.

Sugimoto, Howard H. *Japanese Immigration, the Vancouver Riots and Canadian Diplomacy.* New York: Arno Press, 1978.

Flaming Passion

Bernstein, Gail Lee, ed. *Recreating Japanese Women, 1600–1945.* Berkeley and Los Angeles: University of California Press, 1991.

Ishimoto, Shizue. *Facing Two Ways: The Story of My Life.* New York: Farrar and Rinehart, 1935. Reprint, Stanford, CA: Stanford University Press, 1992.

Kato, Taka, and YWCA Tokyo Japan. *Emma R. Kaufman and the Tokyo YWCA.* Tokyo: YWCA, 1963.

Macdonald, A. Caroline. Papers. United Church of Canada Archives, Toronto.

Prang, Margaret. *A Heart at Leisure from Itself: Caroline Macdonald of Japan.* Vancouver: UBC Press, 1995.

Royce, Marion V. *Women as Achievers in Canadian History: Focus on Emma Kaufman, 1881–1979.* Toronto: YWCA of Canada, 1979.

Tsurimi, Patricia. *Factory Girls.* Princeton, NJ: Princeton University Press, 1990.

The Great Quake and Commerce

Cameron, W.D. "Japanese Earthquake, 1923, Descriptive Letter" and other reports. Sun Life Assurance Company of Canada, Corporate Archives, Toronto.

Campbell, Duncan C. *Global Mission: The Story of Alcan, Volume 1 to 1950.* N.p.: Ontario Publishing Company Limited, 1985.

Drushka, Ken. *H.R.: A Biography of H.R. MacMillan.* Madeira Park, BC: Harbour Publishing, 1995.

MacKay, Donald. *Empire of Wood: The MacMillan Bloedel Story.* Vancouver and Toronto: Douglas & McIntyre; Seattle: University of Washington Press, 1982.

Robinson, Captain S. "Official Report on the Japanese Earthquake and the Fire" (n.d.). Canadian Pacific Railway Archives, Montreal.

"The First Sixty Years: 1887–1947. A History of the Manufacturers Life Insurance Company" and other reports. Manulife Financial Archives, Toronto.

Sir Herbert and the Legation

Hilliker, John. *Canada's Department of External Affairs, Volume 1: The Early Years 1909–1946.* Montreal, Kingston, London and Buffalo: The Institute of Public Administration of Canada, McGill-Queen's University Press, 1990.

Keenleyside, Hugh L. *Memoirs of Hugh L. Keenleyside, Volume 1: Hammer the Golden Day.* Toronto: McClelland and Stewart, 1991.

———. Papers. Library and Archives Canada, Ottawa.

Kirkwood, Kenneth Porter. Papers. Library and Archives Canada, Ottawa.

MacDougall, Elizabeth. *Blossoming: Days in the Orient 1935–1936.* Montreal: Boarish Press, 1989.

Mackenzie, Hector. "Skelton's Boys: Recruitment for the Foreign Service of Canada, 1925–1941," www.international.gc.ca/odskelton/articles_mackenzie. Originally published in *bout de papier* as an extract from "Recruiting Tomorrow's Ambassadors: Examination and Selection for the Foreign Service of Canada, 1925–1997," in *Diplomatic Missions: The Ambassador in Canadian Foreign Policy*, edited by Robert Wolfe. Kingston, ON: Canadian Centre for Foreign Policy Development and the School of Policy Studies, Queen's University, 1998.

Manion, James P. *A Canadian Errant: Twenty-five Years in the Canadian Foreign Service.* Edited by Guy Sylvestre. Toronto: Ryerson Press, 1960.

Marler, Herbert Meredith. Papers. Library and Archives Canada, Ottawa.

Marler, Howard. *Marler: Four Generations of a Quebec Family.* Montreal: Literary and Historical Society of Quebec, Price Patterson Ltd., 1987.

Rice, Eber H. "Sir Herbert Marler and the Canadian Legation in Tokyo." In *Canada and Japan in the Twentieth Century*, edited by John Schulz and Kimitada Miwa, 75–84. Toronto: Oxford University Press, 1991.

Therrien, Marie Josee. "Canadian Chanceries in Tokyo." In *Contradictory Impulses: Canada and Japan in the Twentieth Century*, edited by Greg Donaghy and Patricia E. Roy, 231–43. Vancouver and Toronto: UBC Press, 2008.

The Dark Valley

Bates, C.J.L. *Understanding Japan*. Text of radio speech on the Canadian Broadcasting System, 1942.

Duggan, James. *Paul-Emile Léger*. Don Mills, ON: Fitzhenry and Whiteside Limited, 1981.

Howes, John, ed. *Nitobe Inazō: Japan's Bridge across the Pacific*. San Francisco, Oxford and Boulder: Westview Press, 1995.

Ion, A. Hamish. *The Cross in the Dark Valley: The Canadian Protestant Missionary Movement in the Japanese Empire, 1931–1945*. Waterloo, ON: Wilfrid Laurier University Press, 1999.

Johnson, Gregory A. "Canada and the Far East during the 1930s." In *Canada and Japan in the Twentieth Century*, edited by John Schulz and Kimitada Miwa, 110–26. Toronto: Oxford University Press, 1991.

Johnson, Gregory A., and Galen Perras. "A Menace to the Country and the Empire: Perceptions of the Japanese Military Threat to Canada before 1931." In *Contradictory Impulses: Canada and Japan in the Twentieth Century*, edited by Greg Donaghy and Patricia E. Roy, 62–79. Vancouver and Toronto: UBC Press, 2008.

Keenleyside, Hugh L. *On the Bridge of Time*. Toronto: McClelland and Stewart, 1982.

Lachance, Micheline. *Le Prince de L'Église: le cardinal Léger*. Montreal: Les Editions de l'Homme, 1982.

Leclerc, Richard. *Des Lys a l'ombre du mont Fuji: Histoire de la presence de l'Amerique francaise au Japon*. Sillery, QC: Editions du Bois-de-Coulonge, 1995.

———. "God's Envoys." In *Contradictory Impulses: Canada and Japan in the Twentieth Century*, edited by Greg Donaghy and Patricia E. Roy, 29–45. Vancouver and Toronto: UBC Press, 2008.

Léger, Paul-Émile. Papers. Fondation Jules et Paul-Émile Léger, Montreal.

Kenny, Stephen. "Kwansei Gakuin and the Canadian Connection: An Historical Reflection on a Unique Relationship." *Kwansei Gakuin University, Annual Studies* XXXVII (December 1988): 97–111.

Nitobe, Inazō. *Bushido: The Soul of Japan, An Exposition of Japanese Thought, with an introduction by William Elliot Griffiths*. Revised and enlarged edition. Rutland, VT, and Tokyo: Charles E. Tuttle, 1969.

Nitobe, Inazō, and Others. *Western Influences in Modern Japan: A Series of Papers on Cultural Relations*. Chicago: University of Chicago Press, 1931.

Robinson, Greg. "Two Other Solitudes: Encounters between Japanese Canadians and French Canadians." In *Contradictory Impulses: Canada and Japan in the Twentieth Century*, edited by Greg Donaghy and Patricia E. Roy, 140–57. Vancouver and Toronto: UBC Press, 2008.

Till, Barry. *Samurai: The Warrior Class of Japan*. Victoria: Art Gallery of Greater Victoria, 2003.

Uchikawa, Eiichiro. *The Life of Inazō Nitobe*. Morioka, Japan: Morioka Nitobe Society, 1988.

Woods, Lawrence T. "John Nelson (1873–1936) and the Origins of Canadian Participation in APEC." Working Paper 18, Institute of International Relations, University of British Columbia, Vancouver, 1997.

War and Reconciliation

Allister, William. *Where Life and Death Hold Hands.* Toronto: Stoddart, 1989.

Banham, Tony. *Not the Slightest Chance: The Defence of Hong Kong, 1941.* Vancouver: UBC Press, 2003.

Cambon, Kenneth. *Guest of Hirohito.* Vancouver: PW Press, 1990.

Dancocks, Daniel G. *In Enemy Hands: Canadian Prisoners of War 1939–45.* Edmonton: Hurtig Publishers, 1983.

East, Charles A. *White Paper: Japanese Balloons of WWII.* Prince George, BC: College of New Caledonia Press, 1993.

Greenfield, Nathan M. *The Damned.* Toronto: HarperCollins, 2010.

Johnson, Gregory A. "Canada and the Far East during the 1930's." In *Canada and Japan in the Twentieth Century*, edited by John Schulz and Kimitada Miwa, 111–26. Toronto: Oxford University Press, 1991.

King, William Lyon Mackenzie. Private diaries. Library and Archives Canada, Ottawa.

Malone, Colonel Dick, OBE. *Missing from the Record.* Toronto: Collins, 1946.

Malone, Richard S. *A World in Flames: 1944–45 (A Portrait of War Part 2).* Toronto: Collins, 1984.

MacDonell, George. *One Soldier's Story: From the Fall of Hong Kong to the Defeat of Japan.* Toronto: Dundurn Press Ltd., 2002.

McIntosh, Dave. *Hell on Earth, Aging Faster, Dying Sooner: Canadian Prisoners of the Japanese during World War II.* Whitby, ON: McGraw-Hill Ryerson, 1996.

Rawling, Bill. "Only if Necessary; Canada's War against Japan, 1941–45." In *Contradictory Impulses: Canada and Japan in the Twentieth Century*, edited by Greg Donaghy and Patricia E. Roy, 101–19. Vancouver and Toronto: UBC Press, 2008.

Roland, Charles G. *Long Night's Journey into Day: Prisoners of War in Hong Kong and Japan, 1941–1945.* Waterloo, ON: Wilfrid Laurier University Press, 2001.

Roy, Patricia, J.L. Granatstein, Masako Iino, and Hiroko Takamura. *Mutual Hostages: Canadians and Japanese during the Second World War.* Toronto: University of Toronto Press, 1990.

Soward, Stuart E. *A Formidable Hero: Lt. R.H. Gray, VC, DSC, RCN*, 2nd ed. Victoria, BC: Trafford and Neptune Development, 2003.

Stacey, C.P. *Six Years of War: The Official History of the Canadian Army in the Second World War.* Ottawa: Queen's Printer, 1955.

Takahashi, Hisashi. "The Canadian Expeditionary Force and the Fall of Hong Kong." In *Canada and Japan in the Twentieth Century*, edited by John Schulz and Kimitada Miwa, 102–9. Toronto: Oxford University Press, 1991.

Verreault, Georges. *Journal d'un prisonnier de guerre du Japon, 1941–1945.* Sillery, QC: Septentrion, 1993.

Vincent, Carl. "No Reason Why: The Hong Kong Tragedy." In *Canada and Japan in the Twentieth Century*, edited by John Schulz and Kimitada Miwa, 86–101. Toronto: Oxford University Press, 1991.

Norman *Sensei*

Bowen, Roger W., ed. *E.H. Norman: His Life and Scholarship.* Toronto, Buffalo,
London: University of Toronto Press, 1984.

——. *Innocence Is Not Enough: The Life and Death of Herbert Norman.* Vancouver
and Toronto: Douglas & McIntyre, 1986.

Copithorne, Tamiko Yagai, Yoshio Nakatani, Cyril Powles, Frank Langdon,
Tsunehara Gonnami, and Allan McGill. "E. Herbert Norman and Japan:
A Hero of an International Tragedy." In *Between Cultures: A Selection of Public
Lectures, 1990–2000,* 162–176. Vancouver: David See-Chai Lam Centre for
International Communication, Simon Fraser University, 1999.

Dower, John W., ed. *Origins of the Modern Japanese State: Selected Writings of E.H.
Norman.* New York: Pantheon Asia Library, Random House, 1975.

Katz, Sidney. "What Kind of Man was Herbert Norman?" *Maclean's,*
September 28, 1957, 22.

Lyon, Peyton. *The Loyalties of E. Herbert Norman.* Report prepared for External
Affairs and International Trade, Ottawa, March 18, 1990.

Maruyama, Masao. "An Affection for the Lesser Names: An Appreciation of E.
Herbert Norman." *Pacific Affairs* 30, no. 3 (September 1957): 249–53.

Menzies, Arthur. "Genji Okubo, Japanese Scholar." *bout de papier* 5, no. 4
(Winter 1988): 24.

Miwa Kimitada. "E.H. Norman Revisited." In *Canada and Japan in the Twentieth
Century,* edited by John Schulz and Kimitada Miwa, 48–58. Toronto: Oxford
University Press, 1991.

Nobuya, Bamba. *The Postwar Years,* adapted by Ōkuma Takayuki and translated by
Peter Currie. In *Canada and Japan in the Twentieth Century,* edited by John
Schulz and Kimitada Miwa, 126–36. Toronto: Oxford University Press, 1991.

Norman, E. Herbert. Papers. University of British Columbia Library, Rare Books
and Special Collections, Vancouver.

Norman, Howard and Gwen. Papers. University of British Columbia Library,
Rare Books and Special Collections, Vancouver.

Price, John. "E.H. Norman, Canada and Japan's Postwar Constitution." *Pacific
Affairs* 74, no. 3 (Fall 2001): 383–405.

——. "Herbert Norman, the Occupation of Japan, and Canada-U.S. Relations:
A Canadian critique of MacArthur and the Occupation." *Japan Focus,*
May 26, 2007, 53–81.

——. "Rethinking the Occupation: E.H. Norman, Canada and the American
Empire in Asia." In *Contradictory Impulses: Canada and Japan in the Twentieth
Century,* edited by Greg Donaghy and Patricia Roy, 120–39. Vancouver and
Toronto: UBC Press, 2008.

Tsuiso Okubo Genji (Recollections of Okubo Genji), compiled by the Publications
Committee of Recollections of Okubo Genji, including contributions by
John W. Dower and Herbert P. Bix. Tokyo: PEROG, 1987.

Woods, Lawrence T., ed. *Japan's Emergence as a Modern State: Political and Economic
Problems of the Meiji Period—60th Anniversary Edition.* Vancouver and
Toronto: UBC Press, 2000.

Allister, William, 200–201, 204–207
Alcan, 144, 150–151
    Asia Aluminum Company, 150
Anglo-Japanese Alliance, 116, 126
Arima Shirosuke, 134, 138, 140
Armstrong, Mary Elizabeth, 66, 199
Art Gallery of Greater Victoria, 91

Bates, C.J.L., 180, 181–182
Bennett, R.B., 128, 160–161
Bird, Isabella, 64–65, 67, 84
Bott, George Ernest and Edith, 198
Bruce, R. Randolph, 172
Bryan, Arthur, 145–146, 150
Buddhism, 6, 21, 47, 50, 52, 58, 71, 73, 186
Bushido, 6, 131, 174–176

Cambon, Kenneth, 201, 207
Cameron, W.D., 144–146, 152
Canadian Academy, 70, 72, 184, 209
Canadian Bank of Commerce, 93, 106
Canadian Legation, 151, 163–164,
Canadian National Railway, 100, 108
Canadian Pacific *Empresses*, 79, 154, 181, 185
    Empress of Japan, 82, 102
    Empress of Australia, 141–143, 146
Canadian Pacific rail and ocean service, 6–7, 26, 77
    advertising, 61, 84–86, 107
    silk trains, 100
Cartmell, Martha, 61–64, 132
Chappell, Mary, 68
Christianity, 43–45, 47–50, 53, 54, 56, 70, 107, 134, 185–186
Coates, Agnes Wintemute, 68–72, 199
Cosgrave, Moore, 196–197
Courtice, Sybil, 197
Custer, Elizabeth, 27–28

Douglas, Archibald, 33–37, 40, 42, 46
Douglas, James, 27, 38

earthquake (1923), 135, 140–144, 146–150
Eaton, Winnifred, 75
Eby, Charles, 52–53
Education
    Canadian role, 5, 13, 24, 34–35, 43, 47–49, 51–52, 62–63, 68–72, 75, 131, 179–181, 197, 213, 219–222
    foreign role, 47, 50–51
    Japanese reform, 42–43, 47, 55, 62
emperors
    Hirohito (Showa), 211
    Meiji, 32, 34, 132, 176
    Taishō, 132,

Fisher, Sidney, 106–107
Fleming, Sandford, 26, 78
Fraser, Hon. John, 188
Fukuzawa Yukichi, 6, 42, 43–45, 47, 54, 55, 99, 131, 214
Fushimi, Prince, 107, 158

Gordon Smith, Richard, 41
Grand Trunk Pacific Railway, 107–108
Gray, Robert Hampton, 190–194
Grey, Earl, 96–97, 106–107, 206

Hamilton, Heber James, 58–60
Hankyū Railway Company, 182
Hays, Charles Melville, 107–108
Hearn, Lafcadio, 90–92
Hirooka, Asako, 133
Hudson's Bay Company
    Columbia River, 13, 15
    Colville, 27, 29, 38
    Langley, 13, 15, 38
    Thompson's River (Kamloops) 13

immigration, 83, 107, 109, 113–118, 120, 123, 125, 128, 176
Inoue Kaoru, 40, 62
Institute of Pacific Relations (IPR), 177–178, 217, 222
insurance companies, 152
    Manufacturers Life, 152
    Sun Life, 144, 146, 152, 178, 230
Itō Hirobumi, 6, 33, 50, 64, 101–103, 111–112

Japan–China dispute, 168–169, 177, 179
    impact on Canadians, 172, 179, 181, 187, 203

Kagawa Toyohiko, 182
Katsu Kaishū, 6, 34, 35, 46
Kaufman, Emma, 135–136
Keenleyside, Hugh L., 6, 151, 154–156, 158, 163–164, 166, 168–169, 171, 176, 186–188
Keio Gijuku/University, 42–45, 53–55, 131, 139, 181, 214
King, William Lyon Mackenzie, 7, 113, 114–125, 127–129, 154, 203
Kirkwood, Kenneth, 58–59, 162, 164, 167–170, 176
Kobayashi, Ichizo, 181–182
Komura, Jutarō, 6, 120, 122, 125

Langley, James A., 151, 164, 169
Laurier, Wilfrid, 8, 107–110, 112–113, 118, 123, 125, 128, 153
League of Nations, 126, 168, 176–177
Léger, Paul-Émile, 185, 187
Lemieux, Rodolphe, 113–114

MacArthur, Douglas, 195, 211–213, 216
Macdonald, Caroline, 6, 130–140, 182
Macdonald, John A., 78, 107
MacDonald, Ranald, 5, 6, 12–30, 38
MacDonell, George, 205–206

MacDougall, Elizabeth (Topsy), 169–171
MacDowell, Elmer, 144, 150
MacKenzie, Norman, 178
MacMillan Export Company, 188
MacMillan, Harvey Reginald (H.R.), 6, 147–150
Malone, Richard, 195–197, 199
Manion, James P., 156, 159, 167, 169
Marler, Herbert, 6, 155–163, 168–170, 172
Marler, Beatrice, 156–157, 162, 169–170
Maruyama Masao, 219–220
McDonald, Archibald, 13–14, 25
McDonald, Davidson, 45–48, 50–52
McGreer, D'Arcy, 172, 220
McLeod, Malcolm, 25–28
Meiji Restoration, 32, 35, 57, 99, 103, 210, 214
missionaries
    Anglican, 42–43, 54, 58, 67, 74, 139
    early female, 61–72
    Methodist/United Church, 45–46, 50–53, 58, 62–63, 69–72, 179, 182, 199, 208
    Roman Catholic, 21, 185, 187
Mitsubishi corporation, 79, 106, 110, 124, 148
Mitsui corporation, 79, 110, 133, 136, 146, 148
Morse, E. S., 87, 89, 91
Muraoka Hanako, 74
Murayama (Moriyama) Einosuke, 21–22, 25

Nakamura Keiu, 47, 48, 51
Nasser, Gamal Abdel, 217
Nitobe Inazō, 6, 45, 131–132, 135, 140, 174–178
Norman, Daniel, 51, 209–210
Norman, E. Herbert, 7, 209–223

Okubo Genji, 220, 222–223
Osaka exhibition (1903), 101–102, 104, 106, 131
Outerbridge, Howard, 180–181

Palmer, Henry Spencer, 38–40, 55
Paradis, Hélène, 185
Paris Peace Conference (1919), 126
Pearson, Lester B., 212, 217–218
Perry, Matthew P., 12, 23–25, 28, 30, 33–38, 117, 195
Pollard, Fred and Isabel, 94
Polo, Marco, 80
Powles, Percy and Ruth, 58
Preston, W.T.R., 109–111, 125
prisoners of war (POWs), 199–201, 203, 205–207

Queen's University, 157, 181

Reid, John, 199, 201
Reischauer, Edwin O., 222
Robinson, Samuel, 141–144
Roosevelt, Theodore, 116–118, 120, 122, 174
Rothwell, Florence, 72–73
Royal Ontario Museum, 93–94
Russo–Japanese War (1904–05), 36, 116, 122, 125, 132, 174

Scidmore, Eliza Ruhamah, 84
Shaw, Alexander Croft, 6, 42–45, 48, 53–56, 137
Shidachi Taki, 131
Shidachi Tetsujiro, 131, 138
Shidehara Kijurō, 168
Shigemitsu Mamoru, 196–197
Shinrinkan, 136–139
Shintoism, 50, 54, 56, 163, 179–180, 193, 206
Shiratori Toshio, 169
Skelton, Oscar D., 127. 157, 161–162
Smith, Donald (Lord Strathcona), 78–79, 109–111
social work, 5, 179, 182, 198

Soward, Frank H., 192
St. Andrew's Church, 54, 137, 158
Stephen, George (Lord Mount Stephen), 77–79, 83–85
Sumitomo, Baron, 6, 72–73
    Sumitomo corporation 110
    Alcan, 150–151

Tamura Shinkichi, 6, 103–104, 109, 125
    Tamura Building, 105
    Tamura Shokai (trading), 103–106
Taylor, Louis Denison, 76
Tokugawa Shogunate, 12, 30
    Tokugawa Iyemasa, 156
    Tokugawa Yoshinobu, 32
Tokyo Imperial University, 47, 51–53, 55, 89, 92, 175
Tomii Shuh, 129
Tōyō Eiwa (young men), 51
Tōyō Eiwa Jo Gakkō (young women), 63, 74, 197
trade, 6, 8
    1920s, 125–128, 143, 145
    1930s, 153, 156, 159–160
    early, 15, 22, 42, 79, 96–113
    protectionism/trade dispute, 153
trade, Canadian imports
    oranges, 46, 100, 104, 115, 153
    silk, 58, 64, 83, 87, 99–100, 104, 108, 115, 147, 153
    tea, 97–98, 107–108, 115, 147, 153
trade, Canadian resource exports
    aluminum, 144, 150–151
    automobiles, 151, 153
    fish, 101–102, 104, 109
    lumber, 101, 147–148, 151
    manufactured exports, 152
    metals and minerals, 151, 153, 187
    newsprint, 152
    wheat and flour, 8, 96–97, 101, 103–104, 106–109, 147, 153
Tsuda Ume, 6, 131–132
    Tsuda College/University, 68, 135, 138, 175
Tsuru, Shigeto, 215–217

University of British Columbia, 177–178, 190, 211, 217
University of Toronto, 43, 58, 130

Van Horne, William Cornelius, 7, 78, 83, 85
    advertising, 84
    collecting, 87–89, Hearn, 90–92
    Montreal Museum of Fine Arts, 92–93
    Morse, 85, 89
    trade, 83, 98,

Walker, Edmund, 93–94, 106
Waseda University, 132, 160, 198
Willoughby, Charles A., 216
Wise Wood, Henry, 109
Women's Christian College, 68, 135, 175
Woodsworth, Harold F., 179–181
    children, 184
Woodsworth, J.S., 182
Wright, Frank Lloyd, 93–94, 154, 213

Yoshida Shigeru, 163, 178, 213
Yoshida Shōin, 30–34

ACKNOWLEDGMENTS

Finding Japan would not have been written without the encouragement of Yuen Pau Woo, president and CEO of the Asia Pacific Foundation of Canada, Paul Evans, professor of Asian international relations at the University of British Columbia, Joseph Kess until recently with the University of Victoria, former Canadian ambassadors to Japan Donald W. Campbell and Joseph Caron and the late John Powles, president of the Canada–Japan Society. I am especially grateful to Arthur Hara, former chairman of Mitsubishi Canada, who not only encouraged the project but also generously shared his knowledge of early Canada–Japan connections.

The book also benefitted from the personal insights provided by the Hon. John Fraser (Pacific War), Tamako Copithorne (Keio University), Sylvia Bews Wright (Harold and J.S. Woodsworth), Cyril and Marjorie Powles (Alexander Shaw and the Powles family), Margaret Prang (Caroline Macdonald), John Howes (Nitobe Inazō), Austen Cambon and the Cambon family (Kenneth Cambon), Terry Milne (Robert Hampton Gray), Frances Woodward (Henry Palmer), James Langley (his father of the same name), the late Gwen Norman (the Methodists, Herbert Norman), as well as the late Arthur Menzies regarding much in general. Ambassador Jonathan Fried, Eric Petersson and Misako Terauchi of the Canadian Embassy in Tokyo also provided invaluable help.

The underlying research owes much to the splendid source material and helpful staff of Canadian archives, libraries, museums and galleries, a list of which appears below, as well as the work of Canadian historians and others who have written in the area, cited under Sources and Further Reading.

Among the joys of doing the book was assembling the splendid collection of images that illuminate the text. I am especially indebted in this regard to Barry Till, curator of Asian Art at the Art Gallery of Greater Victoria for his assistance in identifying suitable colour images, as well as Sarah Romkey and the staff of UBC Library Rare Books and Special Collections, Lisa Glandt of the Vancouver Maritime Museum, Bronwen Quarrie of the Hudson's Bay Company Archives and Nick Richbell of the Canadian Pacific Archives.

It has been a pleasure to see the book come to fruition under Rodger Touchie and the excellent team at Heritage House Publishing, including Vivian Sinclair, Kate Scallion, Neil Wedin and in particular my thoughtful editor Lana Okerlund and designers Kate Moore and Jacqui Thomas.

And to Stephen Heeney and Marlyn Horsdal who provided invaluable advice, an enormous thank you.

Archives and Libraries

Anglican Church of Canada Archives, Toronto

BC Archives, Victoria

Canadian Imperial Bank of Commerce Archives, Toronto

Canadian Pacific Archives, Montreal

City of Vancouver Archives

Library and Archives Canada, Ottawa

L'Oeuvre Léger, Montreal

Manulife Financial Corporate Archives, Toronto

Sun Life Financial Corporate Archives, Toronto

United Church of Canada Archives, Toronto

University of British Columbia Library, Rare Books and Special Collections

University of Toronto Archives

University of Waterloo Library, Special Collections

Vancouver Public Library

Museums and Galleries

Art Gallery of Greater Victoria

Glenbow Museum, Calgary

Japanese Canadian National Museum, Burnaby

McCord Museum of Canadian History, Montreal

Montreal Museum of Fine Arts

Royal Ontario Museum, Toronto

Vancouver Maritime Museum

Whyte Museum of the Canadian Rockies, Banff

When Anne Park Shannon headed the economic and financial work of Canada's embassy in Tokyo, she became curious about Canada's early connections westward across the Pacific to Japan. When did they begin? Who ventured forth and why? And what did people find when they got there? Now, as Asia plays an increasing role in the future of Canadians, she decided to share the outcome of her explorations in *Finding Japan*. Currently living in Victoria, she continues to be intrigued by Canadian engagement with Asia.